Best Tactics for Verbal Warfare

1. **Tension Blowouts**—Breathe in for 2 seconds. Hold it 2 seconds. Blow until you run out of air, thinking of what your enemy said to you. (Repeat three times)

2. **Humor**—Make a joke out of what they said or use a snappy comeback.

3. **Love and Kindness**—Be compassionate, open your heart, smile, and speak tenderly, kindly, and lovingly in soft and caring tones, never returning their verbal hostility.

4. **Direct Confrontation**—Let the person know that you don't feel good about what they said or how they said it to you—that it bothered you. Use calm tones and say how it made you feel. Don't blame or accuse them.

5. **Calm Questioning**—In calm tones, ask them logical questions about why they feel a certain way. Try to ask specific questions to which they will agree (answer "yes"). Ask a series of questions that finally leads them to possibly seeing things from a different point of view, even changing their ideas.

6. **Mirroring**—Sometimes a taste of their own medicine may work. Give them back some of their own verbal medicine in the exact way they gave it to you.

7. **Give 'Em Hell and Yell**—Open your mouth. Don't hold back. Let it roar!

8. **Vicarious Fantasy**—Imagine everything you would like to do to them. Never take physical action and harm them. Just fantasize! Then thinking of them, do Tension Blowouts to get them out of your mind.

9. **Unplug**—Let them out of your life. Get out of their lives. Don't look back. Don't contact them. Don't allow them to contact you. It's over! Finished! Tension Blowouts help keep them out of your mind.

alpha
books

Great Snappy Comebacks

1. Have you ever heard of the word *class*? Of course not, you don't have any!

2. I never forget a face, but in your case, I'll make an exception.

3. For a moment I didn't recognize you, and it was one of the best moments I ever had.

4. Are you always this obnoxious or is this day special?

5. I hope you see a doctor—for your foot-in-the-mouth disease.

6. Did you bathe today?—because your manners stink!

7. You have a fine personality, but not for a human being.

8. Whatever's eating you must be suffering from indigestion.

9. I don't know what makes you tick, but I hope it's a time bomb.

10. You need a checkup from the neck up!

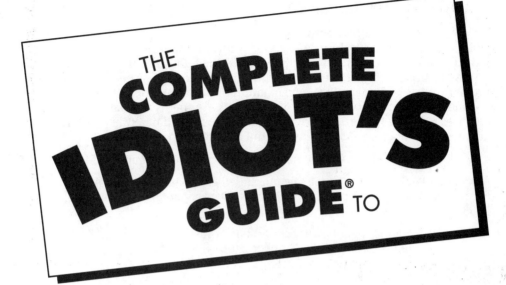

THE COMPLETE IDIOT'S GUIDE® TO

Verbal Self-Defense

by Lillian Glass, Ph.D.

alpha books

A Division of Macmillan General Reference
A Pearson Education Macmillan Company
1633 Broadway, New York, NY 10019

Copyright©1999 Lillian Glass, Ph.D.

THE COMPLETE IDIOT'S GUIDE name and design are trademarks of Macmillan, Inc.

Macmillan Publishing books may be purchased for business or sales promotional use. For information please write: Special Markets Department, Macmillan Publishing USA, 1633 Broadway, New York, NY 10019.

International Standard Book Number: 0-02-862741-5
Library of Congress Catalog Card Number: 99-64466

01   00   99   8   7   6   5   4   3   2   1

Interpretation of the printing code: the rightmost number of the first series of numbers is the year of the book's printing; the rightmost number of the second series of numbers is the number of the book's printing. For example, a printing code of 99-1 shows that the first printing occurred in 1999.

Printed in the United States of America

Note: This publication contains the opinions and ideas of its author. It is intended to provide helpful and informative material on the subject matter covered. It is sold with the understanding that the author and publisher are not engaged in rendering professional services in the book. If the reader requires personal assistance or advice, a competent professional should be consulted.

Alpha Development Team

Publisher
Kathy Nebenhaus

Editorial Director
Gary M. Krebs

Managing Editor
Bob Shuman

Marketing Brand Manager
Felice Primeau

Acquisitions Editor
Jessica Faust

Development Editors
Phil Kitchel
Amy Zavatto

Assistant Editor
Georgette Blau

Production Team

Development Editor
Jessica Faust

Production Editor
Robyn Burnett

Copy Editor
Erik Dafforn

Cover Designer
Mike Freeland

Photo Editor
Richard H. Fox

Illustrator
Kevin Spear

Book Designer
Scott Cook and Amy Adams of Design Lab

Indexer
Tim Wright

Layout/Proofreading
Angela Calvert
Ellen Considine

Contents at a Glance

Contents

Foreword

In the beginning was the WORD. The rest, is as they say, history . . .

Words have had magic power ever since human beings used language to liberate themselves from the constraints of physical reality. Every other life form adapts to the world as it is. Only human beings JUST SAY NO! to reality. Only human beings use words to envision the world as we'd like it to be, and then transform it accordingly. Words are magic symbols by which our dreams become reality.

Words are also the vehicles by which we exchange our thoughts and feelings with others, and in so doing become aware of ourselves (conscious = to know with). The self is literally an ongoing stream of words (psychologists have a variety of terms for this notion; e.g., "stream of consciousness," "inner newsreel," "autobiographical narrative"). So it should not surprise us then, that words are central to the integrity of the self. When someone puts in a **good word** about us, or for us, the self is fortified in proportion to the magnitude of the praise and the importance (in our minds at least) of the mouth from which the good words emerged. Prestige is thus the accumulated good words of others; and the primary meaning of prestige is "enchantment" and "illusion." I told you words are magic power!

But words, like any power, can, and often are, used destructively. We fight wars with words, and over words. And whoever said "sticks and stones can break my bones, but names can never harm me" obviously didn't grow up in my neighborhood in the Bronx in the 1950s, or for that matter, anywhere on earth since the dawn of human history. A **bad word** from the medicine man of many "primitive" peoples is sufficient to kill a person in a few days. We're a bit more subtle in contemporary western civilization, where daily verbal assaults serve to constantly diminish us and condemn us to a slower (but nevertheless ultimately very similar) death. We (observed Martin Luther King, Jr.) "see ominous clouds of inferiority beginning to form in" our "little mental" skies; we become de-moralized and disillusioned: "at a loss for words" precisely when we each need words most urgently to protect our most valuable psychological asset— our self.

All of us have been in situations where words have very much harmed us. All of us have been in situations where the right words, spoken in the right way, at the right time, would have protected us from an especially vicious verbal assault. Words have failed us all at times ("words fail me"), and that's why we all need to read this book.

—Sheldon Solomon, Ph.D., Professor of Psychology at Skidmore College

Sheldon Solomon, Ph.D., has been Professor of Psychology at Skidmore College since 1980. He was recently honored by his faculty colleagues as the 1998 Edwin Mosley Lecturer. As an experimental social psychologist, his interests include the nature of self consciousness and social psychology. His work exploring the effects of the fear of death on all aspects of individual and social behavior has been supported by the National Science Foundation and reported in *The New York Times,* the *Herald Tribune,* the *Boston Globe, Psychology Today,* and *Self* magazine. He is co-author of the forthcoming book *Self-Esteem & Meaning* (APA Books, 2000).

Introduction

Every time you flick on your TV and channel surf, you can't seem to escape seeing one of these self-appointed motivational gurus telling you how you can have a fantastic, phenomenal, heavenly life simply by achieving one or more of the following goals:

Locate your lost powers so that you can have your own zillion-dollar company, tropical island, a closet full of Armani, a limo, yacht, jet, and mansions in every state. Otherwise you're a LOSER! Make marathon love with your partner so that he or she will be faithful! (Who would even have the energy to cheat, let alone walk, after a night of continuous orgasms?) Lose that disgusting fat! Get off your butt and exercise! Confused about which of the zillion exercise machines to buy? Make it easy on yourself. Get them all! The same goes for that "miracle weight loss" food, drink, pill, or diet. Try them all, but stick with the one that makes you puke less. Get hair! Nobody looks good without hair! It doesn't matter if it comes in a can and you spray it on—just get some damn hair! And your skin—UGH! Get rid of those repulsive blackheads, whiteheads, and pus heads! If you don't hurry up and use that lotion, you may end up being someone's weight-loss program, because they won't be able to keep any food down if they look at you.

Even though you may be chuckling at these scenarios, the unfortunate truth is that these commercials and other outside influences in the media unfairly affect the way we see who is pretty, who has a nice body, who is socially acceptable, and who is a winner! Heaven forbid you fall short of the "rules for acceptability." You are then relegated to the position of social leper. The strange thing is that we have all been social lepers at one point in our lives, and we continue to remain social lepers in the eyes of others. Maybe it's a lot of people or maybe it's just a few people. If we weren't perceived so negatively and with such hostility, why would others, even perfect strangers, go out of their way to come up to us just to give us verbal hell?

Even if you have all of the things mentioned in the scenario above—which, by our societies standards make you a "success"—you can still be a social leper. Even if you are a zillionare who's fit, without a zit, and even has hair, some people still won't like you. Who knows why? They just won't. And because they won't, they will try to make your life hell. They will give you dirty looks and try to undermine you, negate you, and say awful things to you.

How do I know this? I know it firsthand from the thousands of people I have seen in my private practices throughout the years who have been devastated by some unkindness or vulgarity someone has said to them. I have received letters and calls from thousands of people around the world who have responded to my book *Toxic People— 10 Ways to Handle People Who Make Your Life Miserable*. They have shared with me their devastation at the horrible things others have said to them. These letters and calls touch me deeply. They bring tears to my eyes as I feel for those who wrote and called.

What You'll Learn in This Book

No matter how much light we make of it, this is a very serious problem. Harsh words do hurt. Mean statements do sting. Insensitive comments do devastate. Prolonged emotional pain due to constant verbal harassment can physically maim and even kill. We often carry negative things people have said to us to our graves. Thus, words can cause us a lifetime of pain, anguish, and agony.

This book however, was not designed to teach you how to start fights or wars! Instead, its goal is to teach you how to defend yourself against those who start verbal fights with you. It will help you recognize who the verbal enemy is and what strategies would work best to defeat them. As you learn the strategies available to you in your attempts to deflect the verbal attacks, you will develop a newfound sense of self-confidence.

It's time to find a solution! It's time to fight back! It's time to relinquish the pain! It's time to never let anyone put their mean words or verbal poison on you again! *It's time to never be a verbal victim again!*

How This Book Is Organized

The chapters in this book fall into six different parts, which take you through the process of how to effectively defend yourself from the verbal dragons of the world.

Part 1, "Identifying the Verbally Venomous Opponent," shows you how to size up your verbally offensive opponent. You will learn the telltale emotional and physical signs of being verbally zapped. It's essential to know exactly what type of person is verbally zapping you. These verbal abusers fall into one of two categories, depending upon the severity of their verbal abuse. I will tell you the characteristics of each of these different types of verbal abusers and how to immediately spot their abuse before it's too late. Knowing this can save you from any emotional and physical torture you could possibly expect from this individual in the future. Finally, you will receive some insight as to some of the underlying psychological reasons someone becomes a verbal abuser and the disastrous long-term consequences of allowing verbal abuse to continue.

Before you can begin to fight your offensive opponent, you need to prepare yourself thoroughly for battle. You need to have all of the necessary equipment available to you. In Part 2, "Preparing to Verbally Defend Yourself," you will learn everything you need to know about doing so. It is not enough that your equipment and weaponry is in functioning order. It has to be in tip-top shape. If it isn't, you must do whatever you can to make sure that it gets in that condition. This section will show you all of the ways to have the most polished equipment, so that it is far superior to and outshines your opponent's.

In Part 3, "Verbal Defense Strategies to Use in Combat," I give you all of the strategies you can use in order to defend yourself against your verbal adversary. These proven techniques range from the benign to the most powerful. You will learn the most effective verbal-defense tactics to use in certain circumstances. You will also learn when it's time to put up the white flag and surrender.

Part 4, "Verbal Warfare with Specific People in Your Life," tells you how to defend yourself against members of the opposite sex—husband, wives, lovers, and co-workers. You will learn the best strategies to use with family members, from children to teens to siblings to parents. Finally you will learn the best tactics to use against any specific opponent who could possibly cross your path. You will learn defense strategies for those you are closer to and must see more often (such as friends, co-workers, and employers), to those you may see on occasion (professionals, police officers, and food servers), to those with whom you rarely have contact (customer-service representatives, attorneys, and store clerks). You will learn the most effective strategies to use based upon these people and what effect they can have on your life.

Part 5, "Verbal Combat Against Verbal Vermin," gets very specific, breaking down the exact verbal defense strategies to use with particular types of verbal vermin. The verbal vermin discussed come in three categories—merely annoying, repulsive and disgusting, and downright lethal. The more threatening the verbal vermin are to your well-being and to you life, the stronger is the verbal weaponry employed. Obviously, the less threatening and more annoying the verbal vermin is to you, the more benign weaponry is utilized. You will learn exactly which type of verbal weapons are best suited for each of the three types of verbal abusers.

In the sixth and final part of this book, "Dodging Verbal Bullets in Specific Battlefields," you will learn exactly what to say and how to say it in a myriad of situations, including getting rid of unwanted phone solicitors, letting someone know you don't want to be used and exploited, dealing with sexist or racist remarks, breaking bad news to someone, admitting your mistakes, confronting someone about their mistakes, and speaking to someone who has a lifestyle you may not support.

You will also learn what to say in life-or-death situations, from calling 911 to discussing AIDS and condom usage to verbally protecting yourself against road rage, violence, and even rape. The end of the book focuses on the power of the word and how what you say about yourself has a profound effect on your world around you. You will learn how to control your tongue so that what you say and how you say it always works in your defense and not against you.

Extras

The Complete Idiot Guide series allows you to learn even more information in a rather unique way. Specific information is presented to you in a concise and easy-to-read manner. These extra pieces or bits of information are categorized into four sections: "Talk Back Tips," "Verbal Vignette," "Bon Mots," and "Listen Up!" Each section is easy to locate because it appears in a gray box on the page.

Verbal Vignette

Verbal Vignette contain information regarding scientific studies, important quotations, and illustrative moments from the world of interpersonal communication.

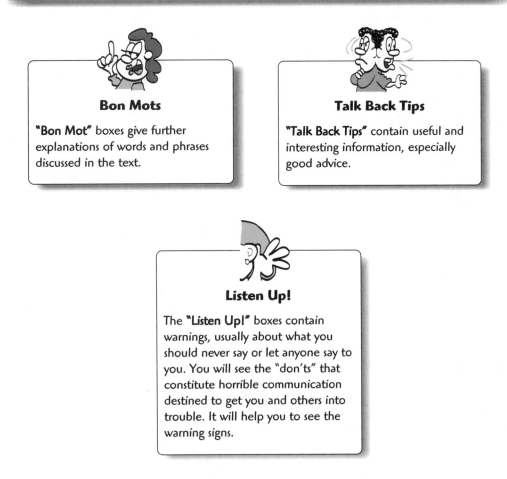

Bon Mots

"**Bon Mot**" boxes give further explanations of words and phrases discussed in the text.

Talk Back Tips

"**Talk Back Tips**" contain useful and interesting information, especially good advice.

Listen Up!

The "**Listen Up!**" boxes contain warnings, usually about what you should never say or let anyone say to you. You will see the "don'ts" that constitute horrible communication destined to get you and others into trouble. It will help you to see the warning signs.

Throughout the book you'll also see special inserts, "Talk Back" boxes. These give samples of conversations that represent both good and bad examples of how to talk with someone. Even though many of the conversations and dialogue may amuse you, keep in mind that people actually do speak like this. People say things that get them into trouble. Perhaps by being a voyeur and seeing what these people say, you'll be more aware of bad patterns and not follow suit. On the other hand, some dialogue in these boxes will also show you how to say it right!

Dedication

To my brother and very best friend in the world Manny M. Glass, who without his incredible wisdom and insight, and a lifetime of being my "mentor" in the area of communication, this book would never have been done. I thank you for your efforts in helping me with the research for this book and for putting your many brilliant ideas and theories into words so that others can benefit from them as I have. As my protector and big brother, you have showed me a lifetime of what it means to speak up for yourself—to say what you mean—to mean what you say—and to say it so that others will hear you. Manny, how lucky I am to have studied the "Art of Verbal Self-Defense" from the master—YOU!

Acknowledgements

To my best friend and mother Rosalie Glass, for loving and adoring me with every inch of her heart and soul. It is largely because of this extraordinary woman that I am able to give back to the world the integrity, warmth, decency, sensitivity, and love that she has instilled in me throughout my entire life! I am blessed and truly grateful for this special gift!

I wish to thank my agent Jane Dystel for being so encouraging and supportive to me in all of my literary endeavors.

To Nancy Mikhail for soliciting me to write this book and affording me the opportunity to help relieve a lot of anguish in the lives of those who will read this book.

To Jessica Faust, my editor, for her insight and professionalism towards this project. Thank you to my developer and editor, John Jones, for his support, kind words, encouragement, and for our thought-provoking conversations; and my copy editor, Erik Dafforn and production editor, Robyn Burnett.

To Tom Brennan, Susan Kaplan, Kevin Thranow, Laura Kovach and Anthony Mora of Anthony Mora Communications, who have consistently proven to be my best PR agents.

To each and everyone of my clients, readers, listeners, seminar audiences, and television viewers who have shared their beautiful words, lovely thoughts, and heartfelt blessings, and by letting me know that in some way, I made a definite difference in their lives! I am both honored and humbled.

And, finally, to all of my dear friends and colleagues in the media, I thank you for your love, affection, and support, and for giving me the gift of be able to do what I love the most: getting my message—Global Peace Through Communication—out to the world.

Feel Free to Get in Touch with Me!

I am here for you! There are other products available to you (books, tapes, videos, and so on) including two new products that have been in enormous demand—tapes and CDs with music and lyrics I have designed to both entertain you and to make you feel good.

They are readily available to you and can be ordered at the back of the book. You will receive them as soon as possible.

In addition, because of the numerous requests I have had from people all over the world, I have made e-mail and telephone consultations available to you. Now you can feel free to call me up or to e-mail me with your specific problem. For a fee, listed in the back of this book, I will consult with you in helping to answer any of your specific questions in helping you to apply the techniques in this book and those in my others. I will help you help yourself in resolving your own specific relationship problems, business dilemmas, or personal and family issues that are bothering you, consuming your thoughts, and holding you back from living a happy, pro-active, and productive live.

If you would like to set up such a telephone appointment, order books, tapes, products, or my music tapes and CDs, e-mail me at **info@drlillianglass.com**, **www.drlillianglass.com, or call (212) 946-5729**. Leave your name, address, e-mail address, and phone number

You can even write to me for more information at one of the following addresses:

Dr. Lillian Glass
c/o Your Total Image Inc.
P.O. Box 792
NYC, NY 10021

Dr. Lillian Glass
c/o Your Total Image Inc.
435 N. Bedford Dr. Suite 413
Beverly Hills, Ca. 90210

I look forward to hearing from you and being of service to you.

Trademarks

All terms mentioned in this book that are known to be or are suspected of being trademarks or service marks have been appropriately capitalized. Alpha Books and Macmillan General Reference cannot attest to the accuracy of this information. Use of a term in this book should not be regarded as affecting the validity of any trademark or service mark.

Part 1
Identifying the Verbally Venomous Opponent

When you "know before whom you stand," you know everything you need to about how to navigate successfully through life. Living becomes so much easier and safer when you know the animal you are around, and then you won't need to feel scared, insecure, or threatened.

The animal kingdom shows a great awareness of "knowing before whom one stands." Animals' very survival depends on it. Is another animal friend or foe? Will one be ignored, played with, or become a meal? We know from personal observation that dogs need a lot of attention and love to play whenever possible. Cats are usually independent, demanding less attention; chimps often mimic whatever you do; pigs usually roll around in dirt; and goats eat just about anything you put in front of them. You just know that an iguana will never cuddle up to you and that a large boa constrictor can wrap itself around you, squeezing your guts out. We also know to beware of a hissing cat or a dog bearing its teeth, growling, or foaming at the mouth.

By knowing the behavior of animals, you know what you can expect from them so that you can act accordingly. Unfortunately, when it comes to the human animal, most of us rarely pay attention to whom we are in front of. We are often shocked and disappointed by human actions when we find out they have lied, betrayed, or refused to make a decision. Learning to look at or listen to who is standing in front of us, however, teaches us what to expect and saves us untold amounts of grief and disappointment.

In Part 1 of this book, you learn to spot the dangerous human lions and tigers that are ready to attack you—not with their teeth, but with their vicious words.

Chapter 1

Identifying the Verbally Venomous Opponent

In This Chapter

➤ Systematically identifying potential verbal attackers

➤ Facial expressions to look for

➤ Body language to look for

➤ Listening to how they sound when they talk to you

Because knowledge is power, identifying your verbally offensive opponent can provide you with the warning signals that the verbal enemy is approaching and ready to attack at any time. It helps you develop verbal radar so that you know who is most likely to be your verbal opponent and what weapons that opponent will likely use to verbally attack you. By identifying would-be attackers immediately, you will be on guard to either ward off their verbal advances or verbally attack back. Close examination of their facial, body, and verbal language can help you determine whether you are standing in front of a friend or foe.

Stop, Look, and Listen—Sizing Up Your Opponent

How many nights have you stayed awake tossing and turning because of an awful, searing comment someone made to you? As you toss and turn, unable to find a comfortable position, you feel like kicking yourself for not saying this or that in retort to the venomous statement. The more you replay the toxic scenario in your mind, the harder you feel like kicking yourself for not following your "gut" instincts about the person.

If it makes you feel any better, this scenario has happened to just about everyone over the age of 10. The reason why you didn't "go with your gut" and act accordingly is because you didn't take the time to *stop, look,* and *listen.* This basic rule of caution for crossing the street is also the basic rule of caution for verbal self-defense. First, *stop* in your tracks and assess the situation so that you don't blindly walk into oncoming traffic. Second, *look* for any oncoming vehicles. Third, *listen* for any oncoming vehicles that may sneak up on you, maiming or hurting you.

Talk Back Tips

"Looking" means observing many levels of a person's behavior, including body language, facial expression, posture, and movement.

Follow this same procedure with everyone you encounter. First, *stop* in your tracks and assess the situation so that you don't step blindly into oncoming verbal traffic. Then *look* at the entire person.

For instance, observe her body language, the distance she is standing away from you, her facial expression, and shoulder, arm, and hand posture and movement. Now you are ready to open your ears and objectively *listen* to what she says and how she says it to you. This loudly and clearly announces any oncoming verbal assassins who may try to sneak up on you, emotionally maiming you.

20/20 Hindsight

If you would have stopped, looked, and listened, you would have had a good night's sleep. You would have seen that your potential "business associate" could not even look you in the eye when speaking with you. When he did manage to look in your direction, his eyebrows were furrowed, and his lips were pursed, tense, and pulled over to one side. You would have seen that he was always leaning away from you, inching farther and farther away anytime you got close to him. His physical gestures and demeanor towards you were completely opposite of those he showed your attractive, shapely assistant when she entered the room. In that case, he moved closer to her, smiled, and was wide-eyed, unable to take his eyes off her as he made some inane comments to her. Had you "listened" more carefully, you would have heard him clearly through his bravado. You would have noticed that whenever you asked him a poignant question, he never really answered you. He was evasive, continually interrupted you, and changed the subject whenever you tried to probe further.

By stopping, looking, and listening, you would have seen ahead of time what was coming. You would have heard his constant bragging as a cue that he was trying way too hard to convince you of how powerful he was. You would not have been so ready to dismiss his sexist remarks about your assistant and other females you discussed—remarks indicating his disrespect for women. You would have interpreted his evasiveness as a sign that he had something to hide. You would have seen his inability to look at you (especially after you asked him a significant question), his squirming, and his distancing himself from you as indications that he felt discomfort around you. In your 20/20 hindsight, you knew all along that not only was he disrespectful towards women, but he was obviously not being honest with you.

Freeze and Focus

Remember when you played musical chairs as a child? While the music played, you marched around the chairs, which always numbered one fewer than the number of children who marched around them. When the music stopped you were told to freeze and whoever wasn't positioned in front of a chair was disqualified from the game. That moment of freezing allowed you to assess whether you had a chair in front of you. The same is true whenever you find yourself in front of others. You need to freeze for a moment to assess who the person really is. Just be careful not to go into a catatonic stupor and freeze in some contorted position.

Before sizing up your opponent, it is essential for you to initially keep your mind open—a *tabula rasa*.

You must be objective, putting all prejudices aside. Blow out preconceived notions and open your mind so that you can objectively input the visual and aural information into your mind's computer.

Directly face the person. Through your nose, breathe in air for three seconds while you visually take in information about him. As he speaks, continue this breathing pattern of slowly breathing air in through your nose, holding it for three seconds, and then slowly exhaling it for 10 seconds, until you have comfortably expelled all the air in your lungs. All the time you are breathing the air in through your nose, absorb what the person is doing with his posture, stance, body, arms, hands, and face.

As you begin to interact with him, absorb what he is saying and how he says it. As you breathe in the air through your nose, hold it, then slowly exhale it while listening to him. "Stopping" gives you the opportunity to digest and process everything he said. It gives you the valuable time needed to analyze what he is relaying to you and for you to respond accordingly.

Bon Mots

Tabula rasa means "clean slate." In philosophy, it refers to the idea that when a person is born, her mind hasn't yet learned any of the facts and opinions it later acquires. In this book, I use it to mean something we as adults can attain, clearing our minds of extraneous ideas so that we can focus on what is immediately before us.

Reading Between the Lines

We've all heard that you can't judge a book by its cover. While this adage is partially true—you can't judge a book's content by its cover—you can certainly determine a lot of other things from its cover. For instance, when browsing in a bookstore, you can assess whether the book in front of you has been handled by many, few, or no potential readers; and whether it is old or new; expensive or cheap.

Similarly, you can determine a great deal about a person just by objectively looking and observing her. Of course, it is odious to judge and to react to people by the color of their skin, their physical stature, hair, height, weight, body, or facial appearance—things they can do little or nothing about, and that have nothing to do with their character. These erroneous and dangerous perceptions breed prejudice and hatred, the cancer of our society. Furthermore they tell you nothing at all about what the person is like. On the other hand, things people can control—the way they act and comport themselves—are appropriate ways to evaluate people. By observing the way people comport themselves and their bodily and facial actions, you can learn a great deal about them, especially in terms of how they relate to you.

Talk Back Tips

The information presented in this section is not based upon subjective prejudicial opinion, but on current scientific research in psychosocial perception of human behavior.

When you learn to objectively read between the lines, you will see things about the other person you never noticed before. This information often gives you the added advantage during your interactions, because you no longer merely "look." Now you will see the truth—what is actually going on.

Looking Between the Lines Quiz

1. Is he standing too close to you?
2. Is he standing to far away from you? Does he lunge forward when speaking to you?
3. Is his posture hunched over? Are his shoulders slumped?
4. Is his posture rigid?
5. Does he rock back and forth when he speaks?
6. Is she in constant motion?
7. Are her arms and hands in constant motion?
8. Does she gesture wildly?
9. Does she take up a lot of room, invading your space?
10. Is she tentative in her walk?
11. Is he tentative in his movements?
12. Does his jaw jut forward when he speaks or listens?
13. Is his head bowed downward?
14. Does he make gestures opposite to what he says (for example, shaking his head "no" when he says "yes")?

15. Does he clench his jaw while listening to you?

16. Does she exhibit extraneous facial tics or muscle throbbing when she listens?

17. Do veins, vessels, and muscles in her neck stick out when she speaks?

18. Does she have trouble looking at you while she listens?

19. Does she look away when speaking with you?

20. Does she stare?

21. Does he have an icy cold stare?

22. Does he smile when he looks at you?

23. Does he furrow his brow (as if frowning)?

24. Does he gaze upward when speaking or listening?

25. Does he frown when looking at or listening to you?

26. Does she have a blank look when you speak to her?

27. Is she nodding her head in agreement when you speak?

28. Does she shake her head "no" when listening to you speak?

29. Does she have a disgusted look when talking with you?

30. Does she smile too quickly or inappropriately?

31. Does he look askance at you when you speak—with forehead furrowed, mouth pulled to the side, and one eyebrow lifted?

32. Are his nostrils flared when speaking with you?

33. Is his mouth open when listening to you?

34. Does he instinctively raise his hand to his cheeks?

35. Does his face rest on his knuckles while listening to you?

Later in this book, you learn the possible meanings of each of these observations.

Telltale Eyes

We have all heard that the "eyes are the windows to the soul." Eyes tell us so much about another person. Our eyes are constantly moving as we think, observe, or speak.

When someone doesn't look at you, what does it really mean? Do you immediately think there is something wrong with you, that he is not interested in you or that he is insecure or lacks confidence? The answer may be any or all of the above. In the following section you learn what someone is really saying to you as you decipher what his eyes are telling you.

Here's Looking (or Not Looking) at You, Kid!

Eyes also signal when you can answer a question, or when it's your turn to talk. When you wish to speak, you usually look into a person's eyes. When she looks back at you, that indicates that it is your turn to speak. This eye contact is typically broken for a few seconds when you start to speak. Thus, those who may not relate well to you or who disrespect what you have to say might never reestablish the eye contact, which would indicate that it is again your turn to speak, even after you interject a comment. This type of behavior often occurs with toxic individuals who are bullies, narcissists, or unconscious of anyone but themselves. Other people might always look around the room when they speak, never making eye contact or even gazing in your direction. These people may not be socially adept and may feel uncomfortable or insecure in your presence.

If the person looks up toward the sky when they speak, they may be "thinking" or trying to recall something. Looking from side to side may also indicate "thinking" in addition to being unsure or doubting something. If a person's eyes dart back and forth quickly, they might be nervous or uncomfortable around you.

Talk Back Tips

It is largely through analysis of another's eyes that we can determine how that person feels about us. In essence, eyes can be an indicator of a person's emotional state at a particular point in time.

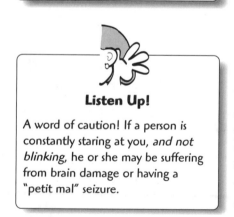

Listen Up!

A word of caution! If a person is constantly staring at you, *and not blinking,* he or she may be suffering from brain damage or having a "petit mal" seizure.

In contrast, constant piercing stares can either debilitate or stimulate. If someone "can't take his eyes off you" and stares right into your eyes without smiling, this is not a good sign. It can be not only disconcerting, but frightening. This person is furious with you or can't stand you. The length of time he or she stares at you in that manner may indicate the degree of hostility towards you, and your personal safety could be in jeopardy. This is often the case in persons who are completely out of control with extreme mental disturbances and a tendency toward violent reactions. But not all forms of continuous staring without a smile indicate that violence is on the way.

Once, when I was seeing a client, he stopped talking midsentence during our conversation and stared blankly at me for what seemed to be an eternity. This was jarring, and my heart was pounding as I was thinking that he might turn violent at any moment. It turned out that he was having a seizure.

On the other hand, constant staring may indicate that a person is madly in love with you. In this case the pupils enlarge due to a chemical response in the brain and the subsequent action of the autonomic nervous system.

When people gaze downward at you, "stare you down," or look you over from head to toe, they are telling you that they think they are better than you. They are putting you in a weaker position during an argument. When a brow is furrowed, the eyes are narrowed as in squinting, you can be assured that the person didn't like something you said, doesn't like you, or is angry with you.

Opening the eyes widely may indicate that the person is either surprised by something you are saying or is trying to be emphatic about what they are saying to you. Looking down may indicate the person is embarrassed, ashamed or saddened, or has poor self-esteem, not feeling worthy or deserving.

Excessive blinking may reflect insecurity about what the person is trying to project. It may also indicate that a person may not be telling the truth. Lying isn't always determined by whether or not a person looks at you. In fact, good liars can unflinchingly look into your eyes and tell a lie, and even continue to look into your eyes after they are accused. Research shows that when most of us are caught in a lie we will look away and if we are innocent will look at the person, but will not stare in their eyes.

A Machiavellian person will constantly stare into the accuser's eyes—an unnatural behavior where they are consciously attempting to appear as though they have nothing to hide. This may be mistaken for honesty. Therefore eye contact is not the only indicator to use in determining a person's guilt or innocence, but it can be a significant factor.

If someone is looking into the distance, at her watch, or is being distracted by another object, chances are she is bored with what you're saying or not interested in you.

Talk Back Tips

If someone is really interested in what you are saying, she will look at your face about 75 percent of the time she is speaking with you. These glances can range anywhere from one to ten seconds in length.

Face Off

Besides a person's eyes, facial movements tell us a lot about how and what people are thinking about us. Approximately 75 percent of our nonverbal communication is done with our face. According to Dr. Paul Ekman at the University of San Francisco, there are approximately six basic emotions that we express through our face: happiness, sadness, anger, disgust, surprise, and fear. No matter what culture you are from—whether New Guinea, China, Africa, or France—these facial expressions are universal. Even though cultural differences still exist, the fact that we all express emotion similarly is one more reason to celebrate the similarities—and not the differences—between people.

Many people, businessmen in particular, have been trained to use a poker face to catch their opponents (and sometimes their colleagues) off guard. If enough time is spent together, however, people's true feelings eventually emerge. The limbic system, located deep within the brain, uncovers our emotions—how we feel. Even if we voluntarily try to control our facial movements to hide our true feelings, the involuntary aspects of the brain eventually take over, unmasking the truth.

The gamut of human emotions is revealed throughout a conversation, so if you pay close attention you will almost always know how the person is feeling at a particular point in the conversation. A conversation might begin with the person's eyebrows raised and head cocked to the side, which reveals that he doubts what you are saying. As you continue to speak, you may then see the corners of his mouth turn up, indicating that he is amused by what you're saying. As the conversation continues, three hours later you may see his slightly flared nostrils, a slightly protruded lower lip, and a perpetual slight smile as you continue to speak, thereby indicting that he has "fallen in love" with you.

Telltale Mouth

The mouth is a barometer of how happy or angry a person is. If someone is grimacing, or tightening or pursing her lips, she is usually frustrated or annoyed with you. If her annoyance with you persists, her facial expression may turn to disgust as she raises her chin and upper lip and wrinkles her nose. If she is unhappy or sad being with you, her face will appear expressionless (with the exception of her eyes and surrounding muscles) and her lower lip will turn downward. If she is nervous around you, you may notice her sucking, biting, chewing, or licking her lips a lot. She may smile nervously, wherein she immediately smiles (often at inappropriate times) and then resumes her normal facial expression.

Verbal Vignette

When approached by a new student who speaks to her through a clenched jaw, world-renowned actress and acting coach Nina Foch usually asks the student which parent he or she is angry at. Her observation that a tight jaw signifies anger has been documented by psychologists worldwide. Therefore, if you see someone's jaw tensing up and their lips tightening, chances are he is mad at you, someone else, or the world.

This is what physically happens to your face when you express the following emotions.

Happiness   Smiling mouth
                                          Cheeks raised
                                          Lips parted

	Jaw slightly dropped Wrinkles around eyes Eyes relaxed and narrowed
Sadness	Eyebrows raised Forehead wrinkled Lower lip depressed—turned downward Upper eyelids lowered
Anger	Eyebrows lowered Hard stare Lips raised Open mouth
Disgust	Lower eyelid pushed up Upper lip raised Nose wrinkled Open mouth Chin raised Eyebrows lowered Eyes tensed and narrowed
Surprise	Eyebrows raised Upper eyelids slightly raised Mouth open Jaw drops
Fear	Eyebrows raised Upper lids raised Lips stretched Mouth open Tense, open eyes

Body Talk

Just as the face tells no lies, neither does the body. Like we use our faces, we use universal signals in order to get our message across, signals that transcend different cultures. The physical distance we keep, the way we stand, our arm and hand movements, our head position, how we shake hands, and how we touch tells us if there is a verbal enemy among us.

Keep Your Distance!

We know whether people like being around us by how physically close or distant they are. People who inch away from you as you inch towards them don't feel the same towards you as you do towards them. They feel uncomfortable around you and want to get away. People who invade your space by getting a little too close may be from another culture, where the norm in communication is such physical closeness, or they may really like you and want to get as close as they can to you.

On the other hand, getting too close may be a power trip, where the person is attempting to be dominant over you. Getting too close and invading one's space is an intimidation technique many business people use to gain the psychological "upper hand" in the situation.

Stand Up!

People's posture can convey their attitude regarding how they feel about us and how they feel about themselves. For example, a person with a low self-image may often slouch. If he doesn't slouch around others, but slouches around you, he may be demonstrating his feelings of subservience or intimidation by "minimizing" himself in your presence. If someone is really attentive to you, he will usually lean forward with straight spine, arms open. If he is relaxed around you, he will lean back with his head positioned upwards and limbs relaxed. A person who is interested in you will have his body turned towards you, while his lack of interest in you will be reflected in his body being turned away from you.

If she is bored or nervous around you, she will usually cross and uncross her legs; rock back and forth while sitting or standing; stretch; or fiddle with her hands, and tap her fingers or feet. Her body may be tense, rigid if she is nervous, and have a seemingly uncontrollable shake. Foot-tapping indicates nervousness and anxiety.

If you have hurt someone or made them sad, his body will be overly loose, with slow and deliberate movements. On the other hand, if he is standing too still or has a rigid posture, he may be uptight and nervous. If his posture is rigid and he is backing away from you, chances are he can't wait to get away from you.

Talk Back Tips

There is some truth in the expression "hand-wringing." When people cup their hands together and rub them back and forth over their knuckles, they are experiencing extreme nervousness and emotional discomfort, unlike when people rub the palms of their hands together. In doing that, they may just be trying to get warm.

Armed with Arms and Hands

Fiddling with one's hands, tapping fingers, rubbing the fingers together, picking the cuticles, or biting one's fingers or nails often indicates nervousness or discomfort in a situation.

Crossing arms often indicates hostility, as does putting the hands on both hips, finger pointing, rapid and uncontrolled arm and hand movements, and clenching of the fists.

Excessive, overly dramatic arm and hand movements may indeed be cultural, but pay close attention, because the person may be expressing irritation with you in trying to be overly convincing in an attempt to sway your opinion.

Crossing and uncrossing the arms usually means that you or what you have just said bore the listener. When someone is really frustrated, he may gesture excessively with his hands and he may point if he is both angry and frustrated. If he is extremely annoyed, he may put his hands on his head and rub the head.

It is essential to note that if someone is just giving up and submitting to you, they may indicate this by throwing their hands up in the air. If someone can't seem to make a decision, they may open and shut their hands, or there may be one hand, then the other, in motion. This act will usually be repeated several times in succession.

Hand-to-Hand Combat

The way that people shake your hand tells you a lot about them and how they feel about you. It is, however, important to note that a handshake is also cultural. In Japan, bowing is the mode of greeting and saying goodbye. When Japanese are forced into communicating with Americans, their handshake is often soft and fishlike. This is because they may feel uncomfortable and tentative, as it is an act that is out of their usual social norm. Outside of the Japanese culture, however, a light and soft hand-shake usually means that the person is timid or unsure of himself, or of you. It may also indicate submissiveness.

In contrast, a firm handshake may indicate self-confidence or confidence in you. If however the handshake is too firm, where the person is squeezing your hand too tightly, they may be trying to establish dominance or power over you. An overly firm handshake may also reflect an inner hostility towards you. Unless the person's arm is disabled, if you extend your hand and she doesn't accept it, or refuses to acknowledge it, she may be saying that she really can't stand you and that she wants nothing to do with you; this is an extremely hostile act.

A clammy or wet hand often reflects nervousness, however there are some cases where the person may have a medical condition that causes excessive perspiration.

Talk Back Tips

When assessing your opponent's body, facial, and vocal language, it is essential for you to realize that no single element indicates a person's behavior or how they are feeling toward you. Instead, it involves a combination of all these factors in order to get the total picture.

Listening Between the Lines

Just as you absorb people with your eyes, you need to absorb them equally with your ears to determine who they are and whether they can help you or harm you. You not only need to listen to what is said, but how it is said. How people speak to you is just as revealing as how they physically act around you.

Telling Tones

After studying the way people communicate for nearly two decades, I have discovered that the tone of one's voice may be the most important factor in determining how someone really feels about himself and about you. What goes on in one's head and in one's heart is clearly reflected in the tone of his voice.

Before discussing what voice and speech pattern may reflect about how people feel about themselves or you, note that many speech and vocal conditions result from genetic conditions or learned behaviors. For example, those who sound nasal may not be lazy, snobby, or condescending people, instead they may be suffering from a cleft on their palate (the roof of their mouth). On the other hand, they may be from an area of the country where the only way they learned to speak was nasal.

For the most part, those who speak in boring, monotonous tones are closed off emotionally and have many unresolved psychological issues. These people have difficulty initiating and maintaining intimate relationships because it is so difficult for others to "get a read on them" and communicate openly and freely with them.

Squeaking or Leaking?

If you encounter women who speak in a high-pitched, breathy, sickeningly sweet, accommodating vocal tone, run for your life! Women who speak to you in high-pitched, little-girl tones usually think they are being cute, girlish, and coquettish. This voice pattern usually reflects a great deal of inner hostility and passive-aggressiveness. If you hang around these people long enough, don't be surprised to hear the pitch of their voice drop down a few octaves. Watch them spew forth verbal lava from their once-delicate mouth.

A woman's high-pitched squeak can be extremely annoying and elicit a hostile reaction from others. I have witnessed this on several occasions.

Verbal Vignette

Once while hearing a squeaky-voiced stewardess giving the safety instructions over the loudspeaker, the audience of passengers mocked her, rolled their eyes, giggled, grimaced, or put their hands up to their ears. When she began taking drink orders, people responded to her with incredible hostility. The person sitting next to me, who knew that I was a psychologist trained as a speech pathologist, suggested that I give her my card immediately.

On one occasion, a squeaky-voiced store manager kept saying things over the loud-speaker until a patron screamed out "shut up, you're getting on my nerves. You sound like a damn chipmunk." Everyone who heard this bold man was in stitches. They felt the same way about her, but they dared not say anything.

When you hear the pitch of the voice (especially a man's voice) rising, you may want to consider the veracity of what the man is saying. This is often a "leakage" of one of the factors that constitutes whether a person is lying or telling the truth.

Tones Ready to Verbally Attack You

People who attack and speak to you in verbal bullets like a machine gun are angry at you, at themselves, or at the world. Stay clear of them. Oftentimes, their verbal hostility makes you react with equally hostility towards them. They may even be unconscious that they sound as hateful as they do and may question why you are speaking in such a hostile tone to them.

The same holds true for excessively loud talkers. In addition to their hostility, unless they have a conductive hearing loss, those who speak so loudly are often insecure, need a lot of attention, and crave to be noticed. This is also the case for men who have deep rich resonant voices but amplify the tone by speaking too loudly—especially in situations where everyone can hear them. Bullies often attack their tones in addition to being loud and obnoxious.

The Mouse That Roars

Those who speak in very soft tones may have hearing loss due to nerve damage, which reflects this type of speech pattern. On the other hand, those with soft voices may be speaking softly because of poor self-esteem and low self-confidence. They may be overly shy and may not feel that what they have to say is very worthy, significant, or important. Because of their low self-worth, most soft or timid speakers can be passive-aggressive. They may use their soft tones in order to force people to listen to them or to get attention from others as they are asked to "speak up." In essence, they may be speaking so low for "effect," in order to gain the upper hand by forcing people to listen closely to what they have to say. By speaking as softly as a mouse, they are usually not letting out any of their true emotions.

Listen Up!

Watch out for the *mice* of this world, because they may unexpectedly turn into lions and roar out the anger that they have stored within them for a long time.

"Tha tha that's all, folks!"

Porky Pig's infamous line at the end of cartoons makes me sick, because I have seen firsthand the devastation teasing causes to individuals who stutter or stammer. There is a lot of controversy about what causes stuttering or stammering (repetition or hesitation of words or sounds). Theories include beliefs that this speech behavior is inborn, reflects a neurological condition, is learned, reflects emotional conflict, or stems from being nervous.

We can see how the "nervousness theory" has become so popular, because most of us stutter or have stuttered at one point or another, especially if we have been around someone who makes us feel less than we are or who intimidates us. We often do it in situations that make us nervous, such as talking in front of others. On the other hand, when people hesitate or speak very slowly, you might want to question whether they are telling the truth, because that is another signal when people lie.

Where's the Foghorn?

Constant hoarse-sounding or raspy voices aren't necessarily sexy. They tend to reflect a person who is harboring a lot of hidden anger. Often these individuals develop growths on their vocal cords because of their constant misuse and anger. As part of their treatment to eliminate these growths or calluses on their vocal cords, they need to work through their inner rage.

Thylvesther the Cat Thaid What?

Like Porky Pig, Sylvester the Cat has tortured many people who lisp. While lisping or whistling *s* sounds may be normal in terms of a child's development or may be due to certain dental conditions, if it persists into adulthood there may be a psychological component.

Verbal Vignette

According to psychoanalysts such as Dr. Paul Cantalupo, those who mispronounce words and sounds as adults are often stuck in a childlike phase in their psychological development. They believe that an adult who mispronounces the *r* sound (not including a regionalism or an accent) usually has many unresolved childhood issues. Similarly, those with lisps that are cute at six are not cute at 26, 36, or 46.

With the exception of those who have dental conditions that lend themselves to lisping (crowns, buck teeth, overbites, underbites, and missing teeth), many cases have not been able to overcome their lisps despite speech therapy. It is not uncommon to find out that these individuals may have suffered some emotional trauma at the age when they were developing the *s* sound, around six or seven.

Slow Down, I Can't Keep Up!

Too fast a talker is usually a hyper person—a type A personality. They are tornadoes trying to do ten things at once with such urgency that they leave a wake of upset, annoyed, and intimidated people. Fast talkers alienate people because they are so difficult to understand. People who listen to them may feel as though they are being cheated, or talked into something, yet the fast talker may have completely honest intentions. For the most part, like the soft talker, the fast talker may be suffering from self-worth issues—not feeling worthy enough to be heard.

Aren't You Done Yet?

There are those who speak so slowly that you can fly from New York City to LA and back by the time they finish a sentence. Unless they are suffering from brain damage such as cerebral palsy or a stroke, or are mentally challenged, too-slow talkers are often self-absorbed. They are so concerned about saying everything correctly that they lose sight of who they are talking to. When you try to interrupt them, they usually ignore you and proceed talking. These people may also be "leaking" and not telling the truth.

Listen Up!

Just as you need to beware of the fast talker, beware of slow talkers!

The Rain in Spain Lies Mainly in the Plain

The hyper-articulate, precise talker is usually very uptight and precise, and everything has to be just so: in Freudian terms, "anal-retentive." They remind you of the stereo-typical old-maid school marm who slapped you on the wrists with a ruler if you kept pronouncing your words incorrectly. (Today this school marm would be doing time for her actions!)

These precise, hyper-articulate people usually have a desire to be noticed and thought of as better and smarter than others. They often act as though they know it all, pontificating and precisely pronouncing every "i" and emphasizing every "t." In reality, their behavior may mask extreme insecurities.

The Least You Need To Know

➤ Stop, look, and listen to people to see what they are all about.

➤ Carefully observe their eye contact, facial movements, mouth posture, body movement and stance, and what they are doing with their hands and arms. Watching each of these aspects of people can reveal more about them than you imagine.

➤ Carefully listen to the way they sound when they are talking to you. Listen for the pitch they use, harshness or attacking tones, softness or loudness, hesitations, hoarseness, lisping, and whether they talk too fast or too slow. All of these elements can say a great deal about people.

Chapter 2

Knowing When You've Been Verbally Zapped

In This Chapter

➤ Learn how to carefully listen to what someone says.

➤ Quiz: Have you been verbally abused?

➤ What happens physically when you're attacked verbally.

➤ What happens psychologically when people abuse you verbally.

Sometimes you get verbally zapped and you don't even realize it until it is too late. When you do finally realize it, you become psychologically and physiologically tortured as the devastating scenario runs through your mind over and over again. You often feel like kicking yourself because of what you could have said. You may start to assault yourself for being "stupid" and "ignorant" and not charging forth to defend yourself against your offensive adversary. By learning how to always be on guard for possible verbal arrows, you will save yourself a lot of grief and physical pain.

What Are They Really Saying to You?

Not only is it important to listen to how people speak to you, such as their tone of voice, it is equally important to listen to everything they say to you and I mean everything!

You need to develop 20/20 hearing—perfect pitch, in a way. You need to hear exactly what people say and process the words coming out of their mouths. You can't hear only what you want to hear or what you think (or hope) they mean.

Steve was devastated when Linda walked out on him. "How could she do this to me? There were no signs. She just left for no reason at all. She took the furniture and everything," said a perplexed Steve during his therapy session in my office. I probed and probed, until he finally realized that Linda in fact had told him she was going to leave him if he didn't start to open up and share himself emotionally as well as physically. After some intensive soul searching, he finally was able to remember one conversation where Linda screamed and yelled at him for not reacting to anything emotionally. He remembered that she called him a "coldblooded lizard with ice running through his veins." She said that she would clean him out of house and home, and then maybe he'd react.

Listen Up!

"I was only kidding" almost *never* means "I was only kidding."

Had Steve really listened to what she was saying, and had he gotten some therapy to help him more freely express himself verbally, the two of them might be together today, and Steve would at least still have a chair on which to sit and a bed on which to sleep! He thought she was "only kidding" when she gave him this ultimatum.

You Were Not "Only Kidding"

Like Steve, many of us think that the other person is only kidding when we hear something drastic or shocking. We tend to obliterate our emotional reaction to these verbal bombs, ignoring the message and dismissing it as a mere joke. We don't want to believe they just said what they said. But the truth is that they did say it, and you had better hear it, or it may be too late. For Steve, it was too late. He quickly learned that there was nothing funny when Linda acted on what she said. You must believe everything that someone says and not dismiss it as mere humor.

Freud once said that there are no jokes, "only truth." Those who say mean things or make cutting remarks are revealing how negatively they really feel towards you. With their shockingly hostile statements, they are actually telling you the truth. When they see the look of shock or anger cross your face, they immediately jump in with "I was only kidding." In essence, they punch you out, you fall down, and by dismissing their own hostile words as a joke, they deprive you of your chance to fight back or retort.

These hostile words will continue to resonate, however, as will the actions. "I was only kidding" is also a form of sadistic behavior. A person sees a flaw or something he doesn't like and relishes it, enjoying your problem in order to make himself feel better. By making the shocking statement to you and verbally slapping you in your face, he tells you how negatively he really feels about you.

We see many people do this to one another; we say that the victim who laughs it off is a "good sport." But there is nothing sporty about being cut down and then smiling about what was said, especially if the words sting you. You need to put a stop to anyone joking with you at your expense.

Common "Jokes" and Their Real Meanings

"Have another cookie, you wear it well. I was only kidding."
Translation: You are fat, so stop eating cookies.

"Were you in a fight? I was only kidding."
Translation: You look like hell.

"They'd never let you in. I'm just kidding."
Translation: You don't look presentable enough to be there. You're not hip enough or cool enough.

"Don't break a leg. I'm only kidding." (In response to you informing the person about your upcoming skiing trip.)
Translation: I'm so jealous I'm not going skiing with you.

"Where did you get that—out of the garbage can? I was only kidding."
Translation: I can't stand what you're wearing. It looks like a cheap piece of junk."

"I'll bet you robbed a bank to get that new car. I'm only kidding."
Translation: Where did *you* ever come up with the money to pay for that expensive sports car?"

"Don't worry about it, things usually work out—but not for you. Ha ha. I was just kidding!"
Translation: What a loser you are! ·

What's the Matter? Cat Got Your Tongue?

There is nothing more disconcerting than attempting to converse with someone who isn't willing to give you any information. They are verbal vampires, trying to suck out all of the information and energy from you and not giving you back anything in return. They are stingy with what they say to you. You might ask them reciprocal questions and hear them not answer, give you a short answer, or circumvent the question entirely, changing the subject and bringing the conversation back to you. These people are very dangerous and often sneaky backstabbers. They acquire all of the information from you and then take advantage of you and the situation.

If someone isn't holding up her end of the conversation, don't let your ego get in the way and think she is "flattering you." Instead, know that she is about to "flatten you." When you hear her deafening silence, shut up and don't give her any more of yourself. Put the ball in her court, no matter how awkward the stillness and quiet become. If she can't give you anything verbal in return, neither can you; end the conversation using techniques that you will learn later in this book.

If He Says He's a Jerk, Believe Him

When I was in college, the women in the dormitory had a rule. "If a guy tells you he's a jerk, believe him. He is!" One classmate argued with a well known jerk, insisting that he was really such a sweet and nice guy, dismissing his claims of being a jerk. But she finally had to agree with him when she saw him hitting on her roommate after he asked her to go steady with him.

The same holds true for women, of course, as well as for people with the opposite claim—those who tell you how *great* they are! Muhammad Ali said he was "the greatest"—he could "float like a butterfly and sting like a bee." He certainly knew what he was saying: he was the greatest boxer of our time.

Even though you might think that they are braggarts or obnoxious, most people who tell you they are the best are telling you that they have plenty of confidence in themselves. Of course, you have to watch out for people who have delusions of grandeur, such as someone who says she is the best singer when she has never taken a lesson and sounds off key. She very well might be the best singer—in her shower, when nobody else is around.

Thus, in addition to seeing the results, you do have to consider some history. Always listen very carefully to what people say about themselves. They are usually right.

Beware, You're Next!

If someone constantly disses (disrespects) others, you can rest assured that you are next on the "diss list." Some people can communicate with another person only when they are trashing someone. It makes them feel as though they are better and have one up on the person. That's why talk shows are currently such a success. If you see someone more miserable than you on television and share what you saw with someone as you chuckle to yourself, you don't feel that your life is in such bad shape after all.

Talk Back Tips

Wouldn't you rather go to a doctor who says, "I am the best in my field and I can definitely help you" than one who says, "I'm not sure about this, but I'll try to help you, even though I really don't know if I can?" The way people talk about their own abilities matters.

In reality, these are people with a lot of inner emotional conflict that hasn't been worked out yet. They are miserable and lonely people. They always put others down in order to build themselves up. These people are often the ones who will be nice to your face and then verbally stab you in the back. If you hear them go after someone one day, their tongue could easily be firing bullets at you the next morning as they make mincemeat out of you behind *your* back.

They Don't Really Mean That!

In their attempts to be civil, not make waves, or to appease you, people often make lame comments that you know may be untrue. They may make typical automatic responses when they really mean to say the opposite.

Now you must combine your newfound knowledge of reading people's body cues, facial cues, and vocal cues with what they are actually saying. Whenever you hear standard phrases such as the ones in the following list, be aware. Observing their physical and vocal manner in conjunction with these particular statements may tell you what they really mean and what they are truly feeling. Watch out for a tight-lipped smile, facial grimacing, a forced smile, a blank facial expression, ridged body posture, a lower pitch, or a monotone when they make these statements to appease you.

Talk Back Tips

Always remember to be aware of both the words a person speaks and the way the person speaks them.

If you observe any of these body cues, chances are that they think the opposite of what they're saying. On the other hand, if the body language, facial movements and voice pattern seem genuine, chances are that they do mean what they say, so "don't worry about it."

Expressions Said but Seldom Meant

1. Don't worry about it.
2. It's no big deal.
3. There's no problem whatsoever.
4. Don't give it a second thought
5. It'll all work out.
6. It doesn't bother me at all.
7. I really don't care.
8. Sure, go ahead.
9. I'm really sorry.
10. It's my fault.

Warning! You've Been Exposed to a Verbal Health Hazard

Remember the innocent mantra you learned as a child? "Sticks and stones can break my bones, but words can never hurt me." Wanna bet? The wrong words said to anyone, especially to a young and vulnerable child, are like glue. They stick to them forever—from ages 3 to 103.

The wrong kind of words can not only hurt you, they can emotionally maim you and even kill you.

The National Committee for the Prevention of Child Abuse and several psychologists who have treated abused children came up with the following list of commonly used remarks with which parents verbally abuse their children. Many parents make these comments, completely unaware of the damaging repercussions and lasting scars these words can have on their youngsters. If you have made any of these comments to your child, never do it again! Apologize to them.

Talk Back Tips

Even though an apology to your child can't take away what you said, it can garner more respect from your child, engender more self-respect, and give back some of your child's dignity, which in turn can enhance self-esteem.

You can also do this with employees. Remember, it takes a big person to apologize, whether a parent, child, sibling, spouse, employer, or employee. Those who can't bring themselves to say they are sorry are often bullies who believe that a kick in the pants is better than a pat on the back. Those who make these cruel statements are often miserable and bitter people with little or no feeling for anyone but themselves. They are often so consumed with self-loathing that they spew forth their toxic bullets towards anyone in their way. Most often, it is towards a defenseless family member, such as a child.

The following are abusive statements you must *never* say.

1. "You look terrible."
2. "Wear something else. You look awful."
3. "You're pathetic. You can't do anything right."
4. "You're so stupid. Can't you ever listen?"
5. "You disgust me. Just shut up!"
6. "If I would have known how much trouble you'd be, I never would have had you."
7. "Get out of here and don't come back."
8. "You make me sick."
9. "You're always wrong."
10. "Who asked you?"

Verbal Abuse—the Silent Killer

Sometimes you may not even be aware that you have been verbally abused. It's often like a silent killer, similar to a gas leak that slowly fills the room and eventually consumes you. You smell something, but you ignore it, thinking it will go away. But it doesn't go away, and then you become unconscious. Unless someone rushes into your home to save you, you will never wake up.

The following section contains a quiz to help you become more aware of whether you have been exposed to verbal abuse. Like the gas leak, the abuse may have taken place slowly until it consumed you. It may have affected your physical health or your emotional well-being, because the verbal abuse seems never to go away. Unless the information and knowledge you acquire from reading this book saves you, your physical and emotional suffering will become worse, until it takes a devastating toll on your body and psyche.

Quiz to Determine Exposure to Verbal Abuse

Answer the following questions with "yes" or "no," then read the section that follows to determine the level of verbal abuse that you've experienced.

1. Have you been told to deny or to minimize your emotions (for example, "don't cry," "keep a stiff upper lip," "stop getting worked up over nothing," "don't get so bent out of shape," and "take it easy")?

2. Were you told how wonderful you were in one breath and then in the next breath how horrible you are?

3. Did someone take the wind out of your sails or diminish what you say (such as, "you'll never be able to do that," "who do you think you are?", or "that's the stupidest idea I ever heard")?

4. Have you been contradicted whenever you say something, even though you know you are correct and have the data or the evidence to prove it?

5. Were you teased in a vicious manner, with the teaser not letting up no matter how upset you got?

6. Did you feel that someone was sadistic by secretly getting satisfaction out of seeing you emotionally hurt or upset?

7. Were you constantly threatened, or did someone hold over your head something that you were sensitive about?

8. Were you ridiculed after you told someone an intimate secret? Did that person tease you about it and constantly throw it back in your face when you least expected it?

9. Did he share your confidence with others after you said not to tell anyone else?

10. Did he speak to you in hostile, harsh, or angry tones?

11. Did she look away when you spoke or when she spoke to you?

12. Did she move away from you when you tried to speak to her?

13. Did he withhold information or neglect to give you vital information?

14. Did he always try to have a "leg up" and try to top anything you told him? Did you feel that he was always trying to compete with you?

15. Did she make you feel wrong, contradict you, or attempt to belittle or dismiss what you had to say in front of others?

16. Did she say something awful or shocking to you and then follow her comment by "I was only kidding?"

17. Did he seem to always accuse you or blame you by making statements beginning with "you never...," "you always...," "it's your fault that...," "you'd better...," or "why don't you ever...?"

18. Does she always try to instigate a fight?

19. Does she curse at you or use profanity?

20. Does he always seem to pick on you, telling you how bad you are and what you did wrong, rarely telling you what you ever did right?

21. Does he call you pejorative names or nicknames that he knows you don't like?

22. Does she constantly bring up something bad that happened in your past or a mistake you made, and never let you forget it?

23. Does she order you around, constantly making demands instead of making requests when she speaks to you?

24. Does he speak so softly that you can't hear him, even though you have heard him speak up when he wants to?

25. Does he bellow out loud and deafening tones when he speaks to you, but not when he speaks to others?

26. Is she always in a hurry or having to go whenever you want to talk with her?

27. Does she answer questions with a question, never giving you a direct answer?

28. Was getting him to talk like pulling teeth? Did he usually give one-word responses to your questions like "yep" or "nope?"

29. Does she say things to make you feel guilty?

30. Does she constantly belittle you or embarrass you in front of others?

31. Does he ignore, dismiss, or reject what you say?

What Do Your Answers Mean?

If you can answer "yes" to any of the 31 questions listed here, then you have definitely been exposed to verbal abuse. To determine the main culprits, write down the names of all those who have committed any of the acts of abuse listed here.

In doing so, you will begin to see a pattern emerge. For the first time, you may see that it is men more than women who are verbally abusive towards you, or vice versa. You may become more conscious of certain people who may be jealous of you or uncomfortable around you. You may see that you are abused with certain family members and not with others. You might see that you were more verbally abused as a child or teenager, as many of the names on your list will be those of people from your early years of life. You may also have numerous names next to one question, which may indicate that you may choose similar types of people who are toxic for you.

This quiz allows you to delve a little deeper and learn more about yourself. Here you can clearly see who your tormentors are (or were) and how they have specifically victimized you.

Ouch, It Hurts! The Physical Pain of Verbal Abuse

As was said earlier, words *do* hurt. Using words as weapons can cause tremendous physical pain, disease, and (as far-fetched as it may seem) can even result in death.

Physical reactions towards verbal abuse take place in stages. When someone verbally slaps you, your system suffers an initial shock. First your cortex, the top layer of your brain, receives the verbal message, which is processed in the appropriate areas of the brain, primarily on the left side, called Wernicke's area. After you have cognitively deciphered what was said, a deeper area of your brain, known as the *limbic system*, kicks in.

When you have been verbally abused your whole physiology changes, becoming different from the state at which you either heard pleasant things about yourself or when you felt neutral.

Now your autonomic nervous system, the system that controls your heart rate, pupil dilation, and blood flow, kicks in. The primitive "fight or flight" response emerges as you aim to physically protect yourself against the predators. Thus, your heart beats faster, the adrenaline flows, and your senses become heightened, making you more aware of what is occurring around you.

Listen Up!

Severe physical problems possibly exacerbated by chronic verbal abuse include ulcers, tempromandibular joint (TMJ) disorder, debilitating back or neck pain, asthma, heart disease, stroke, and cancer.

This is why your heart beats so fast, why blood rushes to or drains out of your face, or why you might develop a sudden headache. It is why you may become dizzy or lightheaded and feel as though you have had an "out-of-body" experience." It is also why you may have difficulty initially catching your breath after you have been verbally zapped and slapped. This is why your stomach tightens and begins to hurt or cramp, why your body becomes rigid, and why the muscles in your neck and back tense up.

If these physiological changes happen to you regularly, a particular area of your body may become weakened due to the added pressure placed upon it. For instance, constant pain and pressure in the abdominal region can cause an increase in stomach acid, which may result in ulcers. This pain can cause such discomfort that it can immobilize you, thereby jeopardizing your work and your interpersonal relationships.

Head Games Lead to Heart Pains

Constant physical stress can also affect the muscles in your heart, thereby weakening the main mechanism you need for life support. Your blood flow may be affected, which may cause heart dysfunction and even stroke. Research has repeatedly shown how added emotional distress can contribute to heart failure, which may kill a person. Similarly, studies have shown that stress can lower the immune system, which can make us susceptible to certain diseases. Among these are cancer, which in most cases leads to death.

The results of verbal abuse, like those of physical abuse, have a devastating effect on the body. This is very serious and should never be taken lightly. When people are verbally abusing you on a constant basis, they are in essence taking away chunks of your life.

Following are several warning signs that often result from verbal abuse:

➤ Shocked or numb feeling

➤ Body or face flinching

➤ Body or face tics

➤ Body or face tremors or shivering

➤ Flushed or hot feeling

➤ Cold feeling

➤ Skin blotches

➤ Head throbbing

➤ Headache in various parts of the head

➤ Neck pain and tightness

➤ Stomach pain and cramping

➤ Diarrhea

➤ Vomiting

➤ Rapid heartbeat

➤ Light-headedness

➤ Dizziness

➤ Inability to catch one's breath

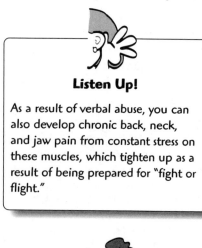

Listen Up!

As a result of verbal abuse, you can also develop chronic back, neck, and jaw pain from constant stress on these muscles, which tighten up as a result of being prepared for "fight or flight."

Bon Mots

The **limbic system** is the area of your brain responsible for your emotions. It regulates all emotions, such as when you are feeling happy, sad, angry, or even fearful.

Shrinking Verbal Abuse—Psychological Pain

When people have been consistently verbally abused, they usually have no other recourse than to get professional help. They need to verbalize their feelings to their clergy, a supportive family member, an intimate friend, a counselor, or a psychotherapist or "shrink." If not remedied, their "shrinking self-esteem" may result in severe self-destructive behaviors leading to a very unpleasant life.

When people are constantly verbally slapped as children, they begin to feel embarrassment and shame. They grow up feeling like less than they are—worthless and irrelevant in the world. People react differently when they have been emotionally traumatized. They may become explosive and let out their emotional pain in some way. On the other hand, they may become implosive, keeping their emotional pain inside of them; this ends up torturing them emotionally. No matter how they manifest their symptoms, the result of their pain is the same—a diminished sense of self brought about by verbally hostile input.

Externally, those who have been verbally abused may in turn become verbally abusive towards others. They may exhibit the same tone of voice or use the same words that they have detested all of their lives. They may do this to keep others at a distance, as they often fear intimacy. To the verbally abused, intimacy is often equated with emotional loss and pain.

They may take out their inner rage on unsuspecting innocent victims, as they themselves were at one time. They may yell, scream, and belittle others. On the other hand, they may become too accommodating or clingy towards others. They may become exceedingly shy and unable to converse with anyone effectively. This further alienates them from others. They may tend to feel hopeless with an attitude of "what's the use of trying? I'm no good anyway". This can eventually lead to lethargy and generalized malaise and can eventually evolve into full-blown depression; in extreme cases, the person becomes "emotionally vegetative" over a period of time.

Verbal Vignette

Empirical studies have repeatedly shown that the verbally abused may turn out to have more psychosomatic manifestations than those who were not verbally abused. They tend to have more anxiety attacks, eating disorders, sleeping disorders, sexual dysfunction, problems with socialization and trusting others, and problems with intimacy.

On the other hand, some of those with such verbal abuse-caused low self-worth direct their rage and anger inward. They feel so worthless and undeserving that they punish themselves by overeating, undereating, bingeing, purging, or starving themselves. They may engage in other self-destructive habits that are a very difficult to break. These include taking drugs, drinking too much, smoking, or self-destructive sexual liaisons.

Practically every patient I have counseled has had the root of his or her psychological problems stem from being verbally abused. This is such a serious matter that it can no longer be minimized or ignored. It prevents people from living their lives to the fullest because a question always rings deep within their psyche about whether the "toxic words and comments" about them were in fact valid. Verbal abuse and violence can create scars so deep and so severe that it can emotionally destroy a person forever.

The feelings of pain and emotional despair can be so severe that it can lead someone with an extremely fragile psyche to commit suicide. Teen suicide has been on the rise lately, going up almost 50 percent. In many cases, it is because these teens can no longer take the verbal tormenting from their parents or peers. In their desperation to be accepted, they find the pressure so enormous that they no longer want to live. The ugly truth is that they were killed by verbal bullets.

The following are several psychological reactions resulting from verbal abuse:

- ➤ Feelings of shame or embarrassment
- ➤ Feelings of worthlessness
- ➤ Insecurity
- ➤ Inability to form intimate relationships
- ➤ Inability to trust
- ➤ Gravitating towards other "familiar" verbal abusers
- ➤ Generalizing anger and inner rage towards others
- ➤ Physical violence
- ➤ Anorexia
- ➤ Bulimia
- ➤ Excessive appetite
- ➤ No appetite
- ➤ Sleeplessness
- ➤ Anxiety attacks
- ➤ Drowsiness and feeling sleepy
- ➤ Diminished sexual interest
- ➤ Increased sexual interest
- ➤ Overly willing to please and accommodate others

➤ Emotional hypersensitivity

➤ Crying jags

➤ Phobias

➤ Withdrawing from others socially

➤ Clinging to others

➤ Generalized malaise

➤ Verbal retaliation

➤ Apathy and lethargy

➤ Excessive drinking

➤ Doing drugs

➤ Smoking despite a doctor's warning

➤ Full-blown depression

➤ Suicide

The Least You Need To Know

➤ Verbal abuse has many forms. Listen carefully to what a person says to you.

➤ You can learn a lot about how people feel about you by their verbal with-holding, insults to you or themselves, and their use of "I was only kidding."

➤ Physical ailments may occur with people who are constantly verbally abused.

➤ Psychological disorders may occur as they result of verbal abuse. The consequences of verbal abuse may be severe enough to end a person's life.

Chapter 3

Verbal Abusers Are Losers

> ### In This Chapter
>
> ➤ The two levels of verbal abuse
>
> ➤ How to identify different types of abusers
>
> ➤ Profiles of abuser types
>
> ➤ How to spot a liar

People who resort to verbal attacks and abuse are full of hostility. They are tortured with rage about issues have nothing to do with you. Usually these issues arise from something traumatic that may have occurred earlier in their lives. If they don't work out their psychological turmoil, the unfortunate person in their path bears the brunt of their tortured souls.

These people have lost out on the quality of life because as a group they are never happy. No matter how much money, fame, or beautiful possessions they have, there is a void. Unless they seek professional assistance to rid them of their demons, they become losers in life. They consistently lose business opportunities and friends, and this further fuels their misery.

Categorizing the Verbal Abuser

In researching this topic, I have concluded that verbal abuse exists in two basic levels. Essentially, the results of both levels are the same: the verbal weaponry stings and hurts. However, the consequences of level one abuses may not be as devastating as those from level two abuses. Both levels of verbal abusers, however, are "toxic people," as identified in my book *Toxic People—10 Ways of Dealing With People Who Make Your Life Miserable* (St. Martin's Press, 1997).

Eleven types of verbal abusers exist in each level. The common thread is self-esteem so low that they have to bring others down to their own perceived level of inadequacy. In level one, the offenders tend not to interfere in your life. They just want to make you miserable or uncomfortable by what they say to you. The people in level two really want to let you have it! They interfere with your life to the extent that they could destroy it.

Level One Abusers

The ten types of verbal abusers in "level one" are more annoying and hurtful to your psyche than those in "level two." You will learn what each particular abuser does and says and red flags to watch out for. Later in this book we will explore ways to handle these types of abusers.

Bon Mots

A **toxic person** is anyone who makes you feel bad about yourself. He or she robs you of your self-esteem and seeks to destroy you. He usually sees the negative in you and tends to get hostile whenever you do well in life. In fact, he may even sabotage your efforts to lead a happy and productive life. His negativity can wear down your resistance and make you physically or mentally ill.

The "I'm Only Kidding" Person

In Chapter 2, I discussed people who always tell you that they are kidding after making some devastating comment to you. They seem like they are erasing what they said, but they really say this only to keep you from attacking them back. If you persist in challenging them about the hostile comment they made, they will ever more loudly insist that they were "only kidding." The more you persist, the more they will resist, by getting louder and using a higher tone. Finally, they may use an exasperated or even sarcastic tone indicating they think you're the one with the problem because you're taking things so seriously. After all, they were "only kidding."

Deep down inside, they really resent you or your actions, but they are too "chicken" to tell you outright, so they disguise their annoyance as humor.

Many young women I speak to experience this type of behavior from dates who want to "get a leg up" on them. If the man feels intimidated by the woman, he may try to gain the upper hand by making hostile and insulting statements to her. When he sees that he was successful in getting a "rise" out of her, he knows he has that power, if only for a moment.

The "Shock 'Em and Rock 'Em" Person

"Shock 'Em and Rock 'Em" people are similar to "I'm Only Kidding" people. Both want to get a rise out of you. They want to shock you by making a bizarre and

Talk Back Tips

Such manipulative behavior isn't the case only with men towards women. It happens with women to men, and with members of the same sex, old and young, parents and children, and bosses and employees.

inappropriate comment to get your attention or see how you will react. Unlike the "I'm Only Kidding" person, they usually don't resent or dislike you. In fact, they may really like you.

Such people are immature in their psychological development. They often have unresolved parental issues. They attempt to keep "pushing the envelope" with you to see if you will still like them even after they are "bad." After all, Mommy and Daddy gave them unconditional love, so why can't you? They fail to realize that you are not Mommy or Daddy, and that when they are "bad," you won't necessarily like them or accept them. If you pass their test and ignore what they said or minimize it, they feel that they "gotcha" and feel that you accept them even if they are being bad.

Listen Up!

Don't expect the sarcastic and sadistic person to pick up on your polite gestures of annoyance. Even if you roll your eyes, tighten up your body, raise your shoulders, squeeze your eyes shut, sigh in exasperation, or cringe, he probably won't even notice it. He is so busy thinking about his next sarcastic comment that he is unaware of your negative reaction.

The Sarcastic/Sadistic Person

These people have a lot of deep-seated psychological issues. Similar to the "I'm Only Kidding" person, they use hostility under the guise of humor because they really don't like you. They don't like themselves and see the world as dark and gloomy.

You can never be happy around these people, because they usually don't let up and are always thinking of something negatively humorous to say in any situation. They rarely take anything seriously. The truth is that they are not funny, and they know it. They know that they are in agony internally. You can rarely have a conversation with them without their resorting to sarcasm. This is most tiring and frustrating to you; you will begin to physically show your frustration with what they say, as you can tell that their dark, unwitty wit is about to invade you.

The Verbal Hammers Person

Verbal hammers won't let up, let alone shut up! They go on and on and on and on. They never let you forget anything bad you ever did in your life. They constantly bring up the past. They verbally torture you to the point where you can't wait to leave them.

Even if you "Shock 'Em and Rock 'Em," they won't be shocked and they won't be rocked. Like the Energizer Bunny, they just keep going! You feel like you're about to explode because there is no way out—they can't even hear you.

You may apologize a hundred times, and they will never hear you. They may stop for a while, but rest assured that they will continue to hammer you at some later date. These people are usually filled with inner rage and have a "victim" approach to life, which makes them feel that people are always doing them wrong. It's virtually impossible for them to break their view of themselves as well as their hammering unless they undergo some major counseling. Often times their hammering has very little to do with you. They may be generalizing a past negative experience (perhaps one they had with another person) onto you.

"My Dog's Bigger Than Your Dog" People

Like the "I'm Only Kidding" person, these people need to get a "leg up" on you, which is quite appropriate because after all, they are "My Dog's Bigger than Your Dog" people. Years ago in a television commercial, a little boy was bragging about his little dog, when a second boy claimed that *his* dog was bigger than the first boy's dog. Although it was a cute commercial, being around people who are always trying to compete with you isn't very cute. It is annoying. Such people are so hungry to show you who they are and what they have that they are relentless in uncovering any morsel of information where they will have a chance to compete with you.

These people may indeed really like you. Perhaps they like you too much—to the point where they envy you and what you have. Their jealousy makes them need to establish an equal playing ground—to play the one-upsmanship game with you to make themselves feel better. They are extremely insecure about themselves and about their accomplishments.

Talk Back Tips

"My dog's bigger than your dog" people don't mean to be obnoxious. Their craving for attention and self-worth, however, makes it impossible to be around them for any length of time.

Perhaps they didn't get enough positive reinforcement when they were children. Unfortunately, they crave it as adults. It becomes the fuel to their existence. No matter how hard you try to build them up, it doesn't matter. They need to build themselves up—mainly at your expense.

They drain you because they try to deflate and negate everything you say. In essence, being with them means constantly listening to their one-upsmanship and being put down. You can't have a conversation with them, you can only have a match where they have to come out the "winner."

The Trashers

These people have to tear down everyone and everything. They, like the Sarcastic Sadist, see the world through dark and cloudy glasses. But unlike the Sarcastic Sadist, they don't try to disguise their verbal venom with humor; instead, they are blunt and open about their feelings about others and everything around them. Like the "My Dog's Bigger Than Your Dog" people, they have a need to build themselves up while putting others down. The only difference is that they don't only try to top you, they also constantly criticize.

If they have only criticized others in your presence and have left you alone, you can bet that you will be trashed either in person at a later date or when you're not around. They have no mercy. Anyone is fair game.

Trashers are miserable people. It is a shame that they have to live with themselves. They go around perpetually tight-lipped and tight-jawed, tense-faced, whiny, and with tones of disgust spewing forth. They are difficult to be around, because nothing seems to make them happy. They will always find something wrong with someone or something. Even though they certainly aren't perfect, they insist that the world around them be perfect.

Perhaps they learned how to be so negative from parents or caretakers who saw the world in the same way. Perhaps they have been so traumatized in life that they have resigned themselves to the bitter Murphy's Law idea that nothing is good and nothing ever goes right. Therefore, they cut down others before circumstances or other people can cut them down.

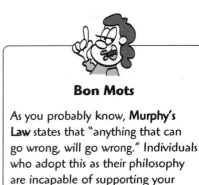

Bon Mots

As you probably know, **Murphy's Law** states that "anything that can go wrong, will go wrong." Individuals who adopt this as their philosophy are incapable of supporting your positive outlook on life.

They are dissatisfied with everything. No matter what you say or do, they cannot be pleased. Like the "My Dog's Bigger Than Your Dog" people and the "Sarcastic Sadists," they are impossible to be around for long periods of time because they drain you. They deflate who you are, what you think, and who and what you like, thereby debilitating your own self-esteem and outlook towards life.

People Who Throw Back Your Confidences

These people are downright vicious. You may have shared something personal with them—something that would embarrass or destroy you if anyone else knew. You tell this person because you trust them implicitly. After all, they revealed their innermost thoughts and deep, dark secrets to you. You feel safe and secure. When there is a conflict or a disagreement between the two of you, however, they will reach for a verbal weapon that is well below the belt, something you shared with them in the strictest confidence.

Once they commit the unforgivable act of throwing back in your face something you're so sensitive about, you can never trust them again! It is dangerous to "forgive and forget." If they did it once, who's to say that they won't do it again? You can never again tell them anything so intimate.

Why did they do it? Because they wanted to use any verbal weapon, no matter how hurtful, to get you back and to win. Deep down, these people may have little or no respect for you. They not only knocked you down, they stomped on you and squished you.

There is another problem with these people: If they threw your confidence back at you, who is to say that they haven't shared your intimacy with others? Obviously, they don't respect you enough to know what is off limits for them to ever bring up.

Some people just can't keep anything inside. They have to tell all about themselves and about anyone who's confided in them. These are people you need to steer clear of. They can verbally destroy you, as they have done to themselves.

Other people tend to know who they are and what they are all about. They don't elicit much respect from others and if you associate with them, you won't elicit respect from others.

The Sugary Fawner

People want to hear good things about themselves, but there is a limit. When you are constantly fawned over and praised relentlessly with extraordinary passion and emotion, you need to be careful.

Verbal Vignette

As the great Chinese philosopher Confucius once said, "when friends are fawning they are harmful." Chances are they are being effusive in their compliments and constantly flattering you in order to hide some inner hostility, resentment, or jealousy towards you.

Sugary fawners have a huge smile and are overly excited to see you, gesturing excessively and hovering around you. They tell you wonderful things about yourself that you know are exaggerations. Most of these sugary fawners tend to be insincere and manipulative. Usually they want something from you, and they will break this news to you well after they are in your good graces. Watch how they turn on you when your answer is "no" or they don't get what they want. Suddenly their sugary words and attitude become salty or even bitter.

Often the Sugary Fawners make you feel as though you are their best friend. This is often calculated, as they most likely want something from you or want you to do something for them. They often pull the rug out from under you either after they get what they wanted from you or don't get what they want. They will continue to be sugary if they think that they can get more from you. Deep inside, they really might not like you, but they are being overly nice to get what they want from you.

These manipulative tactics date back to infancy. The dynamic of many families is that of manipulating or "bribing" a family member to do something. Parents tell their children, "If you are well behaved, I'll buy you...." Children act cutesy in order to get a certain positive reaction from their parents, which results in positive consequences. If their charm doesn't work, they will often cry or throw a tantrum. Many people carry this manipulative behavior into adulthood. This is how some people deal with the world and with people around them.

They are insincere people who are usually backstabbers. They will often become "Trashers" and sing your failures and weak points to others as opposed to singing your praises and strong points. So beware and be aware!

Backhanded Complimentors

These people, like the "I'm Only Kidding" people, have some underlying resentment towards you. They really may not like you and may make a cutting remark. Instead of trying to disguise their hostility with humor, like the "I'm Only Kidding" people, they often disguise it by saying something complimentary to you, followed by a cutting remark in their next breath.

In essence, they are demonstrating an openly hostile attitude towards you. The tone of a person's voice is also a giveaway for Backhanded Complimentors. Their voices usually go up in tone at the end of their truly complementary statement, but will immediately inflect their tone downward, slightly lowering their pitch when they are about to let loose with verbal zingers.

These people really resent you or are jealous of you. They are also negative people who often can't let a person know that the person is "too good." They have to pick on the slightest imperfection. They do it in such a subtle manner that you don't ever know they verbally smacked you until later. Sometimes you don't realize it until moments later, hours later, or even days later.

You begin to mull over what you said and what they said and what you wish you would have said, had you realized what they were saying. This mental mishmash can keep you awake for nights on end. The reason why their zing hits you later is because their initial positive comment is still resonating in your mind as you beam and smile. Then when you have time to think about everything, you really hear what they said.

The Self-Consumed

The Self-Consumed discuss only the topic that is most interesting to them—themselves. They go on and on about themselves with disregard as to whether the other person is interested in what they are saying or not. The Self-Consumed will rarely look in your direction when they talk you. They enjoy reliving their lives' experiences by telling you every little detail about what happened to them.

The Self-Consumed require so much attention from others because deep inside they are extremely insecure about themselves. They need constant validation in order to exist. Their speech is primarily consumed by the word "I." "You" is rarely if ever used. They talk at you, not with you. They are not very helpful or generous, so don't expect them to do anything for you that doesn't benefit them.

In short, be aware of the following level one verbal abusers.

1. "I'm Only Kidding" People
2. "Shock 'Em and Rock 'Em" People
3. Sarcastic/Sadists
4. Verbal Hammers
5. "My Dog's Bigger Than Your Dog" People
6. Trashers
7. People Who Throw Back Your Confidences
8. Sugary Fawners
9. Backhanded Complimentors
10. The Self-Consumed

Level Two Abusers

There are 11 types of Level Two abusers. Unlike the Level Ones, who are annoying, these people are very destructive to you and may be downright dangerous. By learning what they do and how to recognize them, you will be saving yourself a lot of grief in your life.

Talk Back Tips

The self-consumed have the same egocentric view of the world as a two-year-old. In essence, they have not evolved out of that two-year-old stage of development.

Listen Up!

When you start to feel uncomfortable or offended, or you start answering questions you really don't want to, you'll know you have been lured into the web of the interrogator. It is difficult to escape.

Interrogators

After you have been around these people, you feel as though you have been placed under a hot lamp and tortured. It's one thing to be persistent, but these people are relentless. They don't know when to stop. They go on and on asking you questions until they get the answer they want to hear. They will ask you questions in different ways to see if they can catch you in a lie or learn some detail you didn't particularly want them to know. They tend to put you on the defensive, making you feel as though you are guilty, when in fact you might not have done anything wrong. They are also very nosy and want to know everything they can about your business or about your personal life.

These people are so insecure that they need reassurance that everything is the way they feel it should be. When you notice that someone is asking you question after question, nonstop, know that you have met an interrogator.

Certain communities refer to them as *yentas:* they try to suck as much information out of you as they can, so that they can regurgitate it to others. Of course, the information they are giving others is usually misinterpreted and told in the wrong context, which makes you look bad, giving an erroneous impression of who you are and what's going on.

Gossiping, Meddling Instigators

These people enjoy interfering in your personal business by telling you what to do. In order to make situations turn out as they want them to, they will stop at nothing to create their own little soap operas. They often tell you things with an alarmed tone to make you perceive the severity of the problem at hand. To make matters worse, they tell your business to anyone who will listen.

Instigators usually do not have much going on in their own lives—only what commotion they create in the lives of others. They usually begin their wrath by saying things such as "I don't want to pry, but…," "It's none of my business, but…," "I think you should know that…," or "I happened to hear that…." If any of these phrases hit your ears, you know what's coming next. They are usually overzealous in wanting to help or to get involved in your life. They usually speak in rapid tones, which get you enrolled in the immediacy of the situation. Remember that if a person is gossiping to you about others, chances are that you are next on the list to be gossiped about.

Condescending Dismissers

Condescending Dismissers think that they know it all. You can't tell them anything, because they think they have all the answers. Your opinion doesn't matter. They are snob-like in their attitudes as they brush you and your opinions off as if they were lint. The way they ignore you or put you down in subtle and not-so-subtle ways can make you feel two inches tall.

When they speak to you, their tones are impatient and their speech pattern appears to be clipped. They just want to "get on with it." Their tones, along with what they say, are arrogant. They talk at you, not with you. They will usually try to diminish, minimize, or brush off anything you try to contribute to the conversation.

These people have an over-inflated ego and under-inflated self-esteem. Otherwise they wouldn't treat others as they do. In essence, they are very shallow individuals who are closed-minded. You can often detect them from their facial language, as they seem to literally look down on you. There is usually a sneer or a look of disgust on their face when they speak to you.

Listen Up!

Condescending dismissers will often use big words to show off, or try to overwhelm you with information and data.

Sneaky Underminers

These people are some of the most dangerous people you can talk with. They have a lot in common with Instigators; however, they try to undermine you in a more subtle manner. Instead of doing it in front of you, like the Instigator does, they do it behind your back. They smile a lot when they talk to you and usually acquiesce to what you say—all the while trying to pick up morsels of information that they can use against you and stab you in the back with. They try to make you feel so comfortable around them that you can't help but freely open up to them.

They always try to reinterpret whatever you have said, but they use a negative slant. Then they tend to share this misinterpreted data with others. The Sneaky Underminers are passive-aggressive and can never be trusted.

Verbal Vignette

Suppose you make an innocent statement such as "I like tomatoes." The Sneaky Underminer may then say "You mean you don't like lettuce?" You reply, "No, I just happen to like tomatoes better." Some time later, you are at a party where the host is serving a salad. He immediately removes your salad and asks you if you want something else instead, because he heard you hate lettuce. Where did he hear this? From the Sneaky Underminer, of course.

"I Love You—I Hate You" People

You're damned if you do and you're damned if you don't when you're dealing with these people. They appear mostly in romantic relationships and in relationships with children. Perhaps the cruelest thing one can do to a child, something that can leave permanent emotional scars and traumatize the child, is to give love and then take it away with such extreme rage and anger. The roller coaster ride of emotions with these people in intimate relationships can be devastating for both parties involved. Although there are some relationships that thrive on this high drama, it isn't healthy. They really don't hate you, even though they may say they do in a moment of rage. In fact, they may feel extremely passionate, bonded, and close to you.

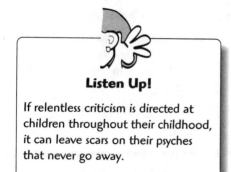

Listen Up!

If relentless criticism is directed at children throughout their childhood, it can leave scars on their psyches that never go away.

These people often have mental problems, such as a bipolar disorder, which means that unless they are medicated, they may love you one day and find fault with you the next. They are emotionally confusing to be around and can drive you crazy. That is why they are often referred to as "crazy makers." Such a person is too flowery and tends to speak on two extremes: things are either black or white. There are no shades of gray.

"You're No Good!" People

Deep down, these people really think that they themselves are no good, so they try to project their own
self-loathing onto you. They are constant critics who attempt to find fault with you. They point out only
your negatives.

Often when a relationship grows close and barriers are broken down, this "You're No Good" syndrome may emerge. It is usually because the person doesn't feel worthy of you or the relationship. They may also be competitors and trying to get a "leg up" on you by showing you every fault you have.

These people are often gloom-and-doomers. They often walk around with a tight and extended lower lip, furrowed brow, and an unhappy heart. They are miserable people who don't have enough self-worth. They often speak in hostile, angry, clipped tones. Giving you a compliment is an extreme rarity. They may speak nicely to others but their verbal wrath is meant for you.

Yellers, Screamers, and Ragers

These people are extremely out of control, to the point that they cannot talk to anyone unless they're yelling or screaming at them. They have a volcano of inner rage within them that they constantly spew forth. Unfortunately, their hot lava melts down everyone they speak to.

You can always tell the Yellers, Screamers, and Ragers even if they aren't engaging in these verbal activities in your presence. They often sound hoarse. When they speak, you can usually see the veins of their neck popping out. They can also be recognized by their loud, clipped, attacking, bullet-like staccato tones. Obviously, these are extremely angry people who need to work out all of their deep-seated inner rage in a therapeutic situation.

Verbal Nazis—My Way or Else!

These people must have order and control in their lives or they cannot function. They don't realize on a conscious level that there is no way that one can control another person. In their frustration, they become angrier and downright verbally hostile. They are definitely not team players and have a difficult time getting along with others, especially in the work environment. These people usually go from job to job. They set themselves up for a life of disappointment as they are never able to "go with the flow."

Bon Mots

Perhaps **Nazis** sound like too harsh a label for this category of verbal abusers, but it is completely appropriate. They try to seize control over others and seek to destroy everything that does not agree with their idea of how things should be. Don't let them destroy *you.*

They are one of the most difficult verbal abusers to be around, as they believe that "it's my way or the highway."

Verbal Nazis are very immature. Like four-year-olds, if you don't do it their way they have a tantrum. The reason why these people have to be in control is that they cannot function in a world where everything is not exactly the way they like it. They are recognized by their adamant and emphatic tones. They are poor listeners and often dismiss or argue with whatever you say, especially if it disagrees with them. Their volume increases when they don't get their way.

They speak in command terms, threaten, and may even scream, yell, or curse at you.

Guilt-Producing Accusers

Guilt-Producing Accusers make you wrong to make themselves right. But unlike the Verbal Nazis, who use anger in their attempt to control you, these people use guilt. They let you know that you made a big mistake and that you should feel bad about it and pay. Often the payment is groveling or saying you're sorry a million times. Still that may not appease them. They usually bring up your "crime" at some inopportune time as further ammunition as to why you made them feel so bad. They are perennial "victims" who feel that everyone is doing them wrong. They try to manipulate you by hitting one of your emotional weak points to make you feel just as bad as they do. They usually hold a grudge against you for a long time.

When you hear phrases like "You always...," "You never...," "You make me...," "Why do you always...," " What you did to me...," or "Why don't you ever...," then you know you have been exposed to someone whose aim is to make you responsible for something in their life that upsets them. They speak in absolute terms. They say just about anything and even resort to crying in order to get you to "feel bad for what you did." It seems as though nothing you can say can appease them, as they tend to go on and on about the woe you "caused" them.

Liars

Liars are one of the most verbally abusive people, because they don't respect you enough to tell you the truth. Liars often lie for different reasons. Some lie to make themselves feel as though they are more than they really are, so that you will have more respect for them. These liars are extremely insecure. Others lie because they are cowardly and can't face the results of their negative actions. Nobody likes a liar. Nobody likes to be fooled, hoodwinked, or disrespected.

On the other hand, people may not tell the truth because they may not want to hurt your feelings. For example, if you have an ugly baby that you happen to think is cute, and you ask people what they think, don't expect them to tell you how ugly the baby is and ask you "where's its tail?" This form of lying can be good and socially acceptable, and we are not concerned with it.

Note that pathological liars are extremely difficult to detect. Being only human, however, they often slip up. If you suspect they are lying, try to check their story by verifying it with other people and by gathering hard evidence.

Verbal Vignette

If you wish to explore the topic of lying in greater detail, ask your bookseller or librarian about works by experts such as Paul Ekman at the University of California at San Francisco, who have determined several ways to detect if a person is lying.

Verbal Icicles

These people withhold their words. They are some of the most difficult people to be around, because you never know what they are thinking. They never seem to react. If there is a building crumbling behind them or they just won a million dollars in the lottery, they remain the same—emotionless. They are so frustrating to be around because you can never get a read on what is going on with them or how they feel about a particular situation.

In actuality, they mostly live in fear. They are afraid to say the wrong thing or afraid to say something that may upset someone, so they keep quiet. They speak when spoken to. As a child, they were often brainwashed by the mantra, "be seen but not heard," or consistently told to "shut up!" They often lack social graces, which further compounds their insecurities.

Even though they are quiet and unassuming, beware! They may unfreeze one day and let out emotions that would scare the most ferocious beast. Withholding words and emotions from you is definitely a major act of cruelty.

To say that they are inexpressive is an understatement. Sometimes you wonder if they are brain-damaged or mute. They often have a vacant look. They are often rigid in their facial and body movements. They speak in monotones or in short clipped phrases. If they should happen to unload, be prepared for someone who won't shut up or who is ranting and raving in loud, uncontrolled tones. As they let out their stored-up verbal poisons, their reactions and words may sound more extreme and hostile than the words of those who let out their emotions regularly.

In summary, beware of the following level two verbal abusers:

1. Interrogators
2. Gossiping, Meddling Instigators
3. Condescending Dismissers
4. Sneaky Underminers
5. "I Love You—I Hate You" People""
6. "You're No Good!" People
7. Yellers, Screamers, and Ragers
8. Verbal Nazis
9. Guilt-Producing Accusers
10. Liars
11. Verbal Icicles

The Least You Need to Know

➤ Most verbal abusers are insecure and have low self-worth and unresolved psychological issues that they haven't dealt with.

➤ There are some people who are annoying or even dangerous verbal abusers: *Be aware!*

➤ Recognize the verbal characteristics of each of these abusers so that you can easily identify their approaching wrath.

➤ Be aware of the signs that someone might be lying to you.

Chapter 4

Verbal Murder— How and Why?

> ### In This Chapter
>
> ➤ Identifying the verbal murderers in your life
>
> ➤ How verbal murder begins
>
> ➤ Common causes of verbal murder
>
> ➤ Consequences of being a verbal murderer
>
> ➤ Consequences of being verbally murdered

What Is Verbal Murder?

Verbal abuse leads to verbal murder—the killing of one's spirit, self-esteem, dignity, and self-respect through emotionally hurtful words and phrases. The aim of verbal murderers is to make you feel bad. The difference between verbal murderers and verbal abusers is that murderers are relentless. They abuse repeatedly until they have done irreparable emotional and even physical damage to their victim. If the verbal abuse mentioned in Chapter 2 continues for any length of time, the result is emotional death—verbal murder.

Who Are Verbal Murderers?

Verbal murderers can be anyone with whom you have ever come in contact who have made you feel less than human, by the constant horrible things they have said to you and about you. They usually are people so full of self-loathing or self-hatred that they spew their venom on anyone who happens to be in their path.

Verbal murderers come in all shapes, colors, sizes, and religions. They cross all cultural, sexual, racial, ethnic, and age barriers. They are from all walks of life and are seen in virtually every profession and in every country in the world.

Half of the verbal murderers know exactly what they are doing. They are very conscious about their motives. The other half murder automatically or unconsciously. Later in this section, we learn both the conscious and unconscious reasons why they emotionally kill.

Bon Mots

The difference between the verbal murderer and verbal abuser is that murderers are relentless. They abuse repeatedly until they have done irreparable damage.

Identifying the Verbal Abusers in Your Life

You might have been verbally abused at one point in your life and not at other points. You may have been abused mostly by men, or mostly by women, or by certain family members and not by others, or by certain friends or acquaintances. Perhaps a co-worker, boss, or employee verbally abused you. You may have been abused verbally as a child without even knowing it.

So do the following exercise. Carefully think back through your life, decade by decade. List people both in your past and in your present. Tally up how many men verbally abused you, as well as how many women. Tally up the number of relatives, employers, friends, and so on. Go through all the categories of people listed on the following chart. In this chart, list the names of people who verbally abused you under each of these kinds of people who were or are in your life. You might discover patterns showing changes over time about who verbally abused you in the past and in the present.

Go down the list of Level One Abusers and Level Two Abusers. To specify the type of verbal abuse you may have received, write the person's name based on his or her relation to you in each of the 21 categories. If you need more room, use another sheet of paper.

Love   Relatives   Friends   Boss   Workers   Co-Workers

Professionals Service Relationships Acquaintances Teachers People

1. "Only Kidding"_____

2. Shock 'Em & Rock 'Em_____

3. Sarcastic Sadists_____

4. Verbal Hammers_____

5. Competitors_____

6. Trashers_____

7. Throw Up Confidences_____

8. Sugary Fawners_____

9. Backhanded Complimentors_____

10. Self-Consumed_____

11. Interrogators_____

12. Gossiping Meddlers_____

13. Condescending Dismissers_____

14. Sneaky Underminers_____

15. Love and Haters_____

16. "You're No Good!"_____

17. Yellers & Screamers _____

18. Verbal Nazis_____

19. Guilt-Producing Accusers_____

20. Liars_____

21. Icicles_____

When Do Verbal Abusers Turn into Verbal Murderers?

Now that you have identified your verbal abusers, go back and, on a separate piece of paper, list all the names of the people on your chart.

Next to each name, write a number from 1 to 3, indicating the frequency that you received their verbal poison. Writing 1 means once or a few times, 2 means several times, and 3 means always. Each number 3 indicates that the named person succeeded in killing something about you emotionally. He went beyond verbal abuse and should now be considered a verbal murderer.

Just like physical murderers, verbal murderers need to be kept away from people and put behind bars. You need to keep them away from you at all times. Bar them from your life.

On the other hand, just as prisoners can often be rehabilitated, if the verbal murderer is willing to get some professional help, or if you can set new limits of ground rules and reestablish your relationship, then the murderer can be set free. He can now become a productive member of society. *Your "society"—your life!*

Listen Up!

The advice I'm giving here is of the highest importance. Every minute, tens of thousands of people are verbally murdered throughout the world! If you don't bar the verbal murderers from your life, they will continue to spit verbal bullets your way—bullets that may eventually kill you.

Why Does Verbal Murder Happen?

People become verbal murderers for several reasons. Some murderers act unconsciously—they couldn't tell you why, but something deep within their psyches allows them to act in such a "toxic" manner. Other murderers are quite conscious. They know exactly why they speak to you the way they do. The following section explores both the subconscious and conscious reasons for verbal murder.

Unconscious Reasons for Verbal Murder

All too often, people who say and do ugly things to you have no idea why they treated you that way. Even if you sit them down and ask them point blank why they act as they do, they can't answer you. They know only that for some unknown reason, you seem to bring out the worst in them, perhaps stimulating their deepest fears.

Hey! Don't Take It Out on Me!

Many people are so frustrated with their own lives that they let out their frustration in the worst way. Unfortunately, that worst way may be towards you. You may be the recipient of the "kick the cat" syndrome. This syndrome is named for the old adage about someone who had a hard day or a misfortune. He comes home and looks to take out his anger on anyone who happens to be there. Unfortunately, the only creature present is the cat. This angry person literally kicks the cat in order to let out his anger and frustration, even though the cat has nothing to do with his frustrations.

Verbal murderers may kick you or someone else who is in their way—not physically, but emotionally. Their boss yelled at them, and they had to take it or risk being fired. Because you are a friend or a family member, however, they have no qualms about taking out their frustrations on you. They do this by being short-tempered with you. For example, you call them at work to let them know that you miss them and would like to take them to lunch. Before you can get a word out, they blurt out gruffly and impatiently, "Didn't I tell you not to call me at work? What do you want?" At this point, the only thing you want is to get off the phone with them and never see them again.

All too often, people who are close to us take the liberty of treating us the worst by unloading their anger onto us. You must never ever let them do this to you. Later on in this book, you will learn what to say in order to defend yourself in this uncomfortable situation.

Hey! We're Not All Like That!

In their emotional pain, they generalize that all people of a certain group act in a certain way. Because of their negative experiences with one particular group, they generalize their ill feelings to everyone who is a member of that group. How many times have we heard women say "men are dawgs (dogs)" or men say "there are no more good women out there?"

After having so many negative experiences, and saying such a thing enough times (whether in jest or not), they come to believe it. Unconsciously, these verbal murderers condemn an entire race, religious group, sex, country, profession, or socioeconomic group for the actions of a few bad seeds.

I'm Not That Toxic Person in Your Past!

Just as a verbal murderer condemns people for the group to which they belong, a murderer will often throw poison verbal darts at someone who reminds him of someone who did him wrong.

Verbal Vignette

A male friend and I were at a party. A very attractive, tall, slender brunette began talking to my friend, but he was incredibly rude to her. I couldn't believe how this normally charming guy was acting like such a pig. Later that evening, when I confronted him about his obnoxious behavior, he was shocked: he realized that the only reason he didn't like the woman was because she reminded him of a girl in high school who would never go out with him!

Most of the time, however, people who dislike someone don't know the reasons why. If you ask them what that person did to them to arouse such disdain, they will be at a loss for words.

Unfortunately, if people have had a series of bad personal relationships (in which they have been cheated on repeatedly, for example), they often might be very suspicious of you and perhaps believe that you are cheating on them as well. Even if you never give them any cause to think that you desire someone else, they might keep insisting that you have been unfaithful.

Green with Envy!

Usually, you are stabbed in the back because of envy. In psychological terms, "envy seeks to destroy." People undermine you or do whatever they can to hold you back because they are green with envy.

Talk Back Tips

Don't chastise yourself by thinking that you are somehow responsible for such people's behavior. *Nothing* you say or do will change their opinion, because you have taken on the identity of the person in their last relationship, the one before that, and the one before that.... In essence, you have to suffer for the sins of past romances.

The envy shows on their face with their tight-lipped smile and hard swallow whenever you tell them something good that has happened or is about to happen in your life. You can actually see the veins tense up in their neck as they have a difficult time swallowing their own venom.

Talk Back Tips

In a survey asking why relationships or friendships break up, close to 60 percent of respondents said that the main reason was "jealousy."

Some people make mean and cutting remarks to you because, consciously or not, they are extremely jealous of you for some reason. You may think that they have nothing to be jealous about, but in their eyes, you are larger than life. They wish to have what you have, or they regard you to be "more" than they are. All this may be a surprise to them, however. If you point out that they are jealous, they might vehemently deny it and profess how much they like, love, or admire you.

I Really Don't Deserve to Be That Happy!

Have you ever met people who had everything going for them? Things are going smoothly for them until they open their big mouths and stick their feet inside, sabotaging everything they worked for.

These people feel that deep down they don't deserve good things to happen to them. They see themselves as impostors who will be "found out" in time, especially if someone gets too close to them. Unconsciously, they feel that the truth about themselves will be revealed. They have low self-esteem and see themselves as losers, no matter how successful they may seem by society's standards.

Because they feel that they don't deserve to be happy or liked, let alone loved, they say rude or mean things to others, including you. They don't realize that this is an attempt to get you to dislike them, so that they can prove that they are unlovable frauds.

A client of mine broke off her engagement with a man because of his verbal hostility toward her. As she put it, he would give with one hand and take away with the other. One small example was when she opened the door to see him and he said "Wow, you look so sexy and gorgeous." She smiled brightly, but her smile turned into a frown when he added, "but I hate the color green. It sickens me and you look like you are sick." He made comments like these constantly. What her ex-fiancé was doing was verbally destroying a relationship that he knew would make him happy. He didn't feel that he deserved happiness, so he talked himself and his fiancée out of it.

I Don't Trust Anybody—Including You!

Just as people project their bad experiences with others onto you, they may also project onto you issues of trust or lack of trust. They may have had trusts broken in their childhood, business life, or personal life. And it takes very little to trigger such people's mistrust—cues from your facial or body movement, or from your voice or what you say. They conclude, rightly or wrongly, and consciously or unconsciously, that you are not forthright, and so they react toward you with verbal abuse. In essence, they are coming across on the offense to subconsciously protect themselves against you.

Conscious Reasons for Verbal Murder

People also have conscious reasons for trying to murder you verbally. They spew verbal bullets when they can't stand you, don't want you to succeed, want to control you, or don't want you to be better than they are.

They Just Plain Can't Stand You!

For whatever reason, some people just can't stomach you. You get on their nerves. This is why they can tell you the worst things about yourself and then say they were only kidding; this is why they can be sarcastic to you. And if you happen to tell them something bad that's going on in your life, they love it!

They Know You Really Don't Like Them

For the most part, the way you feel about a person is the way they will feel about you. If you aren't too crazy about someone, chances are that she's not so crazy about you either. People know when they aren't liked and will often reflect this in their behavior—what they say to you and how they say it.

What's the Use?

Many people resign themselves to a life of despair or mediocrity. Just because things don't go as planned, they feel that their whole life is a mess. They feel like losers; they expect the worst, and they definitely get the worst.

As a result, they don't try anything new. There is no excitement in their souls, as their dull tones usually reflect. Anyone around them who shows a bit of spunk or enthusiasm towards life is regarded as the enemy. Therefore, they always say something to try to discourage you or squelch your dreams or excitement. They figure that if they are so miserable, you should be miserable too. They will rain on your parade, pop your balloon, and deflate your ego. They usually say the phrase "yeah but" when they are going to tear down anything positive you have said. Unfortunately, their hopelessness tends to be contagious.

Talk Back Tips

If you reflect a little, you can probably observe this behavior in your own life. When you sense that people don't like you, you tend to find reasons not to like them.

Gimme the Reins—I Need to Control You!

The control freak can relate to you—or to anyone else for that matter—only if he has you under his control. Sometimes, the control freak can hold money, a certain

Listen Up!

In my practice over the years, I have seen this controlling behavior in so many people, especially women being controlled by men whom they perceive as having power over them. Be vigilant to keep it from happening to you.

lifestyle, or even a job situation over your head to make sure that you are under his thumb.

The most common situation I have encountered is the woman who goes after her dream man—the fantasy Prince Charming with the big bucks who can take care of her financially so that she will live happily ever after. What does he get out of it? He gets the pleasure of controlling her with his big bucks, putting her on a restrictive budget, and dictating her behavior. Yeah—happily ever after! The price is too high when you give up your freedom. It doesn't work—you crumble. Even societies crumble when people are controlled or oppressed. Look at what happened in East Germany and in the former Soviet Union. You can't limit people's creativity and ambition and expect them to flourish.

You're Incompetent!

When people think you're stupid or can't cut the mustard, they usually speak to you in curt sentences, using condescending and impatient-sounding tones. They consistently show their frustration whenever they speak to you directly or speak about you to others.

Often the people around them follow suit. For example, their secretaries, assistants, employees, or friends may treat you and speak to you in a similar manner. They won't show you the courtesy you deserve. Because they so consistently treat you like an idiot, you may find yourself carrying out their self-fulfilling prophecy, believing you are incompetent and acting in accordance to their low expectations of you.

I Just Don't Believe in You!

One client of mine once had a talent agent for her acting career. This agent never got her work and rarely even took her telephone calls. One day, when talking to another client of mine, a director, I heard about a role that she would be perfect for. I told the director about her and he sounded very interested in meeting with her. When she arrived in my office later that morning, I had her immediately telephone her agent in my office. She put the call on speakerphone so that we could both talk to her agent and I could fill him in on the details of the project and put him in direct contact with the director.

After placing us on hold for what seemed like an eternity, the agent finally answered the phone with a gruff, curt, monotonous, disgusted sound "Yeah." She excitedly told him about the project, which he immediately started to pooh-pooh. He told her that the casting agents for that project were looking at a lot of people and that he didn't think she was right for the part. She tried to sound convincing and chipper as she told him what had taken place in my office with the director. I then got on the phone and told him how the director seemed interested in interviewing his client. But in his sour, negating tone, he basically told me that it was too big a role and that they were looking for a name and so wouldn't be interested in her.

When she got off the phone, she was sobbing in frustration. She said that he never believed in her and always talked down to her, negating everything she ever said or suggested. She felt low and worthless, and even began to question her own talents and why she was even pursuing an acting career.

Before she got too down, I got her the meeting with the director myself, and she got the role and "kicked her agent to the curb."

It's better to be alone than to be around anyone who doesn't believe in you. Such people sabotage your efforts by not doing anything to help you— they will neglect you or proactively do their best to make sure nothing good happens to or for you.

Listen Up!

If the people in your life won't support you emotionally, it's time to surround yourself with new people. And if even the people you pay to be on your side don't deliver, kick them to the curb—now!

I Don't Want You to Be Ahead of Me!

These are the ultimate competitors. Unlike those who are unconsciously jealous, these people are fully conscious of who you are and the threat they perceive you to be. They are overt in letting you know that they are the "king," "queen," or "star" and that you should stay in your place.

This is all too common among siblings and spouses. Often, spouses start out being in a subservient role in which they look up to their mate, who makes more money, is in a more powerful position, or is more attractive. When the tables turn and the previously subservient spouse starts to assert himself or herself, when they begin to earn more money, or attain equal or more perceived power in the job world, all hell breaks loose. Lovey-dovey couples who previously cooed accolades and terms of endearment towards one another now roar at and demean one another in their attempts to gain the upper hand.

In my practice, I have seen this scenario repeatedly when people lose a lot of weight, have plastic surgery to improve their looks, or dress differently. People who were supposed to be your "friends"

Talk Back Tips

When there are such dramatic shifts in status, competitive relationships often sour to the point of no repair. It is uncomfortable for one to lose his or her self-perceived higher status, and unacceptable for you not to be treated with the respect you deserve. This parting of the ways is sometimes a healthy result.

aren't too friendly now that you look or feel better. They liked you in your previous role when they had (at least in their minds) more than you or felt they were better than you.

These people make life as miserable as possible for you by exhibiting a wide range of toxic behaviors. These include not acknowledging you, not speaking to you, or ignoring, minimizing, or openly taking issue with everything you say. They may mock you to others and badmouth you. By doing this, they attempt to gain the winning edge of other's favorable perception of them as they perpetuate the unfavorable perception of you.

If this happens in a work environment in which the other person is in a more powerful position than you, there is unfortunately nothing you can do about it. You lose out in that situation, and you have to be the one to leave. In the long run, this is perhaps for the better—who would want to be around such a toxic person anyway?

Listen Up!

You can spot a resenter by his deflating remarks to the effect of "remember what goes up must come down." He doesn't want you around feeling happy when he isn't.

Talk Back Tips

When I became a professor at the University of Southern California, I vowed to break this cycle of abuse. I made certain that all my students were treated with the respect and dignity they deserved, and I urge anyone else in such a position to do the same. Always be aware of your power and try to use it appropriately.

Who Said You Can Be That Happy and Lucky?

Many people are so miserable that they can't stand when someone else is happy or has a run of good fortune. Even if their lives are going well, they resent that yours is, too. Even though they may be smiling at you, they are wishing you ill. Such people either minimize the good things you tell them or try to top you.

They Did It to Me—Now It's Your Turn!

This type of verbal abuse is common in families in which a parent who was verbally abused passes down verbal poison to his or her child, who as an adult in turn passes down this ugly heirloom to their child, and so forth. The old adage "the apple doesn't fall far from the tree" is most appropriate here.

Perhaps one of the worst experiences of my life was getting my first Ph.D., in communication disorders, when I was 24. Thank goodness I didn't encounter the same emotional torture when, years later, I received my second Ph.D., this time in counseling psychology. With a few exceptions, the professors in my first doctorate treated me like dirt. They were rude, condescending, obnoxious, curt, demeaning, uncooperative, unhelpful, unfriendly, and downright awful to me.

I was so depressed over this situation that it took all the energy I could muster just to get up in the morning. I then decided to see a counselor at the university. When I told her my plight, she threw her head back and smiled a smile indicating she had often seen this problem before. She then said, "Don't worry, you are just being initiated into your doctorate the same way they were. Their professors did it to them, and now it's your turn!" As soon as she said that, I understood the game, and I no longer took their abuse to heart.

Consequences of Being a Verbal Murderer

Verbal murderers are usually embarrassed or ashamed about what they say and do to others. They have so much inner anger towards themselves that their poisonous words uncontrollably escape from their lips to attack you. This lack of verbal control often costs them their relationships with friends or family. They find that they are shunned, unforgiven, and untrusted by those to whom they were once close. Social invitations dry up, and people usually stay away from them.

Trust is the essence of any relationship, and when trust is shattered, there is usually no going back. These verbal murderers cannot be trusted, because they may verbally murder again. They cannot keep friends on a long-term basis. They also become the last to know things, because nobody trusts them—sharing one's confidences with these verbal murderers is out of the question.

Another consequence of being a verbal murderer is frequent depression. They are often so bitter at others and life in general that they walk around with a frown, a scowl, or an expressionless face, which further alienates them from others.

They tend to feel so guilty and ashamed of what they have said and done to so many people that they perceive themselves in a negative manner; this in turn permits their low self-esteem. And because they hold themselves in such low esteem, they may act out by being more verbally destructive to others or to themselves. They may drink, smoke, take drugs, or overeat in order to dull and temporarily quiet the pain lurking inside of them.

Consequences of Being Verbally Murdered

When you have been verbally murdered, part of you has literally died, mentally, emotionally, and spiritually. You lose your enthusiasm, your smile, and your inner desires and passions. You feel as though there is no hope left in you.

You become afraid to speak up and share your innermost confidences with anyone. You become close-mouthed, fearful, and withholding around people. Even being around people may become uncomfortable for you because you are afraid to say anything that you feel could sound stupid or ridiculous. Even though such fears are usually unwarranted, you are always "on guard" with others.

This fear cuts you off from the viable communication you need with others in order to have solid and open relationships.

If the verbal murder persists over a long period of time, causing you severe stress, this stress may become so physically devastating to you that it leads to your premature death. You could develop heart disease or even cancer, as research has consistently proven. Suicide is another unfortunate by-product of consistent verbal murder. According to various researchers, the rise in teenage suicide could be due to persistent verbal harassment and feeling so depressed about it that the teen concludes there is no way out.

The Least You Need to Know

➤ Verbal murderers are people who repeatedly make you feel horrible about yourself. They attempt to sabotage your efforts whenever possible.

➤ By examining the verbal murderers throughout your life, you can discover the pattern of abuse and learn to recognize the verbal murder and take the necessary verbal precautions.

➤ People become verbal murderers for a variety of unconscious reasons.

➤ Unconsciously, verbal murderers have low self-esteem, globalize their negative feelings about others towards you, make you responsible for all that have wronged them, are jealous of you, have trust issues, and don't believe they deserve happiness.

➤ Conscious motives for verbal murders include the murderer's dislike for you, jealousy, a need to control you, and lack of belief in you.

➤ The common thread of being a verbal murderer and being verbally murdered is having low self-worth.

Part 2
Preparing to Verbally Defend Yourself

In Part 1, you learned how to recognize the "verbal enemy." You learned how to size them up, and what specific signals to look and listen for. You learned how to recognize whether you have been subjected to verbal abuse. You learned about both the psychological and physical consequences of being subjected to verbal abuse. Finally, you learned about the specific types of verbal abusers and why they do it.

You can never defend yourself against the verbal enemy unless you are prepared. You can't fight a battle and expect to win unless you have the right ammunition.

In fighting back, you must come from a position of power and strength. In order to do this, you need to feel confident that you have all of the equipment essential to help you win the "verbal war."

This part tells you about all the tactics and strategies you need to come out ahead. First, you learn how to objectively analyze yourself as you prepare for verbal warfare. Then you learn how to defend yourself and find out all you need to know about how to gain that added physical, verbal, and communicative advantage against verbally abusive people.

Chapter 5

Analyzing Your Strengths and Weaknesses

In This Chapter

➤ Learn how to objectively analyze your strengths and weaknesses

➤ Discover things about yourself from others' points of view

➤ Discover who you are inside—your likes and dislikes

➤ Learn how you present yourself physically

➤ Examine all of the components related to how you sound

When you know yourself, you know how to effectively comport yourself in the world. You know how to maneuver yourself in any situation, because you are secure enough to know what your psyche or mental makeup can or cannot tolerate. Therefore, you must have the knowledge and the confidence to know how you will react to any given situation. If you know that you tend to act in a certain way, but that way cannot gain you the advantage you need to win the verbal war, you become more conscious of the situation. Thus you can change your usual way of reacting and behave in a more effective manner, which allows you to verbally slay your hostile opponent.

How Others See You Does Matter!

Why would you care what anyone thinks about you? After all, how you look, act, and sound is your business, not theirs. You know in your mind that you are qualified to do any job. You know in your heart that you are a good person and that anyone would be lucky to have a meaningful relationship with you. You are absolutely right. However, unless you look, sound, and act in a way that helps you win friends and influence people, nobody will give you the chance to show how competent you are at that job or take the time to get to know you and discover what a wonderful, sensitive, and generous person you are.

The truth is that we do not live in a meritocracy. In an ideal world, superficial things like appearance shouldn't matter. In the real world, however, it does matter. If people perceive you in a more positive light, they will treat you better. They will have more confidence in you, which will translate into better opportunities for you. More doors will be available to you in your business as well as in your personal life.

Studies consistently show that if you have good posture, a solid walk, an appropriate gaze, the right facial expressions, and a good voice and proper communication skills, you will be perceived as being wealthier, more successful in business, less guilty of committing a crime, more intelligent, friendlier, and more sexually exciting than if you don't possess these qualities.

How Do You Come Across to Others?

To clearly learn about how you come across to others is to ask them objectively what image you give off in general.

Tell them that they won't hurt your feelings, and they would be doing you a great favor in terms of providing you with this information.

I came up with this idea when I was sitting on an airplane next to a businessman who was president and CEO of a highly successful company. He told me that he worked for a company for 25 years and was fired due to downsizing. He was on the fast track to corporate success and suddenly his world fell apart—his job and his marriage. He didn't know who he was or where he was going, so he set out on a quest to find out how others perceived him. He sent out 100 letters to people he knew well—colleagues, acquaintances, family members, and those whom he felt may not like him.

He asked them to take a few moments to honestly write and tell him what they thought of him. He then compiled all of the data and came up with a consensus that he was a doer and innovator, he loves people, and he was personable, friendly, and sensitive towards the needs of others. He spent more time counseling employees than being concerned about the bottom line. He also found out that he was impatient and at times has a bad temper—especially when he doesn't get his way.

Talk Back Tips

Soliciting the opinions of others is more easily done with people who are close to you and who have your best interests at heart.

This information changed his life. He started an employment agency to help scientists and researchers find jobs, since the business employment agencies were tapped out. In his new position he has never been happier in his life—all day long, he counsels unemployed scientists whom he knows he helps. He has made more money than ever before, watches his temper and his impatience, and the best news is that he married one of his scientist clients and is living happily ever after.

The General Consensus About You Is...

In order to make people in your life more comfortable with giving you information about yourself, you may want to ask them to describe how *others* may perceive you. This gets them off the spot; they're less likely to feel they'll embarrass you and themselves, no matter how much you protest that the information won't hurt your feelings.

You may want to do this with your co-workers, employer, employees, spouse, children, friends, relatives, and anyone else who knows you.

Write these comments down in a notebook afterwards and then look at certain personality patterns you have, as well as how they feel you present yourself. Once again, insist that they be 100 percent candid with you so that you can get a true picture of how the world sees you.

Sometimes, people will have already told you how they feel about you. In these cases, you don't need to ask them again. Just include their names on the list along with comments they made about you in the past.

Putting Others to the Test

On each page of a small booklet, write the name of the person to whom you are asking these questions, on the page in your booklet listing with who they represent in your life. Do it with 5–10 people in each category. You can do it with more than 10 people; the more information you get about how several people perceive you, the better equipped you are to learn more about yourself and see if consistent negative perceptions crop up. You may now become aware of them and begin the journey of changing or modifying the negative aspects.

The more you can do to change yourself for the better, the stronger and more powerful you will be in fighting any verbal battle. Following is a sample chart you can fill out to help you learn how people perceive you. You can compare this chart by first writing down how you perceive yourself and see if it is in harmony with what others think of you. If your comments about yourself are widely different from others' comments, this may be a good reality check for you. It may help you modify or amplify your actions or the way you present yourself.

Talk Back Tips

Remember not to get defensive or harbor a grudge against anyone participating in this exercise: in reality, they are doing you a favor by telling you their truth about you—no matter what that truth is.

I See Myself As...

Positive Traits   Negative Traits

1. _____   _____

2. _____   _____

continues

continued

3. _____ _____
4. _____ _____
5. _____ _____
6. _____ _____
7. _____ _____
8. _____ _____
9. _____ _____
10. _____ _____

Family and Relatives Think I Am...

       Name   Comments

1. _____ _____
2. _____ _____
3. _____ _____
4. _____ _____
5. _____ _____
6. _____ _____
7. _____ _____
8. _____ _____
9. _____ _____
10. _____ _____

Now repeat this same chart noting the opinions of close friends, acquaintances, professionals (doctors, attorneys, dentists, teachers), and business colleagues.

Consensus of Opinion of Other's Comments About You

Positive Consensus   Negative Consensus

1. Family
2. Close Friends
3. Acquaintances
4. Professionals
5. Business Colleagues and Employers

General Overall Comment about How Others Perceive Me...

_____

_____

General Overall Comment about How I Perceive Myself...

_____

_____

Equipment You Need to Objectively Examine Yourself

Before you fight any verbal battles, you need to look at yourself very objectively. You need to get emotionally naked and put your ego into your back pocket. You need to step outside yourself and pretend that you are looking at a person other than yourself. Try to look at this person (you) in the same manner as others may be viewing and perceiving this person.

Besides having an objective mind, you need a mirror, preferably full-length (together with an audiotape or a video camera), where you can see yourself soon after you are visually recorded. Both the mirror and audiotape or videotape are ideal devices for observing yourself and keeping a record of the significant changes you make as you learn new and powerful skills to help yourself in your verbal battles. You will be able to see and hear the progress you made from the time you first examined or recorded yourself as part of the exercises in this chapter, to how you are coming across now and in the future.

Mirror, Mirror on the Wall

Walk up to a full-length mirror and examine the person standing there—you! Observe yourself walking to the mirror. Now stand in front of the mirror as you usually stand and look at that person in front of you. As silly as it seems, turn a tape recorder on next to you and talk to a person who is in the room with you. Explain what you are doing so that the person won't think you have gone nuts. If there is no one there, get on the speaker phone (if you have one) so that your head won't be cocked against the receiver as you are speaking and listening to the person on the other line. If your phone isn't next to your full-length mirror, just look in the mirror and start speaking. Ask yourself some questions.

Talk to the "you" in the mirror as you record yourself on the tape recorder. Ask the "you" questions in the second person perspective. For example, don't ask "What did I do today?" but "What did *you* do today?"

If you don't know what to say, the "Talk Back!" section that follows has some suggestions you can discuss with yourself. Talk to yourself while standing up and then while sitting down in a chair.

Talk Back Tips

As you do the mirror exercise, ask yourself several open-ended questions, so that you won't give yourself simple "yes," "no," or "I don't know" answers. This will allow you to probe more deeply.

Perhaps you can ask yourself half of the questions in the "Talk Back!" section while standing and the other half while sitting.

Here are several topics to discuss with yourself in the mirror or on audiotape or videotape:

1. What was the greatest experience of your life?

2. What are your plans for this week and next week?

3. What would be your innermost fantasy for an ideal life?

4. Who are the three people who have most influenced your life, and how did they do it?

5. Describe your ideal mate.

6. Describe an event in detail that you would like to relive.

No Lies on Videotape

Even though the lighting may not be the best, you can still get true representation of how you come across. Use the same techniques that were suggested in the preceding section, "Mirror, Mirror on the Wall." Make sure that when you videotape yourself standing up and then sitting down, the camera lens is adjusted appropriately. If you want to have a conversation on videotape with another person in the room, make sure that they are not shown in the video by appropriately adjusting the camera.

When you play back the videotape to objectively examine yourself, it is best to do it alone, so that nobody can influence or contribute to your analysis. For example, you don't want to objectively observe that your shoulders may be rounded when you stand, then have the other person discount your self-analysis by saying something like, "I don't think they are so rounded."

Talk Back Tips

Much of the vocal frequency and the actual quality of the voice may be somewhat diffused due to the mechanics of the recording device. Therefore, if you want a clearer, more accurate representation of how you sound, invest in a high quality recording device. The same holds true for the video recording device.

Record a Call

Electronics stores sell special tape recorders that enable you to record your telephone conversation with someone else and play it back later. In many states it is a crime to tape record a conversation without telling the other person. If this is the case in your state, let the person know that the call is being taped so that you can examine how you come across on the phone. Assure your partner that the conversation won't be used for any purpose other than your own self-analysis, and that the other person's voice and taped comments won't be analyzed or given to anyone else.

Another way to get the tape recording done is to tape your side of the conversation via an external tape recorder. Make certain that the recorder is located not too far away from you, so that you get a more accurate reading of the way your voice sounds.

A Picture Says a Thousand Words

Sometimes you can determine a lot about the way you come across (for example, your facial expressions and your sitting and standing posture) from photographs.

The reason many people don't like how they look in photos is that there is something about the photos that doesn't present them in the best light. Aside from certain people photographing better than others because of the angles of certain facial features or the way their bodies are positioned, most people know that something about the photos— they don't know what—reflects something negative about them.

On careful inspection of this matter, I did a small study in which I asked people to look at photos of themselves taken over time to determine whether they could spot a pattern in the way they sat, stood, or in the way they presented themselves facially.

To get a clearer perception of people's posture and facial expression, I had them show me some photos of themselves from different times in their lives. Those who consistently hated their photos regardless of when the pictures were taken said that they just didn't like the way they looked. When I further analyzed their photos, I could see that their posture and their facial expression (a consistently tense smile or serious frown, for example) may have contributed to their negative views of themselves. They also may not have liked the way they looked because of poor self-esteem.

Verbal Vignette

Research shows that what is true for videotape analysis holds true for photo analysis. There is an extremely high correlation between our perceptions while observing video tape of a person and perceptions while looking at still photographs of the person. Similarly, what we see and perceive in photographs is not too different from what we observe and perceive about a person in a videotape.

Getting Emotionally Naked

Before you step into your verbal battle gear, you need to shed your previous ego armor. Your first step in removing this armor was established when you found out how people in your world looked at you.

Now is the time to objectively look at yourself and listen to yourself, warts and all. It may be uncomfortable at first, largely because you've never done it before.

Know that after you analyze your body language, facial language, the way you speak, and what you say, and when you learn how to rectify any difficulty you may be having in any of those areas, you are well on your way to having all of your equipment intact. This gives you the proper verbal ammunition to charge forward and defend yourself against any verbal vultures.

Talk Back Tips

This concept is also evident in animals. For example, it is the "alpha" dog—the leader—who has the confident stance, head held high, and tail up with a definite and solid walk that gains the respect of his canine peers. They instinctively know not to mess with this top dog, or the consequences will be unpleasant.

Stand Up and Walk the Walk!

It is well documented that if a person stands and walks like a victim, he will be perceived as weak and helpless. This is why statistics show that the person projecting this weak image is more likely to be victimized in a robbery or assault than the person who stands and walks with a confident gait. These individuals project a "don't mess with me" attitude that usually deters the criminal.

Having a posture and walk reflecting only self-assuredness are extremely vital to your victory in the verbal battleground.

The Stance of Power

"Strand up straight!" "Don't hunch your shoulders!" "Keep your head up!"

Sound familiar? Most of our parents repeated these mantras. Those who took heed have excellent postures today, while those who didn't have carried poor postural habits into their teens and into adulthood.

Because posture is the first thing people see, it is one of the key components to reflect how others who don't know you will initially treat you. If you don't stand straight, giving the impression of self-respect, they may not initially treat you as respectfully as they would someone with better posture.

Perceptual psychosocial studies confirm this. One hundred people were shown photos of people with their head hanging down, rounded shoulders, and stomachs out, while others were shown photos of people with their heads up, shoulders squared and back, and their stomach in. Poor postured people were perceived as less popular, more nerdy, less exciting, less ambitious, and less physically attractive than their straight-postured counterparts.

Look in the mirror or at the videotape of yourself. Now answer "yes" or " no" to the following questions:

Posture Evaluation

1. Is your posture stiff and rigid?
2. Is your posture too relaxed or loose?
3. Is your back hunched over?
4. Do you rock back and forth or are you unable to stand still?
5. Do you stand on one leg instead of two?

The next two questions cannot be answered by observing yourself in the mirror or on video. Therefore, think back to social or business situations you have been involved in when answering them.

6. Do people move away from you when you speak to them because you stand too close?
7. Do people move closer to you because you sit or stand so far away?

If you answered "yes" to any of these questions, you need all the help you can get. Help with your posture appears in Chapter 6.

Those with stiff and rigid postures are perceived as being uptight and inflexible, cold and distant—not warm and inviting. These people tend to alienate others, who find them unapproachable and difficult to communicate with.

While it is great to have a relaxed and inviting stance that indicates self-confidence, a posture that is too loose or over-relaxed is perceived as being sloppy and unconfident. It is alienating—who wants to be around a slob who is overly comfortable around you, even if they just met you?

Rocking back and forth is perceived as impatience or anxiousness to leave the scene. It makes others uncomfortable because your constant movements often contribute to their loss of focus and concentration. Thus, they find it very difficult to talk to you. Other, more compassionate individuals are also uncomfortable and may lose their train of thought around you as they empathize with your anxious need to go to the bathroom or get a drink.

Unless you are a flamingo living in Miami or you are physically challenged and possess only one leg, standing on one leg is highly distracting. You are perceived as being in pain from an injured leg. Instead of thinking about the conversation you are engaged in, the other person is wondering what happened to your leg. People perceive you as immature, because children usually present this stance when talking to others, especially when

Listen Up!

Those who are hunched over or who have stooped or rounded shoulders are perceived as weak and insecure. Such people often don't elicit trust or confidence from others.

they are uncomfortable around that person. Others may also perceive you as being not attuned to the present situation, or too casual. Having others perceive you in this manner does not elicit trust and confidence in you.

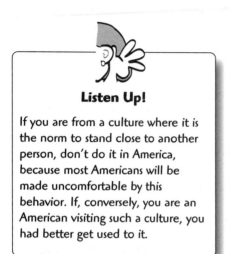

Listen Up!

If you are from a culture where it is the norm to stand close to another person, don't do it in America, because most Americans will be made uncomfortable by this behavior. If, conversely, you are an American visiting such a culture, you had better get used to it.

Standing too close to someone, especially if there is not a mutual love connection, makes people uncomfortable for a number of reasons. First, they may become conscious of their possible bad breath or be repelled by your breath or body odor. Secondly, they may shrink back because they don't want you to get the impression that they are interested in you. They may perceive you as having a lot of nerve or "chutzpah" as you dare to invade their precious space. Remember that in some cultures people stand closer to one another than is comfortable for Westerners.

If someone stands too far away they are perceived as not liking you or being arrogant, snobby, or feeling as though they are better than you. Even if you have a visual problem and can see people clearly only from a distance, no one cares. They still perceive you in a bad light, so move closer!

The Walk of Authority

Videotape yourself walking, or have a friend watch you walk up and down a hallway or across a room. Then answer the following questions.

1. Do you swish and sway when you walk?
2. Do you have a rigid walk, like a soldier?
3. Do you make a lot of noise when you walk?
4. Do you shuffle your feet when you walk?
5. Do you have a tentative, quiet walk?
6. Do you walk too slowly?
7. Do you walk too quickly?

Swishing and swaying while walking has a sexual, seductive connotation. This highly feminine walk may be off-putting to those who are not interested in you sexually.

A rigid, soldier-like march portrays an uptight, alienating, and angry disposition.

People who make a lot of noise when they walk often give the impression of being obnoxious and craving attention. Shufflers are perceived as lazy or insecure or sad and depressed. One who walks too fast appears angry or anxious (always in a hurry). Fast walkers sometimes seem obnoxious, especially if you are walking next to them and they sprint ahead of you. If a man does this to a woman in Western culture, he is perceived as insensitive, chauvinistic, and obnoxious. (Of course, be aware that some people have good reasons for walking quickly. For instance, in the workplace, seeing your boss dash frantically may be a sign not that she's rude but that she overslept for her big sales meeting!)

I Have to Hand It to You

Answer the following questions about your arm and hand movements.

1. Are your arms crossed when you speak?
2. Do your hands and arms flail around when you speak?
3. Do you usually wonder what to do with your hands?
4. Do you use minimal or no hand movement when you speak?
5. Do you use your hands a lot when you speak?
6. Do you always seem to be fidgeting with your hands?
7. Do you feel compelled to touch everything or everyone in front of you, even if they don't belong to you?

Crossing your arms has other connotations besides being closed off to others. It may be perceived as anger and alienation and disinterest in what the other person is saying.

Arm flailers, unless they belong to a culture where this is the norm, come across as angry and hostile. Those who don't know what to do with their hands are perceived as being uncultured, unsophisticated, and insecure.

Those who constantly fidget with their hands are perceived as nervous or anxious. Those who touch everything around them are perceived as annoying, unconscious, unaware, invasive, rude, and out of control.

Talk Back Tips

Westerners who use minimal or no hand movement appear rigid and uptight, unfriendly, withholding, and uncomfortable to be around.

Dead Head?

Watch yourself from the neck up and answer these nagging noggin questions.

1. Do you stick your neck and jaw out when you speak?
2. Is your head usually tilted down when you speak?
3. Do you cock your head to the right or left side when you speak?
4. Do you turn your head just a little when speaking to someone, while keeping your body in a different position (usually straight forward) from your head?
5. Do you constantly nod your head "yes" or "no" when you speak?

When you stick your neck and jaw forward when speaking or listening, you are perceived as being angry. A downward-tilted head spells insecurity, a lack of confidence, and unworthiness. Cocking the head to one side looks like you doubt what the other person has said. It signifies a contentious and suspicious person with an attitude of "I don't believe you—show me."

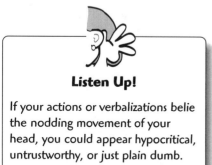

Listen Up!

If your actions or verbalizations belie the nodding movement of your head, you could appear hypocritical, untrustworthy, or just plain dumb.

Turning your head and not your body when talking to a person indicates that you are subconsciously keeping your distance from them. They perceive you as not liking or accepting them.

Unless you are from another culture, you either have a neuromotor problem or are very suspicious and doubtful about what others say to you. You are perceived as negative and unaccepting or disagreeable. Concurrently, if you nod your head "yes" all the time you are speaking to a person, you appear overly agreeable or as if you are seeking approval by giving unmitigated approval to the person to whom you are speaking.

About Face!

Often your facial expressions reflect your feelings more than the words you use. Even though our six basic emotions—happiness, sadness, anger, disgust, surprise, and fear—are reflected through the face, sometimes we may make inappropriate facial gestures, which confuse the listener and detract from the message we are trying to relay.

An exaggerated facial expression can change your facial appearance from attractive to ugly. For example, one noted singer looks very attractive when she sings. When she speaks, however, it is a different story. It is rather disconcerting. Her mouth goes from side to side in a camel-like fashion. In addition to her rapid-fire, hostile-sounding speech pattern, she squints her eyes and furrows her brow, which is perceived as anger and disgust. This particular woman is interested in making the transition from singing to acting. But she has a lot of work to do in terms of controlling and modifying her inappropriate and unaesthetic facial expressions before she hits the big screen (or the little screen, for that matter).

When you wear an incongruous facial expression, people get angry or turned off with you and perceive you as being "weird" or "disconnected" or "not with it." They may also misinterpret your message, as in the case of this successful singer.

As you observe yourself in the mirror or on videotape, answer these questions while paying attention to your facial expressions:

1. Do you mainly seem to have a dull or bored expression when you speak?

2. Do you look angry when you speak, even though you aren't?

3. Do you look sad when you speak, even when you are talking about pleasant things?

4. Is your normal facial expression tense with your muscles showing when you speak?

If you answered "yes" to any of these questions, help is on the way in Chapter 6. Since the eyes and mouth are key elements of your facial language, go back and answer the questions "yes" or "no" as they pertain to your eyes and mouth.

Verbal Vignette

Charles Darwin was the first to discover that "the same state of mind is expressed throughout the world through the face with remarkable unity."

Eye Deal

For centuries people have said, "the eyes are the windows to the soul." Therefore, people can tell a lot about how to deal with you by observing what you do with your eyes.

1. Do you often squint when you speak—furrowing your forehead or knitting your eyebrows together?
2. Do you often open your eyes widely when you speak?
3. Do you look off to the side when speaking?
4. Do your eyes dart around the room when speaking?
5. Do you look people up and down when you talk to them?
6. Are your eyes dull and lifeless?
7. Do you stare?
8. Do you blink too much?

Is Your Mouth Goin' South?

If you don't observe these behaviors in the mirror or on your video, try to recall if you exhibit any of these actions:

1. Do you usually speak jutting your jaw forward, creating an angry look?
2. Do you move your mouth from side to side when you speak?
3. Do you avoid looking at people when you speak to them?

4. Are your lips tense or do you have a strained, pinched smile?

5. Do you have a mask-like smile?

6. Do you curl your upper lip when you speak?

7. Do you hang your mouth open or even drool when listening?

8. Do you spray saliva when speaking?

9. Is there spittle on the corners of your mouth when you speak?

10. Do you clench your jaw when you speak or speak through your teeth, barely opening you mouth?

11. Do you often bite your lips or cheeks?

12. Do you exaggerate your mouth movements when you speak, giving the perception that you have a big mouth?

13. Do you purse your lips together before or after you make a statement?

14. Do you smack your lips before or after you speak?

Air Born

Believe it or not, the way you breathe can annoy others. If you don't coordinate your breathing with your talking in an appropriate manner, it may disturb and distract the listener.

Talk Back Tips

If you answer "yes" to any of the "Air Born" questions, don't worry. Help awaits you in Chapter 6.

1. Do you sound breathy when you speak?

2. Are you out of breath after you speak?

3. Do you take in many little breaths when you speak?

4. Do you sigh, or let out all your air before you speak?

5. Do you sigh, taking in air and abruptly pushing it out when you speak?

Ouch! My Ears Hurt Listening to You!

Research has shown that the way you speak is even more important than the way you look. In fact, the way you speak can affect how you look. Perhaps you have experienced this firsthand. At least once, you have probably seen someone who you found attractive, then, after speaking with that person, suddenly decided that he or she wasn't as attractive as you originally thought. Conversely, as research shows, if a person isn't very attractive but speaks well, that person is perceived as being more attractive.

The way you speak is composed of the pitch of your voice, the quality of your sound, the way you pronounce things, whether you sound too soft or too loud, how fast you speak, how nasal or non-nasal you are, and how you communicate. If you answer "yes" in any of the questions in the following categories, you should know that people are usually not perceiving you in the best light. Just know, however, that your ill-judged talking traits can be fixed in Chapter 6.

Verbal Vignette

Galen, the ancient Greek philosopher, once said, "It is not the eyes that mirror the soul, it is the voice." Modern research has confirmed Galen's findings, showing that the voice is a barometer to determine a person's psyche.

Pitching Your Voice

1. Is your voice too high?
2. Is your voice too low?
3. Do you sound bored or monotonous?
4. Is your speech overly animated or highly dramatic?
5. Are people usually bored or lulled to sleep when you speak?
6. Do you have a squeaky voice?

It's Quality We're After!

1. Does your voice sound breathy?
2. Does your voice sound harsh?
3. Do you attack your sounds when you speak?
4. Do you have a staccato, clipped, machine-gun like pattern when you speak?
5. Do you dislike the sound of your voice?
6. Does your voice sound creaky or crackling, often at the end of sentences?
7. Do you clear your throat before you speak?
8. Is your voice rough and gravely?
9. Does your voice often sound hoarse?

Twisting Your Tongue

1. Are you often asked to repeat what you said?
2. Do you often mispronounce words?
3. Do you mumble?
4. Do you repeat sounds, especially at the beginning of words?
5. Do you mispronounce s, z, ch, j, or sh sounds?
6. Do you mispronounce r or l sounds?
7. Do you distort your vowels?
8. Do people often ask you to repeat what you've said due to your accent?

Pump Up the Volume! Drown the Sound!

1. Is your voice loud and booming?
2. Is your voice too soft, prompting people to ask you to speak up?
3. Does your voice fade out at the end of sentences?
4. Do you have bursts of loudness, especially at the beginning of a sentence?
5. Do you have a loud and disturbing laugh?
6. Do you raise your voice at the slightest provocation or when you disagree?

How Fast Were You Going?

1. Do you speak too quickly, so that people ask you to repeat yourself?
2. Do you sound slow and lethargic?
3. Do you pause too long when starting a new thought?
4. Do you not stop after finishing a thought, immediately going on to the next?

The Nose Knows

1. Do you sound nasal and whiny where there is a vibration or twang in your nose when you speak?
2. Do you sound stuffed up most of the time, as though you have a cold?

Are You Talking to Me?

1. Do you repeat yourself?
2. Do you repeat words?
3. Do you often find that you can't think of words?

4. Do you say one thing and mean another?

5. Is it hard to express what you think?

6. Do you often keep your mouth shut for fear of sounding stupid?

7. Do you often say "I don't know" when asked questions?

8. Is your vocabulary limited and do you not understand the meanings of words?

9. Do you often use words in the wrong context?

10. Do you use improper grammar?

11. Do you always seem to forget what you were going to say?

12. Do you often interrupt others, not allowing them to finish a thought?

13. Do you change the topic midstream?

14. Do you often ignore a question, dismissing the topic someone else brings up?

15. Do you often say self-deprecating things to others?

16. Are you usually saying something negative, especially about others?

17. Do you often put your foot in your mouth?

18. Do you joke around, never serious, or make sarcastic comments?

19. Are you blunt and undiplomatic?

20. Do you usually give one-word responses instead of opening up?

21. Are you overly opinionated—"my way or the highway"?

The Least You Need To Know

➤ Whether you think it's fair or not, others perceive you positively or negatively based on how you act, comport yourself, and sound.

➤ By objectively observing yourself using a mirror and tape recorder, videotape, or even photos, you can learn a great deal about how you come across to others.

➤ Your stance, walk, arm and hand movements, and head position are important components in people's perceptions of you.

➤ Your facial expression, especially your eyes and mouth and the way you speak, can influence how people relate to you.

Chapter 6

Gaining the Physical Edge

In This Chapter

➤ How to have a powerful stance, walk, and posture

➤ How to have an effective handshake, and how touch can give you the upper hand

➤ Using your facial muscles to gain the advantage

➤ The value of "face contact" and how your smile can disarm your opponent

➤ How kissin' gets people to stop, look, and listen

When you fix yourself on the outside, the inside usually follows. I have seen this repeatedly in my private practice. While serving as a communication specialist in my Beverly Hills and Manhattan offices, I discovered that when people learn how to properly comport themselves, they feel more powerful and self-assured. This newfound sense of confidence gives people the ability to function more effectively and live a fuller and richer life, with better relationships in business and private life.

In this chapter, you learn exactly what it takes to present yourself to others so you'll be perceived as a formidable individual. You might even become intimidating to your verbal opponent: you will exude a blinding presence and a newfound sense of self-confidence, which in turn will boost your self-esteem. When your opponents experience your powerful presence, they will often think twice before verbally attacking you. Knowing the actual steps of how to improve the components of your total physical being allows you to win the verbal war and annihilate your opponent.

Postural Defense—Staking Out Your Presence

Because your posture is one of the first things people notice about you, you obviously need to stand up straight. Many people think they are standing up straight when in fact they aren't; you might have noticed your own poor posture when analyzing yourself in the mirror or on videotape. This problem is most common with people who are taller than average. They usually stoop to be at eye level with their shorter counterparts.

Verbal Vignette

Many girls, upon reaching puberty and beginning breast development exhibit poor posture in order to hide their breasts. Not wanting to draw attention to themselves, they hunch over.

If people do this during their formative years of height development, hunching their backs, stooping their shoulders, and bowing their heads can become their normal stance. As we discussed in Chapter 5, this stance elicits less confidence in others than standing with shoulders squared, back erect, and head up.

You must follow several steps if you wish to have a posture that exudes confidence and a "don't mess with me" attitude. By adhering to the following steps, you are well on your way towards looking more powerful when you are standing in front of someone.

Talk Back Tips

As a result of spine alignment exercises, you might experience fewer lower and upper back problems. Note that if you do this exercise and still do not stand erect, however, you should consult a qualified chiropractor. She can do a lot to help you.

1. Stand Up Straight, Without a Leg Up!

Stand up straight with your feet spread apart, parallel to your shoulders. Place both feet firmly on the ground so that your weight is distributed evenly on all parts of your feet. This takes pressure off your toes and the sides and balls of your feet. In essence, you are firmly standing on the soles of your feet. Don't shift your weight from leg to leg or shift your weight to only one leg. This throws you off and makes you feel insecure.

You want a "leg up" on your verbally toxic opponent, but don't take this statement literally.

Unless you're a flamingo living in Miami, never stand on one leg. You'd be surprised at how many public speakers do this when they are behind a podium. They put their weight on one leg while holding onto the podium—and they wonder why they don't feel as confident when they are speaking in front of an audience!

2. Bottoms Up!

Tighten the muscles in your buttocks (your gluteus maximus muscles) by contracting or squeezing your muscles, thus applying pressure to your buttocks. At first this might feel awkward, but eventually you will become used to it and over time, you will begin to feel comfortable. As you exercise and strengthen these muscles, you will have a solid foundation on which to support your erect spine and newfound confident posture.

3. Straighten Up and Back Up!

Next, start at the base of your spine and visualize yourself straightening each vertebrae so that you have a straight and aligned spine. As you visualize your new correct spinal posture, slightly tighten the small muscles going from your lower back towards your upper back. When doing so, you will notice that there is a forward shifting of your upper back that will begin from the middle of your back, around your waist area. This too might seem awkward at first, but as you practice this spinal position, you will feel less pressure in the muscles in your upper and lower back region because your spine will be in better alignment.

4. Heads Up!

Part of attaining a confident posture requires the correct positioning of the head and neck. Pretend that there is a cord or rope softly pulling up the crown of your head. This will automatically allow your eyes to be positioned properly as you gaze at another person at "eye level." It prevents you from protruding your jaw or sticking your neck out. Most of all, it keeps you from bowing your head or from looking down when speaking to someone.

Walk Up!

The way you walk is a vital component of the way you comport yourself. Some have angry, aggressive walks that scream "Here I am" or "Get out of my way." Others walk in a way that says "Just ignore me" or "I'm not important." Some people have a happy bounce, skip, or gallop in their gait, while others seem to shuffle, waddle, and drag themselves along. The only walk that screams "C-O-N-F-I-D-E-N-C-E" consists of the following steps.

Talk Back Tips

To assure that you have a confident walk, you need to wear the right shoes. Specifically, if you are going to do a lot of walking or standing, wear shoes that are one-half to one size bigger than you normally wear. This will accommodate your feet when they swell up. You will never again limp or have a pained look on your face because your feet hurt.

1. Begin with an erect posture, head up, shoulders back, and spine straight.

2. Place one foot directly in front of the other at a comfortable distance so that you have a smooth and even stride. Even though this may seem obvious and elementary to you, you would be surprised at how many people don't do this and end up waddling, shuffling, or slinking along.

3. Walk at an even and steady pace—not too fast and not too slowly.

4. Finally, let your arms move freely and swing naturally as you walk.

Sit Up!

Just as it is important to stand properly, it is equally important to sit in a way that exudes self-confidence. The way you sit in a chair speaks volumes about you, whether you realize it or not. Here are the steps you should follow to make sure this happens.

1. Stand directly in front of your chair.

2. Let your calves touch the seat of the chair.

3. Bend over, placing your buttocks all the way back in the chair.

4. Sit and lean your back against the back of the chair. By placing your buttocks all the way back in the chair first, your spine will straighten out automatically as it rests against the back of the chair. Doing this also prevents you from slouching.

5. Roll your shoulders back and relax your arms, either resting them on the arms of the chair or placing your hands in your lap.

6. Keep your head up. Visualize a string holding up the crown of your head, just as you did while you were standing. Once again, this keeps your eyes focused at the eye level of the person opposite you.

7. If you feel yourself retreating to your old slouching ways, just remember to push your buttocks all the way back in the chair. Lean against the back of the chair and remember to keep the crown of your head up.

Uptight? Lighten Up!

A rigid body posture signifies that a person is uptight, frightened, uncomfortable, nervous, or inflexible. Under certain circumstances, individuals need to be inflexible and follow a rigid code of behavior. But while the order "head up, shoulders back, chest out" works well if you are in the military, it doesn't work in real-life circumstances.

Even when you stand up straight with your shoulders back, you need to maintain a relaxed demeanor. The following shoulder roll exercise is designed to help you release tension in your shoulder region and arms.

1. First, rotate the right shoulder forward, and keep it in that position for approximately three seconds.

2. Keeping your right shoulder in that position, rotate the left shoulder forward for three seconds.

3. Now that both of your shoulders are forward, keep them in this position for about three seconds. Feel the muscles stretch as you maintain this position. It should feel good.

4. Next, rotate the left shoulder back and keep it in that position for three seconds.

5. Likewise, rotate the right shoulder back, keeping it in that position for three seconds.

6. Now that both shoulders are back, leave them there for three seconds, all the while feeling the stretch. This too, should feel good.

7. Rotate both shoulders forward and both shoulders backwards. Try not to rotate them too far back, and relax them.

Now your shoulders are in the proper position to help you maintain a good posture.

Talk Back Tips

Doing these exercises daily helps train you to develop good posture by allowing you to recognize the sensation of keeping your shoulders back in a relaxed fashion.

Up in Arms!

Your arms should hang at your sides in a relaxed fashion. Although arm and hand gestures are essential for helping you emphasize thoughts or ideas, too much movement can be distracting: arms flapping like a chicken's wings and fidgeting with your hands and fingers tend to diminish your total image. As I pointed out in Chapter 5, people perceive you according to the way you comport yourself. Thus, if you move your arms excessively and this isn't typical for your culture, you may be perceived as being anxious, uncomfortable, or even angry or out of control.

Hands Up!

To maintain some control over your gestures, be conscious of your gesturing, and do so only to emphasize key points or ideas. In doing this, it is important to make definite and deliberate hand movements. When you speak, keep your hands in your lap or relaxed at your sides, with your fingers relaxed. Doing this tends to relax the rest of your body.

Of course, this doesn't mean you should sit totally motionless. But the motions you do use should be relaxed. When you use both your hands and arms in a more fluid and open fashion, you are perceived as being warmer and more approachable.

Verbal Vignette

A Harvard University study showed that patients feel a greater rapport with doctors the more the doctors use arm and hand movements when talking with them.

If you notice that you are using your hands too frequently when you speak, try to be mindful and stop or reduce your hand movements. Being conscious of doing something to excess can often help you modify that behavior.

If you still don't know what to do with your hands, adopt the hand posture of the royals, who tend to keep their hands clasped in back of them when they stand or walk. Doing this often suggests to others a sense of security, control, and self-assuredness.

Shake Up!

You can tell a great deal about people by how they shake your hand. In addition, your handshake can reveal your true feelings about the other person. The looser and less firm your handshake, the more you will be perceived as weak, timid, or tentative. All too many men, especially large men, use a soft and wimpy handshake in an attempt to minimize themselves and not appear so threatening. The other extreme, a handshake that is too strong or tight, might express the attempt to dominate in the interaction and compete for control.

On the other hand (no pun intended), a firm handshake, lasting about three seconds, indicates self-confidence, especially when you meet a person for the very first time. In order to shake hands with self-assurance, follow these steps:

1. Be the first one to extend your hand. Do so enthusiastically.
2. Clasp the others person's palm firmly with your palm so that both of your palms are touching one another.
3. Look directly at the person's face using the "face contact" approach discussed later in this chapter.
4. Give their hand about three firm shakes.
5. Then release your grip.

If you really like the person, especially after you meet and get to know one another, you can convey positive feelings toward the other person by using the "cupping shake." For this handshake, cup the other person's hand in both your hands, while placing your left hand over your right hand.

Touch Up!

Ashley Montagu and other researchers and scholars have found that we humans need to be touched to adequately survive in the world. In light of sexual harassment suits these days, however, people must be careful about whom they touch, how they touch, and where they touch someone. A seemingly innocent touch may land you in a courtroom. Sexual harassment suits aside, touching another person is a positive gesture—it shows others that you have bonded or connected with them.

Although some people (most likely those who suffer from some type of psychological disturbance) shun being touched and touching others, research shows that most people enjoy touching and being touched, and they react better to those who touch them than to those who don't.

Verbal Vignette

A study was carried out in which librarians at a major university either touched or refrained from touching a student as they checked out books. In a questionnaire the students received immediately after leaving the library, they were asked to rate the library's personnel and facilities. The students who were touched rated the librarians more favorably than did the students who weren't touched.

Touching can break down barriers between people, especially if tension exists. Here are some rules to follow when touching someone.

1. Never touch anyone who appears by his facial and body language cues not to welcome your touch.

2. Pay attention to how often you touch someone. Touching a person too much is as disturbing to that person as not touching at all. Once again, monitor facial expressions to determine if your touching is becoming annoying to the other person.

3. In business situations, touch people only at the level of the shoulders—never below the shoulders or lower back.

4. In social or personal situations, feel free to touch a person's face, arms, waist, and wherever else you both agree is acceptable.

Verbal Vignette

Studies have repeatedly shown that men touch women more than women touch men. In fact, men touch women four times as much as women touch men.

Face Up!

Remember how when you were growing up, you were told that you should look into a person's eyes when you talk to him? You were told that only honest people can look you in the eye.

This is nonsense. In reality, research has shown that people who constantly look you in the eye without breaking their gaze might not be very honest at all; in fact, they might be lying to you.

You don't need to gaze directly into a person's eyes when you speak to her (unless of course you are in love with her). Doing so can be disconcerting and might indicate that you are taking a hostile or adversarial position against the person.

What you need is not just eye contact but "face contact." If you don't look at the person's entire face along with specific components of the face, how are you going to read all the facial cues of your verbal adversary or potentially toxic opponent?

In order to give someone the impression that she has your undivided attention, follow these steps religiously:

1. Look at the person's entire face for approximately two seconds.
2. Next, look at the person's eyes for approximately two seconds.
3. Switch your gaze over to her nose and look at it for two seconds.
4. Now look at the person's mouth for two seconds.
5. Go back to step 1 and look at the person's entire face for approximately two seconds, continuing on to steps 2 to 4.

You need to repeat these steps for as long as you are speaking and listening to the person in front of you.

People will not think you look weird as they notice you looking at their eyes, then their nose, mouth, and entire face. They won't even notice what you are doing. First, it's only a two-second glance on each of the facial components. Second, the distance from their eyes to their nose to their lips is minimal. It's not a huge football field you are looking at; it's a person's little face.

Most likely, in fact, people will perceive you as being really interested in them and in what they are saying. This technique also tends to soften your gaze, which makes you appear more approachable, more compassionate, and less intense.

Charming, Disarming Smile

We have all heard the expression "a smile speaks a thousand words." It's true. A smile can often disarm the most verbally belligerent person. Don't be afraid to be the first to smile at the other person. And don't be put off if they don't return your smile. Many people are so self-consumed or preoccupied that they will not notice you or your smile.

Don't be reactive to others, just smile sincerely. If you think of all the wonderful things in your life, the people who really love you and the people whom you really love, you will always have a true and radiant smile; your eyes will sparkle.

Oftentimes you can use a smile to defuse a verbal zinger that you will have to retort. Somehow, a smile makes what you are saying a lot less biting and stinging, but also more memorable.

The incongruity of your unpleasant, but strong, words and your soft and pleasant facial expression might throw your opponent off balance.

Listen Up!

When you smile at someone, don't use a tight-lipped smile or a half-smile; this conveys insincerity, and others can detect your insincerity or discomfort as easily as you can detect theirs. So smile with your heart.

Kissin' Up!

In this age of sexual harassment suits, you should think twice about whom you kiss hello or goodbye. Like the cupped handshake mentioned earlier in this chapter, a kiss—especially a final kiss after a wonderful interaction—cements a bond and expresses what a special interaction it was. In film, television, or other parts of the entertainment business, kissing or hugging someone hello or goodbye is the norm. With so many fragile egos and insecurities, and sad feelings due to constant rejection, hugging and kissing help show biz people feel good about themselves and closer to the person they are hugging and or kissing.

Many people outside the entertainment industry, however, don't know how to kiss or don't feel comfortable kissing others as a hello or good-by greeting. These kisses are not as serious as sticking your tongue down a person's throat. But they're more than a boring flat-lipped light touch of the cheek or the phony socialite "air kiss." This is not kissing. A kiss is when you pucker up and actually place your lips on a person's cheek or lips, create suction, and then release the suction a few seconds later. It may seem ridiculous that I am teaching you how to kiss someone hello or goodbye, but how you kiss someone can either charm them or disarm them.

It's very hard not to let down your guard toward an adversary who comes up to you and kisses you. You might even end up liking them. Try doing this after a tense conversation or a heated discussion. Give them a buss on the cheek or a hug, and watch what happens as their tense body and angry face relax.

Talk Back Tips

Nine times out of ten, when you kiss your adversary, you will see his facial expression become softer and feel the tension leaving his body.

This is an excellent and very powerful technique to use in the following situations:

➤ You know someone dislikes you for no good reason that you can think of.

➤ They're jealous of you.

➤ You have just been in an adversarial conversation or heated discussion.

You can't help but smile afterwards as you see how love and your positive attitude can diffuse the most negative energy. That is power! That power contributes to your self-esteem, which in turn translates into self-confidence.

Slipping Up or Messing Up? It All Adds Up and You End Up...!

You should always be conscious of how you come across. You can't slip up on the little things or you will certainly mess up everything. Mindfulness is the key. You need to maintain a constant vigil in terms of what you are doing.

Everything adds up if you want to have the physical advantage over your opponent. You need to have every component of your physical being working in your favor. Not even one part can be missing. You always need to be conscious of how you stand, sit, walk, hold your head, look at people, shake their hands, and how you touch or even kiss them. If you ignore any of these components, you are giving your opponent more of an upper hand in the war of the words.

Step away from yourself consistently and pretend that you are observing yourself outside of your body or from above. You can even imagine that there is an angel hovering over you, watching every move you make. Doing this visualization will make you more conscious of your behavior and comportment and its effect upon others.

The Least You Need To Know

➤ To gain the physical edge over your opponent, you need to have a standing posture, head position, sitting posture, and walk that shout "self-confidence."

➤ The way you shake a person's hand tells him a lot about you and vice-versa. A firm handshake allows you to gain the upper hand in verbal battle.

➤ Focusing on a person's entire face, not just her eyes, makes you appear more interested in her, warmer, and more approachable.

➤ A kiss, a hug, and a warm handshake can not only charm, but disarm a verbally hostile opponent.

Chapter 7

Gaining the Verbal Advantage

In This Chapter

➤ Breathing to gain vocal confidence, clear your mind, and release tension

➤ Gaining the vocal advantage

➤ Speaking more effectively

➤ Eliminating disgusting speaking habits

You're at a party. You spot a gorgeous woman or man at the other end of the room. With every ounce of courage you can muster, you coolly saunter over and flash your radiant smile. Your heart beats wildly, your head pounding like an African drum. You confidently stick out your hand and introduce yourself. The person reciprocates with a handshake and an introduction, saying "Hi, I'm _____." The moment you hear "Hi, I'm ____," you don't care who they are. You don't want to know. Your ears are deafened by a high-pitched, sickening tone that shocks you right back into reality, with your pulse rate returning to normal.

The way a person sounds says it all. Research in psycho-social perception shows that people judge you more by the way you speak than by the way you look. In fact, people who sound good are judged to be more intelligent, sexually exciting, and successful, and less likely to commit a crime than their poor-sounding counterparts.

Those who have poor speaking voices are perceived as weak, defenseless, less intelligent, and more victim-like than those who don't have this voice.

Research in criminal justice indicates that if one walks like a victim, one is more likely to be victimized. The same holds true for talking. If one sounds like a victim, one is more likely to be victimized in one's personal and social life. To verbally defend yourself and have the maximum effect on your verbally abusive opponent, you have to speak in confident and audible tones.

To speak in confident powerful tones to convey your points effectively, you must use your speaking mechanism properly. This mechanism consists of breathing, voice-producing, and speech and pronunciation mechanisms. This chapter will show you how to use these mechanisms to converse with others effectively. You will then learn how to incorporate your new-found speaking skills into confident conversation. Finally, you will learn how to start, maintain, and end a conversation with grace and aplomb.

Defensive Breathing

Did you ever wonder how the world's greatest singers such as Barbra Streisand or Luciano Pavarotti are able to hold those powerful tones for such a long time and still continue to sing so effortlessly? Did you ever watch a pregnant woman use the Lamaze Technique, using her controlled and repeated forceful mouth breathing to cope with the pain of childbirth? Have you ever heard the loud gut-level grunt when a professional tennis player serves a ball or a weight lifter lifts the barbell over his head?

Have you ever become completely mesmerized by a professional speaker, unaware that her melodic and effortlessly flowing tones were responsible for your added interest in what she was saying? How they breathe allows the professional singer to hold that note, the mother to deliver the baby, the athlete to hit the ball or lift the weight, and the speaker's information to glide smoothly into your ears.

Most of us take our breathing for granted. We just know that without it we are dead. It is during times of extreme excitement or stress, however, that we become conscious of how we breathe.

When we are nervous—or, more commonly, when we don't know how to breathe properly—several things can happen.

1. Our inability to focus and think calmly is impaired.

2. We begin to gasp for air because we have difficulty catching our breath as we speak, causing our opponent to perceive us as uncontrolled and desperate.

3. Without proper breath control, our voice sounds shaky and tremulous, giving our adversaries ammunition to perceive us as nervous, tentative, or unsure.

4. Finally, improper breath control can maintain or escalate increased heart rate and blood flow, which can affect the overall status of your health.

The following section on breathing will show you how to breathe to calm down and gain control of your inner being, your listening, and your talking.

Talk Back Tips

There is a lot of truth to the statements "I was breathless" and "it took my breath away." Times of heightened perception and excitement directly affect our breathing.

If you don't breathe properly the following things may happen:

➤ You may have trouble focusing and concentrating.

➤ You may be perceived as sounding desperate.

➤ You may be perceived as sounding nervous or tentative.

➤ Your heart rate may increase, thereby placing you in a more agitated state.

Relaxation Breathing: In—Hold—Out Control!

The Relaxation Breathing Technique is the backbone for all other breathing techniques.

These are the three basic steps for relaxation breathing:

1. Through your mouth only, sip in air for two seconds.

2. Next, hold the breath of air for three seconds without breathing.

3. Finally, exhale the breath of air through your mouth slowly and deliberately for five seconds.

Verbal Vignettes

The breathing techniques I advocate here are not newfangled ideas. They have been around for centuries, designed to create inner peace and tranquillity.

While doing this exercise, you must never move your upper chest when inhaling, and your shoulders must be down, not raised or hunched. All of the movement—the sipping in of air, the holding of the air, and the release of air through exhalation—must take place in the abdominal region. Why? The abdominal area is where we use our muscles to breathe naturally. In fact, if you observe a dog, cat, or small child, you will clearly see that their abdominal area goes in and out as they breathe. A popular but erroneous idea, passed down from singing teacher to singing teacher, is that breathing takes place in our diaphragm. This is not so. The diaphragm is a thin tissue under the lungs that separates the lungs from the stomach and intestines. Whenever you hear someone tell you that you need to breathe from your diaphragm, you will now know that they really mean the abdominal region.

Mind-Clearing Breaths

One of the principles in the martial art of Aikido is called *mushi,* a clearing of the mind.

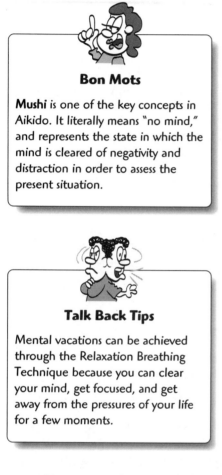

Bon Mots

Mushi is one of the key concepts in Aikido. It literally means "no mind," and represents the state in which the mind is cleared of negativity and distraction in order to assess the present situation.

Talk Back Tips

Mental vacations can be achieved through the Relaxation Breathing Technique because you can clear your mind, get focused, and get away from the pressures of your life for a few moments.

Aikido trains martial artists to gain control mentally over their opponent by clearing their mind of anger. It allows them to clearly assess the situation and the dangers involved and react accordingly. In fact, breath control has been used by ancient yogis as a key to inner peace and tranquility, helping them clear their minds of any negative thought, and allowing them to achieve a higher level of consciousness.

The Relaxation Breathing Technique is essential in clearing the mind and getting rid of anger or "toxic thoughts." What happens when we get nervous or anxious or think about all the people and situations that have made us miserable? We keep taking in shallow little breaths of air that we don't release as frequently as we do when we are not tense. This leads to a build-up of carbon dioxide, which increases anxiety, often producing headaches and light-headedness.

The Relaxation Breathing Technique can be used to clear and focus the mind. Even if only for a few moments, it allows you to have a sort of "mental vacation." Using the principles of the Relaxation Breathing Technique, you will notice that your entire world stops for the three seconds that you hold your breath. It seems as though you are suspended in time and space, which in essence breaks your thought cycle. After doing this exercise for a series of ten times, you will find, as many of my clients have found, that you feel refreshed, re-energized, and clear-headed.

Listening Through Breathing

Because your mind is clearer after doing this breathing technique, it allows you to focus on sight and sounds around you. The next time you are listening to someone speak, take a small (not obvious) sip of air for two seconds. As you sip in the air, sip in the word they are saying. As you hold your breath for three seconds, allow what they said to resonate as you digest and clearly process what they said. As you slowly let the air out of your mouth, you'll become more focused than ever before on what they said. The more you practice this technique, the better your listening skills will become.

Marrying Your Breathing with Your Talking

To speak properly and have good vocal tones, you must sip in air through your mouth (not your nose, since you breathe through your nose only when you are listening), hold it for a second or so, and then speak on the exhalation. It is essential to flow out your tones. To coordinate your breathing with your talking, you must follow the principles of the Relaxation Breathing Technique. However, instead of exhaling air, exhale while saying the *ha* sound for as long as you can.

Vocal Defense

As we noted earlier, Galen, the ancient Greek philosopher, once said that it is the voice, not the eyes, that is the mirror to the soul. When you have an appealing sound to your voice, the whole world opens up to you. Thus your voice is one of your greatest weapons in the art of verbal self defense.

Unfortunately, many people do not possess pleasant sounding voices. In fact, most voices are rather annoying. Studies have determined that if we listen to annoying voices over a period of time, we either become irritable and agitated or we tune out what is being said. This obviously puts you at a disadvantage if you plan to verbally defend yourself with a voice that sounds too soft, too harsh, too loud, too high, or too boring.

This section gives you techniques to effectively remedy these vocal ailments. Before you set forth to improve any vocal problems, however, you must be conscious of factors that might harm your voice. Following is a list of pointers that can contribute to a healthy voice box and a strong and confident sounding voice.

Your Most Overlooked Organ—Your Voice Box

Most of us hardly ever think about our voice box, unless we read about a major singer who can no longer sing or speak because she has injured hers.

Your voice box consists of a little muscle the size of an adult thumbnail. It looks like an inverted V, covered with a layer called a mucous membrane.

The V shape is formed by two separate muscles located side by side and facing one another. They open and close, depending on whether you are talking. When you listen and are silent, this V is supposed to be open; it is connected to a tube, the esophagus, which branches out and connects to the lungs. When the V is open you can inhale and exhale. If the V is closed when you are silent, you will most likely turn blue, pass out, or even die.

When you talk, you speak on the air when you are exhaling. You cannot speak when you are inhaling. The V closes and the muscle vibrates. That is how you make audible tones. The muscles come together and touch in the middle of the V in order to create pleasant and clear speech.

If you use your voice improperly by overly pushing on this muscle when you speak, you produce a hoarse sound. If the muscle swells—for example, when you have a cold—you also sound hoarse, as the two sides of the muscle have trouble coming together and vibrating. If you push these muscles too hard over a long period of time or you put too much pressure on the top part of the muscle when you speak, you will also sound hoarse or raspy. This is cause by two calluses, or nodes, that grow on the top of the muscle. When an actor or singer overstrains her muscle continuously, she develops these nodes and has difficulty singing and speaking.

Verbal Vignettes

If you follow entertainment news, you will often hear about singers who develop nodes as a result of vocal strain. Kim Carnes and Meatloaf are two examples.

Non-actors and non-speakers who talk a lot also develop this problem. Even children develop these nodes if they scream and yell a lot.

Additionally, if one of the vocal cords is paralyzed due to trauma or stroke, the voice may sound very breathy, and it may be difficult to make oneself understood. If you apply constant pressure to your voice box by speaking on the lower end of the V, you may develop what is known as contact ulcers.

Listen Up!

Never, and I mean *never*, go to a teacher who specializes in teaching people how to sing to help you with your problems with your speaking voice. Such a person can cause permanent damage to your voice, because her training is not as extensive and comprehensive as that of a licensed speech pathologist who specializes in treating patients with voice disorders.

A speech therapist or speech pathologist who specializes in voice therapy can usually help you. Before you engage in speech therapy, you must ask the therapist if her specialty is voice therapy and how many voice cases she has seen over the past year. If she has seen fewer than 50 cases throughout the year, or does not have a master's or Ph.D. in speech pathology or speech and hearing sciences, and is not licensed by the state, don't see her!

If therapy doesn't help, you may need surgery to remove these growths on your vocal cords and additional voice therapy to learn how to properly use your voice so growths don't appear again. Coming up, you learn how to care for your voice and how to use it properly, so that you don't have any problems.

The following list gives some rules to follow so you don't damage your voice. The next section of this chapter helps you remedy any speech and voice problems you might have.

Rules for Vocal Health:

➤ No smoking

➤ No drugs (except prescription)

➤ No alcohol

➤ Don't sleep with your mouth open

➤ Don't yell or scream

➤ Don't talk over loud noise

➤ Don't clear your throat

➤ Don't talk too loud

➤ Don't talk too much

➤ Limit consumption of dairy products

➤ Use throat lozenges whenever needed

➤ Drink lots of water

➤ Avoid spicy foods

Speak—Don't Squeak!

If you wish to lower the pitch of your voice, take a small sip of air through your mouth, hold it, bear down on your stomach muscles, like you are going to the bathroom, and speak. You will be surprised at how much lower the pitch of your voice will sound.

Over 60 percent of Gallup Poll respondents found a high-pitched voice to be one of the most annoying speech habits. To ensure a clearer, richer, deeper, and confident sounding voice, bear down on your abdominal muscles while opening up the back of your throat muscles while you speak. You'll learn this next.

Talk Back Tips

To find a speech therapist specializing in voice disorders, call your local university to see if someone there can recommend someone in your area. Or call the American Speech Hearing and Language Association in Rockville, Maryland at (301) 897-5700.

Yawning—Opening Up the Throat for a Smooth Voice

To have a rich and resonant voice, it is essential to open the back of your throat as though you were yawning. Try this as you sip in a breath of air. Hold the air for two seconds, open up the back muscles of your throat, and slowly and gently say the *ha* sound for as long as you can. This exercise is also very helpful for those who have rough and gravely voices or who suffer from vocal nodes, because it encourages the voice to flow smoothly through the exhaled air stream. This exercise can also help to soften a harsh voice.

I Can't Hear You!

According to a Gallup Poll I commissioned to determine the most annoying speech habits, nearly 75 percent of respondents stated that they were frustrated by a voice that is too soft or can't be heard. In order to project your voice so that you can be heard, you must use your abdominal muscles to anchor your tones. Therefore, when you speak you must put pressure on your larger and stronger abdominal muscles, not on your smaller and weaker throat muscles. A good exercise for using these larger muscles is to place your hand on your abdomen while repeating "yes, yes, yes" three times. You should feel a slight pressure on your abdomen as it moves downward when you speak. In order to project your voice, you need to bear down on your abdominal muscles as you speak. This increases the volume of your voice so that you can be heard.

Talk Back Tips

This chart is taken from my book *Talk To Win: 6 Steps to a Successful Vocal Image* (Putnam, 1987). Refer to chapter one of that book for more information on my Gallup poll.

Gallup Poll Results of the Most Annoying Speech Habits

Habit	Annoyed	Not Annoyed	Don't Know
Interrupting	88	11	1
Swear words or cursing	84	15	1
Mumbling, talking too softly	80	20	0
Talking too loudly	73	26	1
Monotonous, boring voice	73	26	1
Fillers "um," "like um," "you know"	69	29	2
Nasal whine	67	29	4
Talking too fast	66	34	0
Poor grammar, mispronouncing words	63	36	1
High-pitched voice	61	37	2
Foreign accent	24	75	1

Stop Turning Me Off!

Besides the sound of your voice, your arsenal must include knowledge of the other major speaking turn-offs discussed later in this chapter. They are monotonous, boring speech, a nasally whine, a too-loud voice, talking too fast, and mispronouncing words. You will also learn how to avoid undesirable and unattractive habits when you are speaking or listening. In this section, I address these issues and show you how to rectify any problems you might have in these areas.

Stop Putting Me to Sleep with Your Boring Voice!

There is nothing more disturbing than to be excited about something you have done, share it with another person, and have that person drone on in a boring monotonous tone how happy she is for you. It feels as though she took the wind out of your sails. She has completely turned you off.

In fact, a Gallup Poll revealed that close to 75 percent of individuals are turned off by people who have no life in their voices. People who speak in a dead voice are emotionally dead. They are not in touch with their emotions, often because they suffered some emotional trauma, repression, or early childhood conditioning. Therefore, if you have a monotone voice I strongly recommend that you consult with a psychologist who can help you uncover and deal with underlying emotional issues.

Physical exercises can also help you reduce your monotonous drone. Make an *"ah"* sound as you express the following ten emotions, while you think back to an event in your life where you experienced these emotions:

➤ sadness

➤ surprise

➤ anger

➤ happiness

➤ fear

➤ disgust

➤ sympathy

➤ love

➤ doubt

➤ boredom

All of your *"ah"* sounds should sound different, some inflecting upward (for example, surprise, doubt, and happiness) and others inflecting downward (disgust, love, and sympathy). Singing also helps you develop your muscles so that your tones move up and down more readily.

I have recently recorded two CDs. Until this experience, I had never sung in my life, except when I was alone in the bathtub or shower. But those who have listened to the CD have unanimously said they were impressed by the quality and sound of my voice. This is the result of all my years as a voice and communication coach and the exercises I did together with my clients, exercises that strengthened my vocal cords.

By listening to my tapes or CDs, you too can hear the results of doing the speech and vocal exercises throughout this chapter. Singing along with the lyrics provided will certainly help you improve the quality of your own voice.

Whining No More

According to a Gallup Poll, 70 percent find whining annoying; it rates as one of the top five annoying talking habits.

With the exception of those who have a physical abnormality such as a cleft palate or a neurological condition, most of the nasal tones you hear are due to people not opening their jaws wide enough when they speak. In essence, they tend to clench their jaws, which makes them talk through their nose instead of through their mouth.

If you sound nasal, never clench your jaws and never allow your back teeth to touch when you speak. I suggest that you pretend there is an imaginary dime holding your back teeth open when you speak. This technique will immediately reduce or completely eliminate your offensive tone.

The following technique is very helpful in getting your jaw and tongue muscles accustomed to opening wider when you speak.

Open your mouth as wide as you can while making a chewing motion. While chewing with your back teeth never touching, repeat the following sounds.

➤ Yah yah yah yah yah

➤ Yo yo yo yo yo

➤ Yu yu yu yu yu

➤ Ye ye ye ye ye

➤ yoo yoo yoo yoo yoo

Talk Back Tips

When doing the jaw–chewing exercises, try chewing gum with wide and exaggerated movements. This can strengthen your jaw muscles. Don't worry about looking silly or disgusting. What your mother taught you about never chewing with your mouth open doesn't apply in this case!

The Stuffed-Up Nose

Just as you can sound too nasal, you can also sound too non-nasal, as though your nose is stuffed up. And your nose may very well be stuffed up, blocking your breathing passages. In this case, it is essential to consult with a qualified ear, nose, and throat doctor. He can provide you with certain medications or may even perform surgery to reduce the blockage.

You may also sound this way because you unconsciously close off your own nasal passages. The following exercises help you eliminate your clogged-up sounds. Repeat each one of the following sounds five times in succession, so that it sounds like you are saying one word (mamamamama, for instance). Do this with each of these separate nasal sounds and repeat five times.

mamamamama

mo ma mu me

nananananana

no na nu ne

ung ung ung ung ung

lung hung sung rung

Tasting Your Sounds

Too many of us slur our words, mumble, and mispronounce our sounds, such as leaving the "ings" off words (such as with "coming" or "going").

As a result, we are often misunderstood or end up making those listening to us feel uncomfortable. The Gallup Poll verified this: over 63 percent of people found these characteristics annoying.

Kicking Key Consonants

Lisping children may be adorable. But as we discussed in the last chapter, studies have shown that people perceive adults who lisp their *s* or *r* sounds (with the exception of a regional or foreign dialect) as not being very bright.

Adult lispers are often made fun of. Those who lisp tend to be perceived as weaker and less intelligent than those who don't lisp. As I have seen throughout the years in my private practice, this can affect one's social and business standing.

Some lisping is due to ill-fitting crowns, dentures, braces or other dental appliances, missing teeth, spaces between the teeth, or the position of the jaw. Other causes of lisping are significant underbites or overbites. If this applies to you, consult an orthodontist immediately.

On the other hand, lisping may be due to poor tongue placement. To make a proper *s* sound, place the tip of your tongue against your lower teeth, slightly open your jaw, and push out the hissing air. To make a proper *r* sound, curl the tip of your tongue all the way back to the roof of your mouth.

Consonants are produced by the positions of the tongue, lips, teeth, and the back of the throat. The following exercises will help improve your consonant pronunciation. Repeat them in rapid succession in the order listed here:

Talk Back Tips

Castillians substitute the *th* sound for *s* sounds. This is not lisping but simply part of their speech.

➤ Lips: pa pa pa ba ba ba ma ma ma wa wa wa

➤ Lower lip against teeth: fa fa fa va va va

➤ Tongue between teeth: the the the thin thin thin

➤ Tongue tip against back of upper teeth: ta ta ta na na na da da da la la la

➤ Tongue tip against back of lower teeth: sa sa sa za za za

➤ Tongue tip against roof of mouth: cha cha cha sha sha sha ja ja ja ra ra ra

➤ Tongue tip against back of throat: ka ka ka ga ga ga ung ung ung

Vowel Control

Vowels are the meat of your speech. They are produced by selectively changing the size and shape of the oral cavity. Here is a spoken exercise to help you with your vowel pronunciation.

➤ beet bit bet bat bought but

➤ boast boot ee ih eh ah aw uh o oo

Demolishing Disgusting Habits

The following sections define additional annoying speech habits and list some possible remedies for the offender.

Listen Up!

Always be conscious of the condition of your lips. There is nothing more distasteful than talking to someone with dry and chapped lips. With Chapstick, lip gloss, and other lip creams readily available in stores, no one has any excuse. When your lips are moist, they'll move better when you speak, and they'll even kiss better.

Say It—Don't Spray It!

Have you ever talked to someone and felt that you needed a raincoat? He spit and sprayed his saliva all over you. If you yourself do this, help is on the way. This may be a casualty of not swallowing your saliva on a consistent basis or having over-active salivary glands. They might also bear down hard on the back portion of your tongue muscles, which in turn press on the salivary gland, thereby causing your saliva to squirt out. You might also do this because of ill-fitting dentures, wearing braces, or having new crowns. In any case, relax your tongue muscles each time you speak. Swallow your excess saliva after you finish speaking, and make yourself take another breath before you continue speaking.

Swallow Already!

If you are listening intensely to someone, you might forget to swallow, and therefore you will drool. Another casualty of not swallowing is ugly spittle that builds up in the corners of your mouth. Both of these conditions gross people out, so it is important to be conscious or mindful of swallowing your saliva on a consistent basis. Swallow whenever you take in a sip of air before you begin speaking. Sipping water on a consistent basis (especially when your mouth is dry) can often remind you to swallow. Mints are also effective in helping you to swallow on a regular basis, so don't leave home without them.

Slow Down! It's Not the Grand Prix

Close to 70 percent of the respondents in the Gallup Poll couldn't stand it when people spoke too fast. Asking someone to constantly repeat what she said is not fun. You may find people snapping at you because they are frustrated by not being able to understand what you are saying. To slow down your speech, do the exercises found in an earlier section, "Marrying Your Breathing with Your Talking." Another way to slow down is to draw out your vowel sounds for approximately one second.

Quiet! My Ears Can't Take It!

Speaking too loudly is often a sign of hearing loss. If you find that people are wincing when you speak or shushing you on a regular basis, you should consider seeing a doctor. The solution may be as simple as having your ears cleaned out.

Spit It Out Already!

According to my Gallup poll, many people were also annoyed by someone who spoke too slowly. You may do this while you are thinking, thus ignoring the person you are speaking to. If you have a boring, monotonous voice, you might tend to exaggerate your vowels. In order to stop this, be mindful each time you speak. As you sip in air before you begin to speak, think of spending only one second on each vowel. This way, you speed up and talk at a rate at which people find it pleasurable to listen to you.

It is also important, especially if you are in a situation where you are expected to do some public speaking, to avoid saying the following words: "like," "um," and "uh." So be mindful of your filler words. Silence is better than making someone listen to these motor-like sounds. Flowing your sounds together and coordinating your breathing with your talking (as mentioned earlier) can help.

Spending one second on each vowel, as well as consciously stopping yourself whenever you want to "um" and "uh," can also help you to modify this negative behavior. Hearing silence is better than hearing your annoying sounds.

Talk Back Tips

To consciously lower your voice, open up the back of your throat muscles and flow out your tones in a soft and relaxed manner. Relax your muscles, especially your throat and abdominal muscles, and spend one second on each vowel when you speak.

Hints to Help Control Your Stuttering

If you stutter by repeating words or sounds, or have episodes of silence accompanied by facial tics, you often can't help it. In many cases, certain techniques I describe in this chapter can help you overcome stuttering. Many of my stuttering clients, including a famed former cornerback of the Oakland Raiders football team, have made amazing progress using these techniques.

The Least You Need To Know

➤ In order to speak well, you need to use your muscles appropriately.

➤ A good voice and relaxed state of mind require proper breathing skills and the ability to coordinate your speaking with your breathing.

➤ Your voice box needs to be cared for, just like any other muscle in your body.

➤ Exercises and techniques are available to reduce and eliminate any of your annoying speech habits. You can improve the pitch, quality, loudness, rate, pronunciation, and quality of your speech.

➤ You can learn how to eliminate numerous annoying habits you might have when speaking or listening to someone.

Chapter 8

Communication Skill Defense

In This Chapter

➤ How self-discovery builds confidence

➤ Connecting with others to gain the upper hand

➤ Feeling more self-confident

➤ Preventing verbal warfare

To win the verbal war, it's not enough to have the proper speaking skills. It is equally important to know how to annihilate your enemy with your radiant confidence. What you say is just as important as how you say it and how you feel about yourself when you say it.

When you can be glib and feel comfortable talking with anyone in any situation, you are halfway to winning the verbal battle against your adversary.

Who in the World Are You?

When you know yourself, you know the world around you and how you fit in. You know what you will and won't tolerate. You will know who and what is good for you and who or what isn't.

Many insecurities come about because we don't really know ourselves, and as a result we aren't sure about ourselves. We know more about others than we know about ourselves. You probably can rattle off your mate's favorite color, food, and turn-ons and turn-offs. If I asked you these same questions about yourself, however, you probably could not answer as quickly, and would most likely have to stop and think for a while.

Why? Because you have never taken the time to really think about your likes and dislikes. Unless you have spent several years in psychoanalysis, you have not closely examined yourself. You haven't invested much time into thinking about all of the parts of you that make you who you are. Now it's time for you to learn as much as you can about the number one person in your life—YOU! It's your chance to become introspective and find out all you ever wanted to know but didn't think to ask about yourself.

Verbal Vignette

When the Greek philosopher Socrates said "Know thyself," he shed some light on what it takes to be more secure in life. Before you can know others, you have to understand yourself.

"Who Are You?" Quiz

In the back of every issue of *Vanity Fair* magazine is a page on which a celebrity is asked provocative questions. If you cover up the celebrity's answer and substitute your own, you will be surprised by the things you can discover about yourself—things that never entered your mind before.

In the following list, you will find a series of questions ranging from easy to some requiring considerable thought. Answer with the first thing that comes into your mind. Enjoy!

"Who Are You?" Quiz

1. Favorite color _____
2. Favorite type of music _____
3. Favorite type of film _____
4. Favorite animal _____
5. Three adjectives describing it _____
6. Favorite smell _____
7. Favorite food _____
8. I like to drink _____
9. My favorite sport is _____

10. My favorite city is _____

11. My favorite books are _____

12. I usually read _____

13. My favorite TV show is _____

14. My favorite actor is _____

15. My favorite actress is _____

16. Favorite season _____

17. Favorite time of the day _____

18. If there was a disaster I would grab _____

19. Favorite male _____

20. Favorite female _____

21. Three things I love to do _____

22. The happiest time of my life _____

23. The worst time of my life _____

24. Three things I would like on a desert island _____

25. Three people I would like on a desert island _____

26. The woman I admire the most _____

27. The man I admire the most _____

28. Three women I admire _____

29. Why _____

30. Three men I admire _____

31. Why _____

32. When I was a child I admired _____

33. Who is my mother _____

34. Who is my father _____

35. People who make me miserable _____

36. Why _____

37. When I was younger _____

38. When I get older _____

39. When I get angry, I _____

40. What upsets me the most is _____

41. I regret _____

42. I never regret _____

43. I am so happy I _____

44. Beautiful women make me feel _____

45. Powerful men make me feel _____

46. Powerful women make me feel _____

47. Handsome men make me feel _____

48. What makes me cry is _____

49. What makes me laugh is _____

50. My biggest fantasy would be _____

51. Whenever I'm nervous, I _____

52. When I look in the mirror I _____

53. The three qualities I look for in a friend are _____

54. The three traits that turn me off in people are _____

55. I could vomit if _____

56. When I get angry, I _____

57. When I get nervous, I _____

58. A perfect mate would _____

59. A perfect life would be _____

60. My three best traits are _____

61. My three worst traits are _____

62. I love _____

63. I hate _____

64. My childhood was _____

65. As an adult I _____

66. I'd never change _____

67. I'd love to change _____

68. I see myself as _____

69. Others see me as _____

70. Next week I want to _____

71. Next month I want to _____

72. Next year I want to _____

73. In the next 5 years, I want to _____

74. If I were President, I would _____

75. If I had three wishes, they would be _____

The Results of Who You Are

There are no right or wrong answers. Your responses merely make up a profile of who you are. How many questions did you have to ponder before you could answer them? How many questions were easy to answer? Examining your answers gives you an even greater opportunity to look inside yourself and even make changes in how you see yourself and live your life. This survey is also excellent to do several times a year, so that you can chart your personal development.

It might also be a good idea to have loved ones fill out the same questionnaire; then you all can share your results. This can bond you closer to the ones you love.

Keys to Gaining the Upper Hand

First and foremost, you need to have a winning attitude and winning ways to communicate with your opponent if you are going to be successful on the verbal battlefield. You have to like and respect yourself enough that the verbal bullets will have a difficult time penetrating your psyche.

You Gotta Like You!

It's not enough to know yourself. You must like yourself as well. If you like and respect you, others usually follow suit. They wouldn't dream of treating you any way you wouldn't treat yourself.

When you like you, you don't let people walk over you, abuse you, or say horrible things to you. You know how you fit into the world. You come from a position of self-respect and in turn demand that respect from others. If you are being treated poorly and consistently spoken to in an abusive manner in your relationship, you are treating yourself poorly by staying in that relationship. The first step to changing this situation is to like yourself enough to get out! Get out immediately! The book *Toxic People—10 Ways of Dealing with People Who Make Your Life Miserable,* which can be purchased using a form in the back of this book, gives you all the steps you need to unplug from this extremely toxic situation.

Don't Like Something About Yourself? Change It !

If you happen to dislike something about yourself, with all the choices available to you these days, you can definitely improve or change it. You might protest, "this is the body or face I was given, so why change it?" In a sense, of course, you are

Talk Back Tips

In my practice, I have seen young women who hated how their noses made them feel ugly and insecure; after getting nose jobs they felt pretty for the first time in their lives. Since they feel so much better about themselves, they put out a more positive vibe. Others tune into their positivity, and soon they have more opportunities both socially and professionally in their lives.

absolutely right! Why change what was given to you naturally? On the other hand, if you're self-conscious about some aspect of yourself such as your nose or body, improving it can change your entire outlook about yourself.

Psychotherapists exist to help you improve your personality, while plastic surgeons, skin specialists, speech and voice coaches, hairdressers, dentists, orthodontists, clothing and makeup consultants, and weight-loss specialists can help you become the best you can be. There are no more excuses! You can be all that you want to be—if you want to be all that you are!

When you really like yourself, are willing to accept everything about yourself, and are working to improve the things you don't like, you become more secure within yourself. As a result you become more powerful. Your power and radiance can be blinding to your verbal adversaries, who might just back off.

Talk Nice to You and Others Will Too

Never be a verbal abuser to the person you need to care for the most—YOU! When you say negative things to yourself, you are unconsciously chipping away at your self-worth, which obviously diminishes your self-esteem. You might think that you are being humble by cutting yourself down or being self-deprecating, but you are not.

Instead you are exhibiting a weakness—a "one-downsmanship" that your verbally hostile opponent can latch onto. In essence, you are giving your opponent more verbal ammunition to use against you. It may feel okay or painless when you make a cutting remark about yourself. When that cutting remark comes out of the mouths of other people, however, suddenly there is a painful sting to their zing! They might even add more verbal poison to the cutting remarks you already made about yourself. They may embellish what you said, thereby making their cut even deeper and more excruciating by hitting one of your most vulnerable emotional spots. Imagine.

The moral of this lesson is this: Don't add to the arsenal of your verbal enemy—don't say bad things to yourself.

Talk Back Tips

It doesn't matter who hears you "cancel your remark." In fact, the person listening may have even more respect for you as he or she witnesses you giving yourself more respect.

Cancel That!

What happens if you forget and end up saying something bad about yourself because you haven't yet gotten into the habit of being nice to yourself? This is expected. What you need to do in this case is to say the words, "Cancel that remark!" Say it out loud. Eventually your negative remarks will become fewer and fewer because you will be more verbally conscious of what you are saying to yourself.

The Power of the Word—What a Surprise!

Whether you believe in metaphysics or precognitions, in my personal research of tragic stories, I've observed that when people utter negative expectations, these usually come to pass. This is called the "self-fulfilling prophecy." If you don't think that you can do something, chances are that you can't or that you won't do it well.

Even if you are feeling a little insecure because you have never done something before, keep telling yourself that you can do it: you'll be surprised at what happens. Many successful athletes and Olympic winners with whom I've worked use this technique. So did the little train in the ever-popular children's story. The little train "thought he could," and by golly, he did get up that steep railroad track!

Thoughts in Your Head

You are what you think! It doesn't matter what others think. It only matters what you think about you. It's as simple as the fact that if you think good thoughts, more good will happen to you, while if you think bad thoughts, more bad will come to you. If you really believe you can do something, most likely you will do it.

If you really want to work to replace the ideas that you are a failure in life and that you are limited in how far you can go, try meditation and affirmation tapes by Guru Ji Pillai, Ph.D. The tapes teach you how to think "vertically"—to think about infinite possibilities in your life. This is in contrast to horizontal thinking—going along with the status quo and being stuck in a rut. Guru Ji says that only by expanding your thoughts and your awareness can you manifest your goals and life dreams. His philosophies and concepts are so effective that popular author Dr. Wayne Dyer has incorporated Guru Ji's unique technique in his best-selling book *Manifest Your Destiny*.

Open Your Mind!

To gain the winning advantage over your verbally vicious opponent, you need to deflate all prejudices or preconceived notions you have about him or her. Begin each interaction with a fresh new outlook.

This might seem a Herculean task, and indeed it does require a lot of practice and inner harmony to accomplish. I'm not telling you to forget about how awful they can be. I am not telling you not to be on guard. What I am telling you is to follow the same approach used by martial artists. When they face their opponents, they show no fear or anger towards their opponents and clear their minds of any previous feelings toward them.

A closed mind begets closed life. An open mind, on the other hand, results in an open and exciting life filled with the excited anticipation of what is going to happen next. An open, non-prejudiced mind allows you to deal with any situation or person that may come your way because you are free of preconceived notions. You are ready for any surprise!

Open Your Heart!

When we are angry or upset, our body, especially our hearts, react much differently than when we have good and positive feelings about a person.

Here is a technique that can help you open your heart, even toward a verbal adversary. Try to imagine that person as a sweet and innocent baby. Try to find one good point about him and focus on that thought. If you can't find at least one good thing about him, you haven't looked hard enough.

Opening up your heart towards the adversary may often result in diffusing his hostility and anger. Don't hesitate to make the first move—whether you smile at him, put out your hand for a friendly handshake, or make a kind remark. If the situation is befitting, you can even offer a short and warm "hello" kiss. You'll get a lot of satisfaction from taking him off-guard.

Listen Up!

Even if you didn't intend to do so, you unknowingly have used some words that can make anyone see red. In other situations, you may have sloughed off a misinterpreted comment said to you and kept it in until it festered and you ended up detesting the person who said it. Verbal battles often arise when someone is ignorant—he doesn't mean to stick his foot in his mouth, but he can't seem to avoid it.

Your loving and heartfelt gestures often diffuse others' anger and hostility towards you. So don't be surprised if you see a 180-degree turn in their behavior. Watch them metamorphose from mean to nice in less than 10 seconds.

Congratulations, you have just won the first battle in the verbal war!

Tactics Used to Promote Verbal Peace with Others

So much of verbal warfare is brought about by miscommunication and by misconceptions of what was said, and by misinterpretations of words and perceived rudeness from the other party. The rest of this chapter is devoted to ways you can avoid potential verbal attacks.

Speak Up Immediately!

No festering allowed! No shoving what they said, and your emotional reactions to it, under the table! No more keeping things in. Speak out immediately. The best phrase for you to use when you are miffed by what someone had just said is, "Excuse me, what did you mean by that? Explain what you mean."

If you heard right the first time, and they said what you thought they said, take immediate issue. What happens when it's 2 A.M., and your thinking about a perceived negative comment keeps you up? Call the person first thing in the morning when she gets into work, and deal with it then. Otherwise, if it's a reasonable time in the day, call her as soon as the comment starts to bother you.

Monitor Your Mouth

Just as it is essential to know when to speak up, it is equally important to know when to keep quiet. You can do this by observing your opponents clearly, as was discussed throughout Chapter l.

If you stop, look at them, and really listen and empathize with them, you will be surprised at how much less frequently you will say the wrong thing. You will become more conscious of your words.

If you stop and suck in air for a moment before you speak, you will never make a faux pas. Mistakes like these are usually made when you are not thinking about whom you are speaking to and what you intend to say.

Pay Attention to Trigger Words and Phrases

Sometimes, things are going along fine, and then all of a sudden you hear a word or a phrase that sets you off, starting a full-scale war. These words and phrases can cause long-buried negative emotions to resurface.

The following list gives some phrases you should never use. They are destined to trigger a negative response and put someone on the defensive. When a sentence or conversation begins with any of these phrases, the person has automatically tuned you out, is ready to attack, or is ready to verbally defend himself.

1. You should have _____.
2. You never _____.
3. Why don't you ever _____?
4. Why didn't you ____?
5. You'd better _____.
6. I don't believe you.
7. That's not true.
8. Don't you ever _____?
9. How could you ever ____?
10. You make me _____.

Instead, you might want to substitute the phrases listed here with the following phrases, which are destined to get the person to hear you and perhaps do what you want them to do:

1. Perhaps you could _____.
2. I'd appreciate it if you would _____.
3. It would be in your best interest if you would _____.
4. Have you looked at it from this point of view?

5. I don't mean to contradict you, but have you also considered _____?

6. Perhaps we could both _____.

7. May I suggest _____?

8. I would prefer _____.

9. It hurts my feelings when you don't _____.

10. Do you think it would be a good idea if _____?

11. I would never criticize you, but don't you think that perhaps _____?

Terms of Endearment

A verbal pat on the back is only a few vertebrae away from a verbal kick in the pants. When you want to maintain good relationships with people who you like, always incorporate terms of endearment. "Please," "would you mind," "I like [or "love," if appropriate] it when you _____" are musts, no matter how familiar you are with the person.

Listen Up!

We often take our loved ones for granted by not speaking these words of affection and kindness. When they are said to a potential verbal adversary, they can often defuse or even reverse the negative way in which those people speak to you.

"Honey," "sweetie," "baby," "dear," "love," and "darling" are great terms to use when you have just been in verbal battle with a loved one. These terms often reassure the person that no matter how angry you both got at one another, you still feel tremendous affection towards her. On the other hand, the consequences of speaking these words to the wrong person in the wrong context can be disastrous. They can land you in front of a judge in a sexual harassment suit or get you fired, not to mention generating a lot of unnecessary hard feelings.

Southerners and older people who see nothing wrong with calling someone they like "darlin'" have to be extra careful, since their use of terms of endearment are a way of life.

The moral of this story is to be always mindful of whom you are going to verbally endear.

Let Them Speak Their Piece

If you really want to aggravate people, just keep interrupting them when they are trying to make a point. As I explained earlier in the book, people who interrupt are considered to be extremely annoying as well as toxic.

To curb your tendency to interrupt someone constantly, do the following:

1. Take the tip of your tongue and stick it between your two front teeth.

2. Bite down hard on your tongue (not so hard that you bite off your tongue or make it bleed).

3. Stick your tongue back in your mouth.

The stinging and lasting pain you experience from having bitten your tongue will serve as reminder to keep your tongue in your mouth and let the other person speak.

Enough About You Already!

Constant talking about yourself angers people who are forced to listen to you. They might react by becoming short-tempered with you or by making fun of you. You might, however, be so self-consumed that you won't hear them anyway, or don't care even if you do care. Eventually, in addition to avoiding talking to you, they will use you as the brunt of jokes with their friends. The bottom line is, share the stage! Don't hog the conversation!

You will learn more about the art of having a great conversation in Chapter 9.

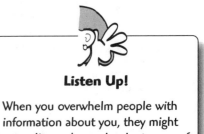

Listen Up!

When you overwhelm people with information about you, they might act polite and even laugh at some of the amusing details of your experiences. After a while, however, they will grow tired of hearing about you.

Mind Your Own Business!

Don't impose; don't get too detailed. Read their body, face, and verbal cues. Don't ignorantly and unconsciously keep asking questions. Let them volunteer. Don't invade their privacy or personal space. If you pay close enough attention, you'll know when you have done so. If you have, back off immediately!

Don't offer advice unless you are asked. This is a sure-fire way to alienate people, especially if they don't like your advice. You will feel bad that they didn't heed it. And they in turn will feel bad that you are judging them, when in reality you were only trying to help them.

Minding your own business means keeping confidences. Even though we all love the dirt, it's ugly when someone tells you something that is her personal business. Therefore, mind your own business and not everyone else's, even though you may know more than you need to know.

Respect Should Be Your Mantra

We throw the word "respect" around like a Frisbee, but nobody pays much attention to what it really means. When you respect, you appreciate, cherish, honor, and admire.

Talk Back Tips

Respect other people's word. Respect everything they say, and out of that respect, keep everything in the strictest confidence, no matter whether they've just shared a juicy a piece of gossip.

In essence, you look up to the person. That doesn't mean that you look down at yourself and hold him in higher esteem. Instead, it means that you honor who he is. With "respect" comes the complete consciousness and awareness of the other person. You need to always be aware of his time. That means when he says he has to go, let him go. Don't keep him.

When people say they're going to accomplish something no matter how large or small the project is, respect them enough to assume that they will accomplish what they said they would accomplish. Don't give any reasons why it can't be done. Don't even think about negating or diluting what they said.

Don't Like the Answer? Then Don't Ask the Question

Too many people bait you by trying to get you to commit to an answer or get your opinion even though you may be reluctant to give it. Then, if they don't like what they hear, they will take it out on you or on themselves. Often they can never forgive you. In order to avoid giving them an answer they may not want to hear and to circumvent the dilemma of being damned if you speak and damned if you don't speak, be diplomatic. If you sense that they will hold a grudge against you for life, think carefully about answering them. It may seem like the cowardly thing to do, but it is your judgment call. Trust your instincts. Another tactic is to change the subject or excuse yourself from the room for a moment (go to the bathroom, for instance). This might buy enough time that they will forget and go on to another topic. If they persist, tell them that you feel uncomfortable and don't want them to hate you if they don't like the answer they are about to hear.

If you are the recipient of the news, take full responsibility for asking the question, and most importantly, "don't kill the messenger."

The Least You Need To Know

➤ When you know yourself, you know the world. The more you learn about yourself, the more confident you will become.

➤ If there is something you don't like about yourself, change it! These days, you have many options available to you.

➤ Change negative thoughts and words about yourself when you communicate with others.

➤ There are ways to avoid verbal warfare, including being a diplomat, letting the person speak, and not using words and phrases that negatively trigger someone's emotions.

Confident Conversation

The Real Secret of Talking to Anyone

You can read a million self-help books on how to have a great conversation. In fact, I know of about five books on the market with similar titles about how to speak to anyone about anything. Television interviewer Barbara Walters released one of these books in the '70s; more recently, talk-show host Larry King had one published.

You can sum up this entire topic up in just four words: *Be interested—not interesting!*

Listen and ask sincere questions, and you'll be surprised at how many successful business liaisons you will develop and how many friends you will make. No matter how you deny it, everyone—you, me, and everyone else in the world—loves to talk about their favorite and most interesting topic—themselves! When you stimulate that topic, they like it, and in turn they like you!

Understanding the Four Steps of Confident Conversation

Now that you have the tools for a great verbal mechanism, you have to put them to use. What better way than to have a conversation with others?

In this section, you learn about the four basic steps to holding a confident conversation.

First, you will learn about pre-conversation, what to do before you even approach someone and initiate a conversation with them. The second step is initiating the conversation. This involves the key questions to ask once you have approached someone and subjects to avoid. You will also learn how to maintain the conversation once it has begun, and finally, the key to exiting a conversation with confidence.

When you are done reading this section, you'll have all the tools necessary to be confident enough to talk to anyone, any time, and under any circumstances.

Talk Back Tips

When you initiate a conversation with a stranger and get rejected, everything is not all right. You feel bad. In fact, you might feel so bad that every instinct you have tells you to turn around and go home, pull the blanket over your head, and sleep it off for a few days. But guess what? You've got no choice! You have to initiate those conversations.

Confident Pre-Conversation

Whether you realize it or not, your conversation begins well before you have even opened your mouth. Those with a lot of experience dealing with people—such as a salesperson or a social butterfly—find it second nature to meet and greet people. But most people feel uncomfortable going up to a stranger and talking to them. The thought of doing it leaves most people either paralyzed or with a sick feeling in the pit of their stomach. So, if you can relate to this, rest assured you are not alone. Everyone gets rejected and feels bad, so join the club.

Only this time, you have pre-conversation tools to help you gear up for the gut-shaking event about to take place. Before you begin, you have to visualize something good happening with the prey that you have picked out to experiment on.

Ending the "I Think That You Think That I Think" Game Forever!

For the most part, who cares what people think about you? Even if they don't like you, before even meeting you, they won't have laser beams coming out of their eyes to burn you. Usually, what a stranger thinks about you is irrelevant and none of your business. As long as *you* like you and feel secure with yourself, that's what counts.

So stop making yourself nuts playing the "I think, you think, I think" game. The truth is that they aren't even thinking about you or anything else. They may have a sourpuss expression on their faces because they are hungry or their tummy hurts.

If your mind starts to play the "I think, they think" game, stop yourself immediately using the "cancel that thought" technique. Only instead of doing this technique by speaking out loud, think it silently to yourself.

Verbal Vignette

In rare circumstances, someone's initial impression of you can cost you a potential job or a relationship. A woman I know went to audition as co-host for a television show. Everyone took to this sincere woman—except for the host, who had the final hiring decision. As soon as she walked into the room, she noticed his scowl and refusal to shake her hand, and her audition didn't even take place. She was out before she got in the door. But remember that it is rare to experience insecurity so extreme that the other person has to act in such a toxic manner. There is nothing you can do about it, so breathe out and move on!

Smile All the While

Stop! Look and smile, and keep looking and smiling! That is the best way to meet someone you are attracted to. If someone looks at you, smile back out of respect. If you are not interested, make it a short, curt smile and then look away. This shows that you have politely acknowledged him or her. If you are attracted to the person, no matter who looked at whom first, simply smile a little longer and say hello. If they return your hello, you have a golden opportunity to start talking and to make a new friend. I have met so many people this way, especially in airports, and many of them have turned out to be some of my closest and dearest friends.

Granted, at first it may be very uncomfortable for you to make this behavior part of your life. But with practice it will become a habit, and a pleasant one at that.

Do It Anyway!

Come on—just smile! Even though you don't feel like it, do it anyway! Nine times out of ten, the other person will smile back .

If you're having trouble kick-starting your smile, simply visualize yourself smiling at them and them returning the smile, accepting you, returning your

Talk Back Tips

In a study at Temple University in which 16,000 people were observed in public places, results showed that women and younger people smile more than men and older people.

compliments, and engaging you in conversation. Visualize yourself having them as a potential client, employer, employee, friend, lover, or even mate.

Now visualize the reverse. See the situation being a disaster, with them paying no attention to you, giving you dirty looks, and walking away from you. Did you die? No, you survived, with all your parts intact. So what's stopping you? What's the worst that can happen? Let's say that the person rejects you. There is nothing bad that can happen, not even bruised ego, because this is also an exercise in seeing reality—the reality that not everyone will be attracted to you nor will you be attracted to them.

After your positive and negative visualizations, enter the situation with a clean slate, erasing from your mind every pre-conceived notion about the person and about yourself. Remember to do the Relaxation Breathing Technique before you make your move. Now go for it! Do it! *Smile!*

You Die When You're Shy!

You both connect with one another, you've returned glances and smiles, but what to do you next? You're paralyzed with fear. You rationalize that you are feeling this way only because you are "a shy person." Well, if that's what you want to believe about yourself, you may as well crawl into a hole and live there.

Life is to be lived. Opportunities are to be taken and people are to be met. If you have ever felt like kicking yourself, even years later, for not making that first move and saying something, you are not alone.

To make sure this situation never happens again, re-label yourself and remove the word "shyness" from your vocabulary. You have nothing to be shy (insecure) about anymore.

Of course, you have to have something to say, and in the rest of this chapter you'll learn what to say to break the ice.

Only a Fool Plays It Cool!

There are those who think they are being cool by acting aloof. Even if they are chomping at the bit or drooling at the mouth and would give almost anything just to meet the person across the room, they don't. It's not because they are shy and intimidated, it is because they are trying to act "cool."

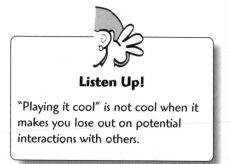

Listen Up!

"Playing it cool" is not cool when it makes you lose out on potential interactions with others.

This coolness takes the form of not looking at people or returning their glance or smile. It's looking down or pretending to be very animated in conversation with someone else. It's designed to let someone know that you are cool—a catch—albeit difficult to catch. Acting cool is quite common among young people in their teens and twenties, but it often continues into adulthood. It's a power game that establishes who's going to be in control. Just remember, the people who play this game ultimately lose.

The cool people may lose an opportunity to enhance their professional lives. The person they have snubbed may have been an important conduit towards success in their career.

Initiating a Confident Conversation

Coolness aside, here are some things not to do when initiating a conversation. Otherwise your conversation will end before it begins.

➤ Don't tell lame jokes or a joke where there is a 50 percent chance people won't like it.

➤ Don't excessively fawn over the person.

➤ Don't make sarcastic comments or cutting remarks in an attempt to appear cute. There's nothing cute about being obnoxious.

➤ Don't lie to give someone a compliment, and don't use a standard line they've probably heard a thousand times before.

Instead, here are some icebreakers guaranteed to help you initiate conversation.

➤ Give people a sincere compliment without fawning over them.

➤ Bring up a current news event (the juicier the better!).

➤ Speak positively about people whom you both may know.

➤ Tell people you observed them and thought that they

   a. Resemble a friend, relative, or famous person.

   b. Look like they are from _____. (This can be whatever you decide. Just don't say Mars or make a lame comment.)

   c. Work out or are in good shape. Ask if they are athletic.

Maintaining a Confident Conversation

So many people become mute after they say "hello." They have succeeded in getting the person to acknowledge them and to make that first contact. Now they freeze, go blank, and stand there like a deer in headlights, not knowing what to do or say and mumbling about something stupid.

If this scenario sounds all too familiar and you've been there/done that, help is on the way!

The reason you acted like a vegetable is that you began to focus on yourself instead of paying attention to the other person. You were more concerned about things working out right and about being interesting, witty, and clever than you were about what the other person was all about. In essence, you were not *interested*. You may try to contradict me here by saying "of course I am interested, or I wouldn't have approached them

You don't ever want to ask someone their weight, how much money they have in the bank, or about their most intimate sexual experiences. Unless they volunteer this particular information, never ask!

in the first place." True, you were interested, but you were interested in *you* making a good impression. If you shifted your attention away from yourself, you would never have felt so awkward and out of place.

Ask, Ask, and Keep Asking!

The first rule is to ask questions, but not invasive ones. What I am actually saying is to think before you speak so that you don't put your foot in your mouth and embarrass or insult everyone, including yourself. Instead, try to find some common ground as you continue to ask questions and relate to the person.

Elaborate—Don't Interrogate!

In the Elaboration Technique, you ask the person who, what, when, where, and why—questions. Use techniques developed by journalists. Remember to ask your question and then elaborate on the person's answer by asking another question related to their last answer.

This is a wonderful technique that helps you uncover things you both might share in common. If their answers are curt, if they seem annoyed, bored, or disinterested, ask another question, or cut the conversation short, it's a hint that they may no longer wish to speak with you. So leave!

Remember to maintain eye-to-eye contact at all times. It gives you a better opportunity to observe a person and react to what you see. In doing so, you will make the person feel important and make yourself aware of their facial and body cues. These invaluable messages will also let you know, in a non-verbal way, that they wish you'd leave, or that they couldn't bear it if you left. The example in the "Talk Back!" section on the next page clearly illustrates how a compliment about a dress initiates the topic of travel, which results in the two people realizing they have something in common, which is further elaborated on to find another commonalty, and so on and so on.

Studies have shown that the more you have in common with someone, the more likely you are to begin a relationship. Thus, the Elaboration Technique is just the tool you need to discover potential friends.

Talk Back!

Hillary: I like your pretty dress. It's so colorful.

Adrienne: Why, thank you.

Hillary: Did you buy it locally?

Adrienne: No, I got it on my trip to Italy in Capri.

Hillary: This is unbelievable! I just came back from Capri last week. My husband and I were there to see his family; they have a jewelry business and one of the largest jewelry shops on the island.

Adrienne: Really? Which one?

Hillary: It's the one in the center of town across from the plaza.

Adrienne: I know the place! I was there! Look, I got this bracelet there.

Hillary: What a coincidence! I can't believe it! Why were you in Capri?

Adrienne: I was there on my honeymoon!

Hillary: So was I!

Here are some extremely important tips for maintaining a conversation:

➤ Be interested, not interesting.

➤ Be mindful of your own body and facial language so that you don't invade the person's space.

➤ Cultivate a wide range of conversational topics that you acquire through the media.

➤ Have a sense of humor, but don't be a jokester or obnoxious.

➤ Don't interrupt!

➤ Be enthusiastic, but not so overly animated so that you come across as phony.

Getting Deeper and Deeper

Let's say the conversation is going quite well. You discover more and more about one another. You're learning about your similarities as well as your differences. If you understand the person and can relate when you talk about specific topics or philosophies, there is a greater chance that this person will feel more favorably towards you—even become part of your life. If you enjoy the same topics and can speak each other's language (and that doesn't just mean standard English!), you're both doing well.

What Shall We Talk About?

Topics of conversation come in three categories, from the more basic and superficial to the deepest. Studies have shown that the deeper the level of conversation and the more numerous the similarities, the deeper the bond will become. Following is a list of the three categories, from most shallow to deepest, and the topics within each one.

Category 1—Basic Needs

➤ Food (restaurants, preparation, recipes, favorite meals)

➤ Travel (vacations, where you're going to go, where you went, likes and dislikes, what you saw and bought and ate)

➤ Clothing (styles, shopping, bargains, where to go, accessories)

➤ Shelter (homes, location, areas, decoration, values, real estate)

➤ Safety (weather, protection, crime prevention, natural and unnatural disasters, dangerous areas)

Category 2—Relationships

➤ People/family/interpersonal relationships

➤ Good, bad, and former relationships

➤ Dating

➤ People in the news, celebrities, and other high-profile people

➤ People you have in common (both those you like and dislike)

➤ Employers, employees, and co-workers

➤ Other interesting people you have met

➤ Foreigners, people you have met in your travels, and people from different cultures

➤ New information about specific people

➤ People you admire, people who revolt you (for example, odious newsmakers)

Category 3—Interests, Achievements, and Opinions

➤ Travel (culture, history)

➤ Past history of nations

➤ Political situations in countries

➤ Attitudes and opinion towards specific news events

➤ Value system

➤ Job challenges, career development, past career achievements

➤ Achievements, failures

➤ Arts and entertainment opinions and information (film, plays, music)

➤ Politics and religion (preferably if they are in common with yours)

➤ Health issues, fitness strategies

➤ Relationship philosophies and personal application

Know What You're Talking About!

"A little knowledge is a dangerous thing," so make sure you know quite a bit about a subject before you spout off. If you're giving someone information, make sure it's the right information. Otherwise keep quiet! There is nothing more annoying than a "know-it-all" who knows nothing.

If you're unfamiliar with a topic, don't be afraid to say so and ask questions of people.

If they are impatient with you or act as though they think you are stupid for asking, let them know in no uncertain terms that they are out of line. Their intolerance certainly tells you a lot about how toxic they are. So watch out for them! Their actions may have revealed that they are a person from whom you need to keep your distance.

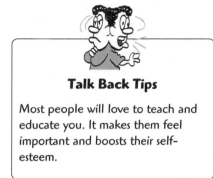

Talk Back Tips

Most people will love to teach and educate you. It makes them feel important and boosts their self-esteem.

Bingo! You Got the Lingo!

There is perhaps nothing more embarrassing than trying to relate to someone while using the wrong words or lingo in the wrong context. People will laugh at you, think you are not hip, or think you're trying too hard to relate.

So what are you supposed to do if you don't know what a word means? Don't be embarrassed. If you don't know, ask "what do you mean by ____?" This way, you add a new word to your vocabulary.

If you can speak a person's language, you usually have that person on your team, because you can identify with one another and know what the other is really trying to communicate. When I first started doing talk shows I didn't always understand the language that was spoken. However, as time went on, I have learned how to both speak and understand some of today's hippest words. I have learned how to talk "street."

Chillin' does not mean sticking something in the refrigerator. It means to relax or hang out. *Fly* doesn't mean that pesky insect that sits on your hamburgers when you're picnicking. Instead, it means great looking—sexy. If someone thinks they are *all that,* they are full of themselves and think they're *fly. Bad* means good. *Homey* does not mean a cozy house, nor do *homes* mean a group of houses. Derived from the word *homeboys*, neighborhood gang members, it means buddy or close friend. An even closer friend is a *bro,* which can also be used as a greeting. "Hey bro wuss happenin' man" means "Hello, how are you?" When you *kick 'em to the curb,* you aren't literally using your feet to push them over the edge of the pavement. Instead, you are getting rid of someone with whom you haven't had a *happenin'* (good, working) relationship.

Talking Ethnic

In order to bond with someone from a different culture, it's best to know what certain words mean before you use them. An American ice skater went on Australian television and said "when I last skated, I fell on my fanny." To an American that's not funny at all, but to an Australian, it's hysterical! Translated into Australian, she said "when I last skated, I fell on my vagina." So you have to be careful. To help you, I have come up with a list of some common ethnic words and phrases (many familiar to you) so that you will know what people are talking about when you hear them. If necessary, I list their pronunciation after the term.

Latin Terms Commonly Used in English

➤ modus operandi (MO)—method of procedure

➤ modicum of decorum—way of behavior

➤ per diem (per DEE um) or per annum—by the day or by the year

➤ in absentia—in one's absence

➤ status quo—the present state of things

➤ de facto—in actuality

➤ ex post facto—after the fact

➤ pueris enternis—man refusing to grow up

➤ per se (per SAY)—in itself, intrinsically

➤ persona non grata—person not welcome

German Terms Commonly Used in English

➤ wunderkind (VUN der kind)—talented, precocious child

➤ angst—foreboding or anxiety

➤ doppleganger—mirror image

➤ verboten (vayer BOAT tin)—forbidden

➤ gesundheit (gez ZUNT hite)—to your health (said after one sneezes)

➤ zeitgeist (ZITE guyst)—spirit of an era

➤ wanderlust—yearning to travel

Yiddish Terms Commonly Used in English

➤ mishigas (mish shig Goss)—insanity

➤ shlep—drag

➤ mensch—a person who does good by others

➤ yenta—gossipy person

➤ chutzpha (HOOTS pah)—a lot of nerve

➤ klutz—clumsy person

➤ shlock—cheap stuff

➤ nebbish—weak, unhip person

➤ kvetch (kuh VECH)—gripe, complain

French Terms Commonly Used in English

➤ vis-à-vis (VEE zah VEE)—in relation to

➤ déjà vu (day zhah VOO)—illusion something happened before

➤ double-entendre (on TAWN druh)—expression with a double meaning

➤ malaise (mal LAYZ)—a blue mood or funk—not feeling well

➤ nuance (NOO wawns)—subtlty

➤ passé (pass SAY)—out of date or style

➤ pièce de résistance (PEE yes dah ree zis TONCE)—the best of something

➤ voilà (vwah LAH)—There it is!

➤ crème de la crème (krem day lah krem)—The best of the best

➤ c'est la vie (say lah VEE)—oh well, that's life!, that's the way it is

➤ tres chic (tray SHEEK)—fashionable and sophisticated

➤ avant-garde (ah vawnt gard)—ahead of its time

Italian Terms Commonly Used in English

➤ ciao (chow)—goodbye for now

➤ incognito (in kog NEE toe)—in disguise

➤ al fresco (all FRES koe)—free

➤ terra firma—solid ground

➤ que sera sera (kay suh RAH suh RAH)—what will be will be

It's Over—I Wanna Go Now

As the old saying goes, it takes two to tango. Just as the person you are talking to might be turned off to you, it goes both ways. The other person may not be all that *you* bargained for. The main thing is to maintain your dignity and that others maintain theirs. Never be a hypocrite and say that you'll call or get together with them if that is not your real intention. This makes for ill feelings in the long run.

If you never intend to see someone again, just tell him that you enjoyed speaking with him. If you want to move on and talk to someone else, do so, but do it graciously. Say: "I'm glad we had the opportunity to chat. Would you please excuse me, because I need to speak to someone over there." If you just want to mingle, tell them: "I'm glad we

Talk Back Tips

If you tell someone you're glad to meet her, you aren't lying, even if you really weren't "glad." You *were* glad to meet her to find out that you didn't want to have anything more to do with her.

met. I am going to mingle now" (or "meet some other people"). Always remember, the last thing you say leaves a lasting impression, so be gracious and leave with a firm handshake and a smile.

Don't Be a Liar—Follow Up Immediately!

If you said something during the conversation that requires a follow-up, then follow up. Forgetting is no excuse! Write yourself a note and put it in a place where you'll be sure to see it. Do it! Whether it's giving someone a business call, placing her in contact with another person, sending him an article, or anything else, act immediately on what you said!

Never Say You'll Call If You Don't Mean It!

I can't begin to tell you the number of people whom I have seen with broken hearts, people who have literally waited by the phone for that expected call and never received it. Even if they had a phone answering machine, they sacrificed going out somewhere to personally pick up the phone to hear the promiser's call. So if you don't intend to call, don't say you will! If you think that by saying it you're being polite, you are not! In reality, you are being extremely rude and potentially hurtful! You have even elicited negative feelings in the person whom you promised to call.

In the same vein, don't say "let's get together" or agree to get together if you don't intend to do it. It is usually taken seriously and can elicit negative feelings about you from the people you misled.

The Least You Need To Know

➤ Approach with a smile whenever you see someone you want to communicate with.

➤ Don't freak out if someone is not interested in you. After all, how many people have you not been interested in? Not everyone will be attracted to you.

➤ Be sincere, and don't make lame comments that can initially turn someone off.

➤ There's always something to talk about. Just keep asking questions and elaborate upon what they said. Be *interested*. Don't worry about being *interesting*.

➤ When you've had enough, be classy in your exit. Above all, be honest! When you say you'll call, do it. Follow up!

Part 3
Verbal Defense Strategies to Use in Combat

In earlier chapters, you took a good look to determine who your verbal enemy might be. You learned to identify certain characteristics of these wild and savage verbal beasts who are dangerous to both your physical and emotional health. You should now feel confident in your abilities to spot these beasts as you wander through the jungles of life.

You have prepared yourself for defense in every way possible. You are now verbally armed to the point where nobody should mess with you—or else! You have the strongest weapon imaginable, which can guarantee that you have the winning advantage in fighting a verbal war. It is a weapon so precious that your adversary can never get his or her hands on it. That weapon is self-confidence.

Now that you've assembled all of your equipment, this part of the book shares with you all you need to know about which verbal and non-verbal strategies to use and how and when to use them. You will also learn how to use more sophisticated verbal weaponry if needed. You will learn the signals to alert you to the fact that the verbal war is over.

No matter whether you win or lose the verbal war, there is always the aftermath of emotional devastation. Thus, you will learn how to pick up the pieces and rehabilitate yourself after leaving the verbal battlefield. You will find out how to heal your emotional wounds. Finally, you will learn how to deal with the aftereffects of post-traumatic verbal shock syndrome.

Chapter 10

Verbal Defense Strategies

In This Chapter

➤ Knowing when you have entered the verbal combat zone

➤ Learning the Imaginary Conversation Strategy to practice verbally defending yourself

➤ Seeing the similarity between fighting a verbal battle and an actual battle

➤ Knowing that choices are available to you when dealing with verbal abusers

Entering the Verbal Combat Zone

You need to be prepared for everything and anything as you learn the art of verbal self-defense. You might not be looking for a fight, an argument, or any problems. For example, you go out to walk your dog, and a perfect stranger walks by and tells you a dead dog story—something you don't want to hear, especially at 7 A.M. Then you go to the corner to buy a newspaper. As you put out your hand to pay the vendor, someone in line curses you because she says she was there first, even though you know that you were there before she was. Next, you unsuspectingly go to get a cup of cappuccino at an upscale coffee shop on the corner. You are met by a nasty, abrupt, impatient server who looks at you in disgust when you hand him a ten dollar bill and he is forced to make change for you. As you sit down, you see someone sitting alone at the next table. You smile and say good morning, she looks away as though you were invisible.

Your day is filled with meetings, but before it begins your boss is barking out commands devoid of "please" or "thank you," or, for that matter, any terms of politeness. He shouts only about the few things you did wrong, ignoring the fact that you did everything else right. In fact, you have done things so right that you are still the number one salesperson in the company over the past six months.

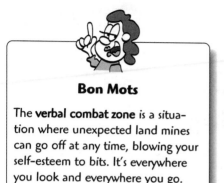

Bon Mots

The **verbal combat zone** is a situation where unexpected land mines can go off at any time, blowing your self-esteem to bits. It's everywhere you look and everywhere you go.

As if your day couldn't get any worse, you finally get to go home and relax, only to discover that you are getting the silent treatment from your spouse for something you must have done. No kiss, no hug, nothing. Perplexed, you ask "what's wrong," only to hear "nothing's wrong!"

Could things possibly get any worse?

Guess what? You have just entered the *verbal combat zone!* But there is good news—you need not be a victim anymore! Help has finally arrived! The pages to come will show you how to effectively strategize to defend yourself against these foes. You will never be a verbal victim again.

A Verbal Weakling No More!

Remember the cartoon where the big buffed-up bully kicks sand in the face of the 90-pound weakling? Then the little guy works out and pumps up. Now he's the one who kicks the sand kicker's behind as he's bigger and stronger after a regimen of weight training and diet.

You are in the same position as the little guy. You are going to be trained and fed with the proper verbal nutrients—the right words to say to any adversary in any circumstance. This in turn will allow you to pump yourself up and kick some verbal butt!

Verbally Pumping Up

Just as the boxer, wrestler, and karate champion have to do a standard workout before they get into the arena to defend themselves against their opponents, you have to do the same.

They have a daily physical exercise regimen that requires exercises to stretch and build up the muscles in their upper and lower body. They do this every day to make themselves stronger, more limber, and more confident in their physical abilities.

Similarly, you need to have a daily verbal exercise regimen that prepares you for any verbally venomous opponent you will encounter. You need to work out the physical, verbal, and communication skills discussed in Chapters 6, 7, and 8. Doing exercises for posture, breathing, voice, jaw, nasality, pronunciation, and communication skills will help you become more verbally limber and more confident in your communication abilities.

Imaginary Conversation Strategy

You need to practice what you are going to say to your verbal adversary. You need to imagine yourself talking to him, playing out every possible scenario in your mind. Then, when it comes time for you to face the real situation, it will be a piece of cake for you. You will have already rehearsed what to say in every possible outcome so that you are no longer nervous when you have to have a face-off on the verbal battleground.

As you talk to yourself, imagine asking out the guy or girl you like.

Imagine them saying "yes." Then imagine them saying "no." Finally, imagine them saying "maybe." Practice what you would say in each of these possible outcomes.

Now, in your mind, ask your boss for a raise. Picture yourself sitting down in the chair in front of his desk. See yourself sitting with the confident sitting posture you learned about in previous chapters. See yourself looking directly at his face as you say, "Mr. Brown, I have been with the company for over four years and have brought in thousands of dollars of new business every month. This is why I feel comfortable talking with you about the possibility of raising my salary."

Talk Back Tips

Repeated training and imagination are powerful tools on the verbal battleground. The more you do this exercise, the better at it you become. Remember—practice makes perfect!

See yourself, hear yourself, feel yourself going over and over the scenario. Going over it while picturing yourself gives you confidence. Do it over again and again, until you are devoid of stammering and mumbling. Bear down on exactly what you want to say until it is committed to memory. Practice until saying what you want to say becomes second nature to you. Now again, visualize your reaction if the boss says "yes," then your reaction and response if he says "no" or "maybe." By the time you have to actually sit down in front of your boss and ask him for a raise, you will be 150 percent prepared.

Use this strategy to practice telling someone off or confronting someone who has betrayed you. After examining every possible scenario in your mind, you will know exactly what to say and how to say it to your verbal adversary.

Chapter 11 explains how to use each of the verbal strategies available to you. Then you can effectively use this "Imaginary Mirror Technique" with a specific verbal strategy that you have picked.

Through the Looking Glass

The best way to practice the Imaginary Conversation Strategy is while you are looking into a mirror. That way, as you talk to yourself, you will be more conscious of your facial expressions, posture, voice, and how other people see you. You might want to put a tape recorder near you as you rehearse the various scenarios while looking in the mirror. It can serve as a barometer to let you know how you come across vocally during certain levels of anger or excitement.

The very best time to practice is in the morning when you are already looking in the mirror to either shave or put on your makeup. Why not take a few extra moments to practice your strategy? You can even do it in your car when you are alone, perhaps while driving to and from work.

Knowing When to Attack Back

It is only when you really know yourself (which you probably do by now, having read Chapter 8) that you become utterly confident and secure that you are doing the right thing. You automatically know when to take matters in your own hands and attack back! You know what your limits are. Nobody else but you does.

Talk Back Tips

Some people may come up with only a few situations, while others could probably fill notebooks. Make this an ongoing process; find a notebook specially for this assignment.

In order to feel more comfortable attacking back, think of all the times in your life when you *didn't* attack back or respond to your verbal adversary. Think about how you felt immediately afterwards, two hours later, during your sleep (not being able to sleep, or having a bad dream about it), and when you got up the next morning. In the following chart, put an X next to the times of the day when someone said something that bothered you. Write down as many situations as you can remember, even from childhood, where you took the verbal abuse and didn't react immediately.

Immediately afterwards	2 hrs. later	During sleep	Upon awakening	2 days later	1 week later	1 month later	1 year later

Specific Situation:

1. _____
2. _____
3. _____
4. _____
5. _____
6. _____
7. _____
8. _____
9. _____
10. _____

What Your Answers Mean

Do you see a pattern here? Do you think immediately afterwards about what happened? If you do, that's good. It's a normal reaction. You obviously need a few minutes, even up to a half hour, to digest exactly what they said. You probably wish you had said something back, but it's too late and you let it go. Your letting it go and really forgetting about or not paying attention to what happened is not lip service. You have a productive and healthy way of dealing with toxic individuals.

If it's still in your mind two hours later, that's starting to be a problem, because it's wasting time that you could have spent thinking about more positive and productive things.

If it has kept you awake, or tossing and turning, you are in big trouble. If it's giving you an upset stomach or heartburn, makes you throw up, or makes you feel like unzipping your skin and jumping out of it, then you are also in big trouble. Now the fact that you didn't respond has affected you physically. That is dangerous. If it happened in two situations or more, then you have developed a pattern of making yourself sick over not taking action. You are literally "kicking yourself," causing yourself pain and agony because of your non-confrontational behavior.

If you have ever thought about the situation as soon as you got up in the morning, you have probably awakened with either a headache or nausea. Even if you are feeling just a little nauseous, it's still nausea. The toxicity of the situation and your not dealing with it has crept into your internal organs—namely, your stomach and your brain. It has affected your blood flow, not to mention consuming your thoughts. If you woke up with the problem on your mind, chances are that you will likely be thinking about it periodically during the day or perhaps all day long. Now your poor internal organs are being tortured by your lack of dealing with the situation.

Two days have gone by, and you are still undergoing mental torture. Every time you think of what happened, you get restless, and your face has a tense and angry expression. By now you have told everyone what happened, to get some relief and support so that you won't have to carry this heavy burden all by yourself. Some of the people you tell take your side; you lose respect for and get mad at those who don't. Now you have two problems—the one that's been bugging you for two days and the loss of some people you thought were your friends. In your mind, they proved who they are and you plan to drop them like a hot potato.

Two days pass, now a week, and you are still thinking about what you could've, should've, or would've done if you had it to do all over again. By now you have developed chronic head and stomach pains, in addition to back and neck pains. Every time you think about it, you literally get sick. This is the time to see a therapist. You not only need to get treated for your physical back and neck pains by a chiropractor. You need to be treated for your mental pain by a psychologist.

Listen Up!

Never forget that verbal toxicity creates physical toxicity. I can't "stress" this enough.

Keep Your Eyes and Ears Open at All Times

The first thing you need to do when dealing with a toxic situation is get your head out of the sand and face the situation directly. If you don't do this the only one who is going to get hurt is you.

The first step of any martial arts training is to keep your eyes fixed on your opponent so that you can anticipate any move he or she makes. This way you can block his kick, and take him off balance by leaning back or going forward. The same is true in the verbal arts. You need to keep both your eyes and your ears on the alert at all times.

Listen Up!

You are not an ostrich, so you have no need to hide your head in the sand to avoid seeing or hearing all the negativity going on around you. Guess what? You can't ignore it anyway! It's there right in front of your eyes and ears. You have to see it, hear it, and react to it. Otherwise, there will be no "you!"

It's time to come out of the closet! It's time to admit to yourself and to everyone else that you are a human being. You are a human being who both requires and deserves respect—respect from others, and most important of all, *self-respect.*

A self-respecting human being would never allow the earlier scenario to go so far. She would nip it in the bud immediately! When a soldier is engaged in actual battle on the battlefield, does she wait two hours, a week, a month, or a year to deal with the enemy who has just attacked her? Of course not! It goes without saying that she would be dead if she didn't handle the situation immediately!

Make a Choice and Make It *Now*

The soldier has choices, but he has to make those choices in a split second. His choices determine the outcome of his well-being. He can run for his life, he can hide, he can shoot back, or he can use a hand grenade and blow everything to bits. He also has another choice, and that is to do nothing and die in battle.

This scenario would never have happened at all had the leaders of the two opposing sides sat down in an attempt to make peace with one another.

Even though this is a rather harsh analogy, it's the naked truth! After all, this book is about defending yourself against the enemy—the verbal enemy!

The strategy for verbal self-defense is no different from the one the soldier uses. You, like the soldier, have to make choices—and immediate choices at that! The choices you make determine the outcome of your well-being. You can run for your life and never look back (the Unplug Strategy). You can shoot back (Mirroring Strategy). You can really let the verbal enemy have it, by verbally blowing him or her to bits (Give 'Em Hell and Yell Technique). Finally, you can do nothing. You can simply remain silent and allow the verbally abusive enemy's toxins to fester inside you, to the point that it makes you mentally or physically ill. If the verbal abuse takes place over long periods of time, the end result can even kill you!

Verbal Vignette

Scientists all over the world have repeatedly proven that stress contributes to life-threatening conditions such as cancer and heart disease.

Picking Your Strategy

Now that you know that you have to make a choice, because your life can literally depend on it, you need to know that you are in complete control. You are in control of picking the right strategy to use at the right time with the right verbal enemy. If one strategy doesn't work, know that you have others from which to choose.

The thing to remember in picking your verbal weapon is that, like the martial artist, you are never initially on the offensive. The black belt in karate keeps her lethal weapons (her hands and feet) under wraps until she must defend herself.

Similarly, you too need to keep your verbal weapons under wraps until the point that you have to verbally defend yourself.

The Verbal Artist Has Complete Control!

In order to be in complete control, there are four things you need to remember, no matter what:

1. Enter every situation in the verbal battlefield with an open mind.
2. Observe "what is."
3. Take a moment to pick your strategy.
4. Go ahead and defend yourself.

In the first step, you, the verbal artist, come into any situation "clean" and weaponless, with no hidden agenda, like the martial artist. You leave your ego at the door. You have no chip on your shoulder. You are just "you"—open, honest, and not offensive in any way. This means that you never initiate an attack, consciously saying anything that is verbally toxic to another person. You, like the martial artist, are calm, open-minded, pleasant, and accepting of everyone who crosses your path.

When using the second step, by simply observing what "is," you, like the martial artist, are not concerned with the past: you deal only with the present, experiencing the here and now. Therefore, neither you nor the martial artist is burdened by excess baggage.

You both have learned to let go. You have learned not to take a toxic situation from the past into your present time and space. As a result, peacefulness and pleasantness reside in your demeanor, your body language, face, language, verbal tones, and in everything you happen to say to others.

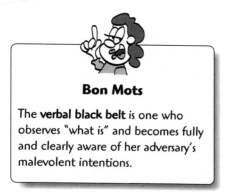

Bon Mots

The **verbal black belt** is one who observes "what is" and becomes fully and clearly aware of her adversary's malevolent intentions.

For the third step, while continuing to take control over the situation, make certain that you are in absolute conscious control by controlling your breathing. In Chapter 11, you learn how to effectively control your breathing using the Breath Control Technique. This technique gives you the split-second timing to reach into your bag of "verbal self-defense strategies" and pick the one appropriate to that particular situation.

Picking the right verbal weapon with which to defend yourself does take a lot of skill. But don't worry. With a lot of practice, you, just like the black belt in karate, will learn to develop the skill to become a verbal black belt.

The martial arts expert is well-versed in his stances, blocks, and kicks. By having control over the situation, you are equally well-versed in your stance (head and body posture), moves (facial, arm, and hand movements), and kicks (verbal self-defense strategies). The martial artist has physical advantage over his opponent; you now have vocal advantage over your opponent.

Now for the fourth step. When the martial artist decides to kick back, *watch out*. The results are not pretty. Neither are they pretty when you decide to "kick back" verbally, as your opponent will definitely get a dose of his own verbal poison. He might even get more than he bargained for. Because he will be completely disarmed, rest assured that he will definitely think twice about attacking you—the verbal black belt—or anyone else, for that matter.

The Least You Need To Know

➤ Without realizing it, you enter the verbal combat zone every day.

➤ People can be rude and obnoxious, invading your space and overstepping their bounds.

➤ Fighting a verbal battle is no different than fighting a physical battle.

➤ Your life literally depends on how you choose to deal with the verbal abuse.

➤ You are in total control when you begin to verbally defend yourself.

Chapter 11

Letting Them Know They've Overstepped Their Verbal Boundaries

---

In This Chapter

➤ Using silence to your advantage

➤ Communicating directly

➤ Using the weapon of laughter

➤ Using the weapon of love and kindness

If you are to gain an advantage over your opponent, you must have both the knowledge and the ability to choose and use verbal self-defense techniques, depending upon which ones are called for.

Techniques range from silence to taking extreme verbal measures. The key is letting someone know that she has clearly overstepped her boundaries.

Learning each of these verbal strategies is so important because it helps you rid yourself of any toxins that might reside in your system as a result of keeping the verbally venomous person's poison within you.

In Chapter 10, you learned that you must never keep any of the verbal venom inside of you, and that doing so can be deleterious to both your physical and mental health.

Silent, Expressionless, Blank Stare

The silent, expressionless, blank stare occurs when you immediately stop everything you are doing and freeze as you blankly stare down your opponent. This often throws your verbal adversary so off balance that he doesn't know what to do.

In this case, silence is truly golden. You most likely grew up with this technique being done to you. As a child, all your mother or father needed to do was to give you that "look," or rather, "non-look." First came the expressionless stare, followed by silence, followed by a furrowed brow and then, the verbal reprimand. After some time and many blank stares, it got to the point where all your parents had to do was to give you that look and you immediately knew you had to behave. Teachers often use this technique to get their students to be quiet and to pay attention.

Verbal Vignette

People in law enforcement sometimes use the "blank stare" technique when they are interrogating a suspect. In many instances, the silence is so uncomfortable that the suspect begins speaking automatically. Often as suspects ramble on and are left to their own devices, they provide the detective with enough information to throw them in jail.

It's most disconcerting to see a face that is usually full of expression and life turn mask-like. It's so disconcerting to be shocked by this out-of-context facial non-expression, that you tend to stop whatever you are doing, just to make sure your eyes are not deceiving you.

Now that we have established that this technique definitely works, you need to use it as part of your repertoire in verbal defense. Imagine that someone says something really insulting to you. Here are the steps you need to take to stare him down.

1. Immediately stop whatever you are doing.

2. Take a small breath of air in through your nose. It is important to aid in your silence that you not inhale through your mouth. Because you are not going to be speaking, you don't need to fill your abdominal area with air. You are not going to be making any rich sonorous tones.

3. Hold the breath. By holding your breath, you are slowing down your heart rate as well as focusing your thoughts, so that you are in total control of the situation.

4. While still holding your breath, relax every one of your facial muscles. Visualize your forehead relaxing, along with your eyelids, nose, cheeks, lips, jaw, and chin. From the top to the bottom of your face, feel your muscles relaxing so much that your face becomes expressionless.

5. Now look in the direction of the verbal perpetrator. Just stare at him. Try not to blink; just stare. Usually after 3 seconds, he will feel so uncomfortable that he will

most likely say "What's wrong?" or "What are you looking at?"—with a small chuckle and an uncomfortable tight-lipped smile.

6. Do not speak! Just keep staring. As soon as he has spoken, you know you have gotten the upper hand in the situation. See how fast the tables have turned. Now it is you who are in control. His attempt to overpower you by his toxic words is nullified. Your facial shield protects you from giving him any satisfaction for trying to annihilate you with his verbal bullets. Now, he is the one squirming, not you.

By the way, as soon as he starts speaking, which he will do in a matter of seconds, you can release your breath so you don't turn blue and pass out.

Listen Up!

Research has shown that staring into someone's eyes can be threatening to the person being stared at. It might be considered an act of aggression and hostility. Animals know this. When two animals stare at one another, the one who looks away first is the one who has relinquished his status to the other.

The Look of Disgust Strategy

The Look of Disgust Strategy is very much like the Silent, Expressionless, Blank Stare Strategy. Instead of having no expression on your face, however, you have an expression of disgust. This technique is especially disconcerting to your opponent because he was not expecting this—someone scowling at him in disgust, staring at him, and saying nothing.

Now he is really thrown off balance. He might start to furrow his forehead and knit his brows together, tightening up his jaw as he says, in a defensive tone, "What's the matter?" or "Why are you looking at me like that?" If he is really uncomfortable, you might hear those infamous four words, "I was only kidding." There is no way he was "just kidding." You know it and he knows it. And now he knows that he can't speak to you the way he did. Your facial expression speaks volumes.

To make the Look of Disgust:

1. Raise your upper lip.
2. Wrinkle your nose.
3. Open your mouth.
4. Raise your chin.
5. Squint your eyes.

This is a universal expression. People from every culture use this facial expression to reflect the emotion of disgust.

Let It Go—Breathe and Blow Strategy

When doing this strategy you must remember the importance of never *ever* allowing any of this verbal venom to fester inside of you and poison your psyche. As I mentioned in Chapter 2, venomous words are like glue—they stick. They will always stick to you unless you are able to release them mentally and physically.

Therefore, the next strategy is designed to give you complete control over your emotions. This strategy underlies all of the other strategies presented in this chapter.

When someone aggravates, your adrenaline begins to flow. Your heart beats faster, your head begins to throb, your face reddens, and your eyes bulge out as you hold your breath. Because you are so shocked, you in essence forget to breathe. In this case, I'm not talking about strategies where you consciously hold your breath in order to achieve a specified effect. I'm talking about uncontrolled cessation of breathing. Here is how you can effectively use the Breathe and Blow strategy to *oxygenate* yourself.

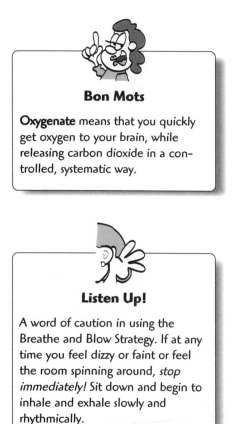

Bon Mots

Oxygenate means that you quickly get oxygen to your brain, while releasing carbon dioxide in a controlled, systematic way.

Listen Up!

A word of caution in using the Breathe and Blow Strategy. If at any time you feel dizzy or faint or feel the room spinning around, *stop immediately!* Sit down and begin to inhale and exhale slowly and rhythmically.

1. Take a small breath—a two-second sip of air into your mouth.

2. Next, think of your verbal adversary. Recall all the awful things he said to you. Hear his voice spewing forth poisons. Do your recalling in the three-second period where you will be consciously holding on to your breath. In this case, you are in complete control of your breathing because you are fully conscious of what you are doing.

3. As you keep this "verbal violator" in your mind, blow him out through your mouth, exhaling with all your strength.

4. Keep blowing out this breath until you have completely run out of air.

5. Now stop for two seconds and do not breathe.

6. Repeat this exercise a second time. As you literally blow what he said out of your mind, you are ejecting this person from your system.

7. Repeat this procedure once more as you continue to blow out all of the toxic negativity and ill feelings the person's words have brought you.

8. Now stop and take a big breath in through your mouth, filling up your lungs and exhaling normally.

While using this strategy, you may feel a bit light-headed. Not to worry—this is quite normal.

Calm, Calculating, Questioning Strategy— Like Columbo

Remember the popular television series *Columbo?* Detective Columbo would calmly ask invasive questions in such a matter-of-fact, unassuming way that the criminal would unsuspectingly cooperate and answer his seemingly benign—but really quite calculated—questions. Then, of course, Columbo was able to solve the crime and save the day.

Just as Columbo caught his criminal by throwing him or her off balance, you too can use the same approach to throw your verbal opponent off balance.

If you use this technique, you must use a non-hostile, non-angry, unassuming tone. You will have more successful results if you take the following advice.

The purpose of this strategy is to ask someone a series of questions that require either a *yes* or *no* answer in a logical progression. It's kind of like a courtroom lawyer who attempts to make an important point by having his witness respond to a succession of questions. In your case, however, you aren't hostile.

In questioning, you have to begin by asking the most absurd question, which is guaranteed to elicit a *no* answer. Then keep going, asking less and less bizarre and over-the-top questions until the person gets the point. Eventually, he is put in a corner and is forced to see how wrong he is. The "Talk Back!" section gives a clear example of what I'm talking about. The ignorant man who made a generalized racial slur did a complete turnaround in his thinking as a result of this strategy.

Talk Back Tips

This strategy can be used in all sorts of situations and with all sorts of people—not just racists, but those who are toxic about the sexes, other cultures, and so forth.

Talk Back

Here is the Calm, Calculating, Columbo-Like Questioning Strategy in action. This is a dialogue between an ignorant, prejudiced, narrow-minded bigot and a level-headed, open-minded, people-loving person. The bigot has made a pejorative comment about people of color. The Loving Person takes control, as you will see.

Loving Person: You mean to say you can't stand every single black person in the entire world?

Bigot: No, I didn't say that.

Loving Person: Do you know of any black person that you do like?

Bigot: I can't recall anyone.

Loving Person: Do you like sports?

continues

143

continued

Bigot: Of course, doesn't every man?

Loving Person: Do you respect any sports stars?

Bigot: Yes.

Loving Person: Who?

Bigot: Muhammad Ali and Michael Jordan.

Loving Person: How about in politics or music?

Bigot: I don't know much about politics, but I like BB King and Aretha Franklin.

Loving Person: Is there any one black person whom you ever thought was intelligent or talented?

Bigot: Sure, Oprah Winfrey, that guy on *60 Minutes*...Ed Bradley.

Loving Person: Have black people as a whole ever done anything to hurt you personally?

Bigot: No, not me. Not personally.

Loving Person: You seem like a hard-working man who takes care of his family. Do you think that there are some black people who work hard for and care about their families as much as you care about yours?

Bigot: Of course there are!

Loving Person: Do you personally know a lot of black people?

Bigot: No, not personally.

Loving Person: Have you ever worked with any black people?

Bigot: Of course I have.

Loving Person: Did you hate every black person you worked with?

Bigot: Of course not. In fact, one of my best buddies at work was a black man.

Loving Person: Have you ever felt that if fewer people hated one another and got to know one another better as individuals, just like you got to know your buddy at work, that there would be less hatred and ignorance in the world?

This strategy is so powerful because it makes a person become accountable for what verbal toxin he has spewed forth. If you practice this strategy and learn to do it well, you can not only make your point, you can even change the other person's way of thinking. As an active participant in the communication process, he is clearly able to take a good look at himself and see how ridiculous he has been.

The Naked Truth Strategy

Because it is such a rarity in this day and age, direct, bold honesty can blow someone out of the water! When someone makes a nasty and hurtful comment to you, you have the option to tell her the "naked truth." If you decide to use this strategy, you will definitely have thrown her off balance. No way was she expecting to hear how repulsive you think she was being when she said what she said to you.

Most likely, she will be intimidated by your direct honesty as you deliver the message to her in a projected and well-modulated tone, with an upright, heads-up posture. This is a perfect situation to illustrate how your daily verbal workouts can assist you in each of the strategies you choose to use. Incorporating good posture, direct facial contact, and a sonorous voice—techniques you learned about earlier in this book—are essential if you want to be effective in getting your verbal message across to verbal abusers.

The Naked Truth Strategy often prevents verbal bombs from being hurled at you in the future. Your verbal adversary usually gains a newfound respect for you, because you have let her know in no uncertain terms that you are on to her verbal games and you will tolerate none of them.

In essence, your self-respect—speaking up for yourself—made the verbal enemy have more respect for you as well.

"The Joke's on You"—Funny Bone Strategy

Another sure-fire way to throw your verbal enemy off-kilter is to make fun of either him or yourself. Sometimes it's difficult for you to come up with something funny, especially after the other person says something that almost leaves you crying, not laughing. Once again, take that lifesaving sip of air in through your mouth for two seconds. Hold it for two seconds, and then start rolling with some humor. The four seconds buys you some time to think of a joke.

It's best to make a joke related to something negative the person said to you. By retorting in a positive and humorous vein, you gain the upper hand and control over the situation. On the other hand, you can add insult to insult. This will definitely throw him for a loop! He may think he "gotcha" with his zing when in reality, you "gotcha" self with an even better zing!

The key here is to say something even more outrageous than he did.

Verbal Vignette

Suppose someone who knows you are highly sensitive about your weight says something like "You've put on a little weight lately." That's a sting—here's another insensitive ignoramus criticizing your body. At first you might want to break down in tears, but instead, use the Funny Bone Strategy. Reply: "Oh, thank goodness. I am too *skinny*. I need to put on 60 more pounds, and then I'll look really good!" Now smile, keep smiling, and don't say a word. Now watch his jaw drop! He is stunned and squirming! It's amusing to see someone fall down after trying to put you down.

Another humorous technique is to fight fire with fire. He zinged you—zing him back! He says you need to lose weight; you say he does too. Chances are, this insensitive clod isn't exactly *Baywatch* material either, right? Tell him that. Now his big mouth must weigh a ton.

Using this strategy, it doesn't matter what you say, as long as you say something that's funny to you.

Later on in the book you learn how to use some snappy comebacks that apply to specific verbally noxious people in specific situations.

Love 'Em Up Strategy

"A pat on the back is just a few vertebrae from a kick in the pants."

Anyone who has to resort to spitting out verbal venom usually lacks the basic element for survival—love. Those who lack enough love and support from others usually become insecure, jealous, and angry, and they don't really feel good about themselves. Deep down, they really want to reach out but can't, so they go the other direction and act hateful and spiteful. This behavior is, of course, due to their inner rage of not feeling loved enough.

Listen Up!

"Turning the other cheek," a tenet of many religions, may be one of the most difficult things to do, especially if you thoroughly believe in the "eye for an eye, tooth for a tooth" philosophy. It takes a great deal of inner strength to turn your anger at others into love. For some people, this is nearly impossible to do.

If you look at them in this vein, you won't have as many bad feelings towards them. They really need to be pitied more than hated. They need more compassion than aggression.

Therefore, instead of being angry at them you actually need to diffuse their anger with love and kindness. This is a Herculean task for anyone who has been verbally shot, maimed, and blown to bits. If you find you just can't do it, not to worry. This is just one tool of many in your arsenal of verbal defense weapons.

If you think of the common phrase "kill them with kindness," you might feel a lot better about employing this strategy more often.

Below are six sub-strategies of the Love 'Em Up Strategy for verbal defense. Try them! They are actually fun to do and very empowering.

Gentle-Toned Name Repetition

In his bible of the times, *How to Win Friends and Influence People*, Dale Carnegie mentions that the sound of a person's name is the sweetest music to her ears. Why? It's the same as what was said earlier in this book—people love to talk about their favorite subject, themselves. Softly saying people's names over and over in a loving tone certainly gets their attention, especially if they are in a rage. It helps to calm them down. Your control over the situation allows them to get in control of themselves. It disarms them. They can't help but stop and listen. Instead of being seen as the verbal battering ram, you become a warm, soft verbal cushion, making yourself "user-friendly" to them. By the way, this is a standard technique mental health care professionals use in their attempts to gain some control with autistic children.

Hush Hush Strategy

This technique is similar to the preceding one, except that you substitute the term "hush hush" for the person's name. It's virtually the same technique that you would use with a crying baby in softly telling her to hush as you hold her. Your steady calming tone as the air produces the "hush" sound elicits calmness.

This is an excellent technique to use when a person won't shut up. If you keep repeating "hush hush" in a calm and steady voice, on a continuous basis, he or she will eventually stop yelling and carrying on. In essence, these people are like big babies who need their mommy or daddy to comfort them.

Let the Baby Have Her Bottle Strategy

Speaking of babies, remember when you were a child and another child would cry or get upset when you played with his her toy? Oftentimes, to save face and rationalize your little feelings (which were actually big feelings at the time), you retorted with "Okay, let the baby have her bottle." The little perpetrator was usually taken aback by your comment. She didn't want to be referred to by that evil four-letter word, B-A-B-Y, so she often relinquished the toy to you or shared it with you. Little has changed since your youth. Oftentimes, when you yield to your verbal opponent, she becomes powerless and you gain back the control.

If you counter what the verbal abuser says by agreeing with her, she has nowhere to go. She is taken off-balance and loses her verbal footing. She has no idea where you are coming from and no idea of what to say next. Obviously, she can't fight with herself, so she is silent. This quashes her verbal venom.

Bon Mots

Yielding is a key concept in the martial arts, especially in Aikido. In **yotto**, you yield to your opponent by moving in her direction. For instance, when she pushes you, you lean back, going in the direction of her push; if she pulls you, you go in the direction of her pull. This throws her off-balance. She loses her footing and falls to the ground.

Hand-Holding Fighting Strategy

This strategy, which I personally devised for my clients, is one of the best techniques to be used in relationship therapy. It's obvious that the couple loves one another, but they keep fighting and bickering over stupid and ridiculous things. They end up saying mean and ugly things to one another that devastate both of them. As you learned earlier in the book, words stick—especially ugly words! So, I tell the couple, as difficult as it may seem, as soon as they start this stupid bickering, one has to immediately grab the other's hand and hold it and continue to bicker.

They usually start laughing and stop fighting, becoming softer and more affectionate with one another. As they continue to hold hands, each one often starts to communicate his or her side of the issue in a calm and loving manner, so that each mate is able to really hear what the other has to say.

It's a very powerful tool for effective communication between couples as well as friends.

By the way, the one who takes the other's hand first is the one who has the control over the situation.

Heart-in-Hand Strategy

Listen Up!

We've all seen exaggerations of the "heart-in-hand" gesture in silent films, where the star puts his hand over his heart in an attempt to profess his love towards the fair maiden. It's easy to parody this gesture, but its serious value should not be overlooked.

Dating back to ancient Roman times, when Rome was busy trying to conquer the world, anyone who met up with the Romans was concerned about weapons they might be hiding. Thus, when the Romans placed their hand over their heart to express their sincerity, respect, and liking toward the person, one could readily see that the person was safe (at least at that moment), because there was no weapon in the potential opponent's hands.

In this century, this gesture has come to express extreme passion and feeling toward another person. More currently, it expresses passionate love but also despair, a "heaviness of the heart." Therefore, when you lovingly converse with your verbal opponent with this gesture, especially one whom you really love, you have the advantage. Subconsciously, they are getting the cue of how deeply they have affected you. Usually this mitigates their verbally toxic behavior.

"What's Good About You" Strategy

If you tell your child he is good even if he is a little terrorist tormenting everyone and leaving a path of destruction in his wake, he often acts better, especially around you. Since you have good expectations for him, he will often follow suit.

This is no different when you tell grown-ups how good they are and discuss their good points. Doing so, you gain the upper hand and control over the situation. Who wouldn't want to hear good things about themselves? This usually stops them in their tracks and they begin smiling. Even though they know they have been bad, the fact that you still manage to see something good in them makes them feel pretty good about you. If they are feeling good about you, it is more difficult for them to verbally attack you.

The Least You Need to Know

➤ Silence can definitely be golden if you use the right facial expressions to match your silence. Whether a blank stare or a look of disgust, it makes your verbal enemy stop and look.

➤ The direct approach is often the best approach. Since most people aren't bold enough to be brutally honest, you can easily throw your opponent off-balance: they aren't expecting to hear the bare-bones truth.

➤ A laugh a day keeps verbal adversaries away. Who can verbally abuse you when you are humorously verbally abusing yourself? It usually stops them in their tracks and makes them smile—something verbal opponents rarely do.

➤ Even though it's difficult to find anything good in people who have been verbally abusive to you, let alone love them, such techniques are surprisingly powerful.

Chapter 12

When More Powerful Weaponry Is Needed

The strategies in Chapter 11 work quite well if you are dealing with basically civilized people with whom you can communicate at least on a basic level. Others need to be shaken up a bit more. Even though I recommend first using the "pat on the back" philosophy in dealing with verbal venomites, sometimes you have no choice but to give them the "kick in the pants" in order to get them to finally hear you.

This chapter explains when you really need to implement this kick in the pants approach. These strategies are most effective in defending yourself against those verbal bullies.

Never Walk Away When You Have Something to Say!

Ask a group of people what they would do if someone had just verbally assaulted them and continued to verbally abuse them. Inevitably you will hear the following, unfortunately very common response. "I'd just walk away." If you give them a clearer, more descriptive picture of the verbal perpetrator's heinous actions, the response would still stay the same, only some people would probably pipe up "I'd ignore them!"

Well, guess what? You *can't* ignore it! It's there. It's right in front of your eyes. It haunts you later. You hear the voices, you see the vision, you feel the pain. If you ignore it now, it will come back to haunt you later through physical and mental anguish.

Protecting the Other Cheek

Perhaps they say that they would simply walk away because they feel that they are "peace-loving" people and that's what peace lovers should say—at least publicly.

Listen Up!

If you say that you can simply "walk away" from a verbal tormentor, you are kidding yourself. Where are you walking, and what are you walking away with? Emotional pain that you haven't dealt with? You must deal with the situation head-on.

There are others who walk away because of their religious teachings. They have been raised to turn the other cheek when someone doesn't treat them right.

I don't want to sound cavalier or irresponsible or insult anyone's religious views. In fact, I endeavor to respect everyone's religious views. So do not in any way misinterpret what I am about to say.

Turning the other cheek does not mean to turn the other cheek so that you can be slapped again on the other side of your face. As I and many people in the clergy see it, turning the other cheek means turning the other cheek away from the verbal tormentor so that you can be proactive and move on, and never let anyone verbally abuse you again.

Don't Just Stand There—Do Something!

Whatever you decide to do, do something. Even if you choose to simply walk away, don't ignore how the verbal abuser's words made you feel. Unless you are a zombie or an alien from another planet, you have feelings that will emerge following this psychologically traumatic event, although you might not realize it at first as you slough off what happened.

Talk Back Tips

Just having someone agree with you about what a jerk someone else was can help you release verbal toxins.

Later on, you might develop a type of post-traumatic verbal shock syndrome. If you don't deal with your feelings immediately, you will have to deal with the emotional consequences later. So talk about what happened to you—what awful things someone said to you and how he or she said it. Tell all your friends, your family, your clergy, and your therapist. These people will support you.

Verbally Setting Firm Limits

Frequently, those who become victims of verbal crime are in the situation they are in because they don't set strict verbal limits with the verbal perpetrator. If they do set limits about how a person can talk to them, they often won't enforce those requirements. As a result, the verbal perpetrator loses respect and doesn't take what the person says seriously.

One of the biggest miscommunications occurs when a verbal victim cries out, "I told him time after time not to say what he says to me and cut me down, but he keeps saying it anyway." When you first hear a victim report this, you feel like punching the verbal perpetrator in the nose. However, upon closer examination you find out that although the victim really did tell him to stop bringing up that sensitive topic and stop putting her down, she neglected to report that she made this request while giggling and laughing, using a coquettish girlie tone.

In no way was the message conveyed to "Cease and desist! Immediately!" At times (like when she began to cry), he would get the message, but then he would retreat to his old ways. He never took her seriously. In fact, upon questioning him about her tears in regard to his verbal abuse he sloughed it off by saying, "It was probably her PMS kicking in."

Granted he sounds like a jerk, and granted it is not appropriate to blame the victim. But in this case we see how, if she doesn't adamantly stand up for herself so that he truly hears her, thereby causing him to show some verbal respect for her, the effect is that she will continue to suffer hearing his verbal abuse.

She needs to speak up—not giggle and laugh—but really speak up in a manner that will perk up his ears once and for all and cause him to change his obnoxious behavior. Most important of all, she needs to be consistent if he falters and attempts to revert to his old ways.

The tone and words you choose definitely let the person know that you mean business. It lets him know that he can never again say what he just said to you.

The upcoming "Talk Back!" section illustrates how this is done. Julia, an investment banker, has a conversation with one of her male colleagues. Julia, who usually dresses in corporate-style clothing, runs into one of her colleagues, James, at a disco. There is nothing corporate about her appearance at the club. She is wearing a short, low-cut, skin-tight, black Lycra spandex dress that shows off her ample cleavage and long, sleek legs. As she leaves the disco, she runs into her colleague on the street. Here's what happens next.

Talk Back

James: Oh my God. I am going to have a heart attack! Julia, this can't be you.

Julia: Well, it is me!

James: You... you... you certainly don't look like this at work.

Julia: Well, I should hope not. When I'm at work, I'm not out clubbing.

James: Whoa, I can't wait to tell everyone about this at work tomorrow.

Julia: [Smile immediately changes into serious scowl while looking directly at him. Voice becomes low-pitched and she projects her voice loudly.] My social hours are mine! My work hours are the company's! Get it?

James: Don't get so bent out of shape, I was only kidding!

Julia: Well, I'm not kidding. You have no business discussing my personal business with anyone! We both need to be respected by everyone in the office if we want to get anywhere, wouldn't you agree?

James: Sure! No problem.

Verbally and vocally, Julia left her light and comfortable, friendly, social speaking style and turned to her corporate style of speech, which was more projecting, lower pitched, and more serious. James obviously got the message. Later, he tried to avoid Julia whenever he saw her at the office.

"This Is Unacceptable!"

This is the best phrase to use when someone is trespassing your verbal limits. Say it in a firm, projected tone so that you will be heard! Do not laugh when you say it! Do not smile or have a "matter of fact" expression on your face! Do not giggle! Do not use a high pitched voice! Don't say it as a question, sounding tentative as you go up at the end of the word "unacceptable." Do not pepper this phrase with filler words such as "like," "um," and "you know!" Finally, do not mumble. Draw out your vowels when you speak these three words.

Talk Back Tips

If you need a reminder on gaining your vocal advantage so that you effectively get your point across, go back and study Chapter 7.

In continuing to let someone know that he has overstepped his bounds, you can then go on to explain what it was that you didn't like about what he said to you. Try not to get out of control, screaming and yelling. Instead, talk calmly, yet firmly, so that there is no question that you meant what you said and said what you meant. Never deviate from what you said!

Therefore, you need to watch out for verbally toxic behavior that someone may once again repeat.

"Excuse Me? Are You Talkin' to Me?"

Even more intimidating to the verbal perpetrator is using the classic lines that Robert DeNiro's character, Travis Bickel, spoke in the Martin Scorsese film *Taxi Driver:* "Excuse me? Are you talkin' to me?" indicating that he was armed and ready for action.

It has become a catch phrase. In basic terms, it is a warning signal. It means "I heard what you said. You disrespected me. I didn't like it! So don't even think of talking to me like that again."

This immediately lets people know that you are serious and you have no patience for their ill verbal treatment of you. This being the case, do not smile while you make this powerful statement or give a nervous laugh afterward. Say it loud and clear so you will be heard. Your loud, clear voice resonating these words in their ears are destined to wake them up, shake them up, and shut them up!

Strategy of Loud Verbal Explosions!

Speaking in a loud and clear voice gives you a lot of verbal and vocal power. People listen. In order to get a verbally abusive person to curtail hurling her abuse in your direction, you can often deflect her verbal bullets with sound, especially if that sound is loud and booming.

You will definitely throw her off balance, which, as in martial arts, is a winning move! It certainly gets her attention and shocks her into stopping—at least for the moment.

Her startled response has been put into action, causing her nervous system to work overtime and to be thrown off balance. She is thrown off balance mentally as well. She saw you in one speed, and here you go changing gears! She definitely wasn't expecting that! Unless she is completely deaf, you have gained the upper hand and come out ahead in another verbal battle.

Talk Back Tips

Verbal Explosion is even more effective when you have been silent for a while, listening to someone's verbal abuse. As you come out of your period of complete silence, bellowing out your unexpected retort in a loud, booming voice, you are shocking her both physically and mentally.

Fight Clean and Fair!

A verbal warrior who fights dirty is the absolute worst! With a dirty fighter, there is little or no hope in your attempts to win the communication battle.

Dirty verbal fighters can cause a melee. Often they will hit you so far below the belt that you'll reel in emotional pain forever.

In the boxing ring, if a professional fighter fights dirty by hitting an opponent below the belt, or does something really dirty (like biting off an opponent's ear), that fighter will be disqualified.

Keep It Above the Belt

Sometimes, the public's rage at the fighter's injustices to the other fighter become so inflamed that the fighting extends to those outside the boxing arena. Look what happened at Madison Square Garden when fighter Riddick Bowe was repeatedly punched below the belt by Ron Goletta, a known dirty fighter who was warned about his tactics. Each time Bowe was hit in the groin, the fans felt his pain too. After Goletta was finally disqualified, all hell broke loose, literally. Fans mobbed the ring. Chairs were flying. Managers and fight personnel were beaten. Innocent bystanders were physically flung out of the ring. Countless fights broke out in the stands, with stranger pummeling stranger. People were injured, people were arrested, people were jailed, all because of dirty fighting—literally being hit below the belt.

Hitting someone below the belt is not confined to the boxing ring. It happens on a daily basis in people's homes, offices, at social gatherings, and even on the street. We know all too well about hitting below the belt in communities that suffer extreme gang violence. A verbal insult about someone's mother or girlfriend, which is definitely hitting below the verbal belt, can result in the insultor being killed.

In anger, people bring up things you never knew about (for example, your husband's three-year affair, communicated to you in hostile, angry terms). They bring up things you thought they never knew about (the time you went to jail for stealing a car when you were 18, for instance) They bring up and uncover horrible things that happened in your life where only extensive psychotherapy or religious devotion have allowed you to cope with the guilt and live one day at a time (such as when your girlfriend got killed in a motorcycle accident, while you were driving).

These verbal cuts are the deepest and hurt the most. In many cases, these cuts will never heal. There is too much resulting pain. There is so much blood coming from the verbal wound that your relationship is gone forever—dead!

Even if someone is a dirt bag of a fighter, you don't have to join in and follow suit. It's not going to make you feel any better throwing verbal bombs at him. He has to live with the devastation he has done to you. Don't add insult to your injury and have the additional burden of living with the emotional devastation you caused them. Take solace in knowing that what goes around usually comes around.

Never, Ever Use Physical Violence!

Your hands, legs, body, and teeth are completely off limits! The only time you can use your teeth is when they are used in conjunction with your tongue and your lips and allow you to speak to someone—never to physically hurt someone.

Never use physical violence!

No matter how angry you get at what someone said, the consequences of physical violence are not worth enduring. There is no excuse whatsoever for physical violence. If you feel as though you are coming close to beating someone up over what they said, *please don't do it!* Before you get ready to do it, take your breath in, hold it, and blow, blow, blow all your air out instead of blowing someone's brains out!

Verbal Vignette

A terrific LA radio personality once told listeners that he was going to beat up the morning radio personality for saying something bad about his girlfriend. Most people assumed it was merely a publicity stunt. The next morning he beat the morning host (on the air) so badly that an ambulance had to be called. The station was in disarray, the police were called, and the evening host was arrested. A promising career ended. He went to jail, had to deal with the legal consequences of his actions, and worst of all, his girlfriend left him. All for what?

Fantasy Strategy—an Alternative to Physical Violence

If you are so angry that you can spit nails, or you feel as though steam is coming out of you ears and you are thinking that no matter what happens to you, you're gonna do someone in—*don't!*

Instead, use this strategy immediately! Fantasize about what you'd like to do to them. See it in your mind, feel it, hear it. *Just don't do it in real life!* I can't give you any specific ideas here in terms of what to imagine. These fantasies must come out of your own mind and your own anger. If they are gruesome, run with it mentally. As you see the images in your mind, you will be surprised at how much better you will feel and how much less enraged, even relieved. You will feel like you have released the pressure-cooker tension from your physical being.

Another alternative is to watch the fights on television or even to go and see a boxing match. As the winner is punching the loser with repeated blows, picture your enemy's face being pummeled by the winner. Don't think this is weird. We have all unknowingly used the Vicarious Fantasy Technique when we watch our favorite superstar heroes beat the living daylights out of someone on screen. Next time you're watching one of these films, just think of what a thrill it would be to see the hero doing what he's doing on screen to your adversary. It's a lot more acceptable than living this scenario in real life.

Never Threaten One's Basic Needs!

"You'll never work in this town again." "I will ruin you." "I will make sure everyone knows about this." "I will get you fired." "I will sue you for everything you've got." "When I'm done with you, you won't have a penny left to your name." "You'll be living on the streets." "I'll make sure you starve to death."

These types of verbal threats are often made in anger. People making these threats don't even think twice about the implications of what they have said. They just know that they are hopping mad and that these threats are the best way for them to let off steam. They have no clue about the impact of their words or the possible resounding consequences.

Bon Mots

The **fight-or-flight** mechanism is a response triggered when our survival is threatened. The flight mechanism causes us to flee to find other places to get food and shelter; the fight mechanism causes us to fight to preserve our food and shelter. These are the essence of biological survival.

It is extremely dangerous to threaten people by holding the threat of their basic existence up to them. In the classic book *The Hierarchy of Needs*, the famed psychologist Abraham Maslow discusses human being's basic need for air, food, and shelter.

When these basic needs are threatened, the consequences can be devastating. Biologically, it triggers basic survival instincts, such as the *fight-or-flight* mechanism. When this happens, the results are not pretty; they are pretty devastating. Through the ages, people have been killed for making verbal threats against one's basic needs.

To repeat: Never, under any circumstances, make threats to people, especially when it pertains to their livelihood! Tempers can flare to the point that they become out of control, and the results can be deleterious.

Keep Your Cool

If your livelihood has been threatened, never resort to physical violence or perpetrating physical harm against someone. Reread this section. Other alternatives are more effective and more productive! So read on and you will discover what these alternatives are and how to use them.

In light of the repeated school killings in which young students (children) have shot their peers to death, threats should *always* be taken seriously, whether or not they are just made in the moment of anger. We have, unfortunately, seen the aftermath of what happens when threats are not heeded.

The moral of all of this is that, no matter how angry you get, never threaten anyone—not even in jest. You are risking being taken to jail. You are risking the financial ruin of having to go through a lengthy court battle. And most important of all, you are risking your life!

Verbally Mirroring the Foe Strategy

In describing the strategy of Verbally Mirroring the Foe, many of you might argue, "I couldn't do what they did. I would never think of stooping to their level." I understand your point. However, guess what? If you don't stoop to their level, how are they going to hear you? How are they going to know when their verbal behavior is unacceptable?

By stooping to their level, you are forcing your verbal perpetrators to see their ugly words reflected back to them. You are, in essence, their "verbal mirror."

One of my attorney clients was negotiating a deal over the telephone with another attorney who was verbally hostile and abusive. My client could not get a word in edgewise as the verbally toxic adversary hogged up the entire conversation, shouting obscenities, and screaming and yelling. All of a sudden, my client pulled the phone away from his ear and began to bark like a dog. Stunned, the abusive adversary stopped talking and asked "What did you say?" My client continued to bark like a dog. He then stopped and said, "That is exactly what you sound like—a barking dog. Now Mr. Jones, you and I are both highly qualified, well-trained, civilized professionals. Let's act that way and speak intelligently and quietly so that we can each listen carefully to what the other is trying to say and come to an amicable resolution."

My client merely gave Mr. Jones a glimpse of himself in the verbal mirror. He certainly didn't like what he heard. It was obvious that Mr. Jones had no clue that he sounded like a barking dog when he negotiated. But he certainly became aware of it and has subsequently made it a point to listen and not "bark" at other attorneys—at least not as much as before!

A taste of their own verbally toxic medicine is often all they need to make them aware of how poorly they come across to others. In fact, because they often don't even realize it, look at using this strategy as doing them a favor!

Talk Back Tips

When you "mirror," don't beat abusers over the head with the mirror so that they understand how ugly they sound. Verbal mirroring is about giving them just a glimpse of their verbally toxic behavior. This is all they need to become conscious of how they are talking to you.

Talk Back

Here is a conversation of an employee mirroring her boss. A word of caution before using this technique on your boss: There's only a 50 percent chance that you will still have a job after using this strategy on someone who has more clout than you do. Ann was lucky her boss responded well. I don't know how your boss will take it, so it's strictly up to you whether to use it or not.

Boss: [in loud and gruff monotone] ANN, GET ME THE JOHNSON FILE AND BRING ME A CUP OF COFFEE—CREAM AND SUGAR!

Ann: [mirroring his exact loud and gruff tone] OKAY, I'LL GET YOU THE JOHNSON FILE AND BRING YOU A CUP OF COFFEE—CREAM AND SUGAR!

Boss: Why are you yelling? Why are you talking so rudely to me?

Ann: Well, Mr. Thompson, that's exactly how you talk to me.

Boss: Really, I had no idea. Well, I apologize. Thanks for pointing it out.

"Give 'Em Hell and Yell" Strategy

Similar to the Mirror Strategy, the Give 'Em Hell and Yell Strategy allows people to see how verbally toxic they are. Although we have been conditioned that it's not nice to scream and yell at people, there are times when you have no choice. You are at your wit's end. You've tried everything else and the verbal vulture still doesn't "hear" you.

There is nothing else to do but "let 'em have it!" Go for it! Be as loud and angry as you want. Let your face turn red and the veins in your neck pop out and pulsate. Yes, you can even say a four-letter word or two and contort your face to look like a monster. The key is to say anything (short of threatening their livelihood or their life) to get out the anger and frustration that you have towards them. Don't keep any of it in! Open the flood gates and let it roar! It gives you permission to act like a wild tiger.

Talk Back Tips

Mark Twain once said, "Under certain circumstances, profanity provides a relief even denied to prayer."

Yes, you read correctly, I said that it was okay to use cuss words (but don't make a habit of it). Doing so, and "shocking" them into listening to you, might be the only way you can get them to finally hear you.

A big word of CAUTION! Never use any of these strategies in conjunction with your hands, arms, fists, legs, feet, or teeth. Never use any weapons (knives, forks, guns, rifles, machine guns, or hand grenades) whatsoever, even if it's only done for effect, to threaten or scare your verbally offensive opponent. The potential consequences can be horrific!

The Least You Need to Know

➤ You never have to take anyone's verbal abuse. Set limits in terms of how people can and cannot speak to you.

➤ Never hit below the belt in verbal warfare. Never bring up something that hits a raw nerve, just to get back at someone. It's unfair and its consequences are beyond repair!

➤ Never use your fists, or any weapons for that matter. Physical violence is not an acceptable way to handle your verbally toxic enemy. Instead, fantasize (*only* fantasize!) about what you would like to do to them.

➤ You take your life in your own hands when you threaten people's family, basic needs (food and shelter), or livelihood. Never threaten anyone. If your threats are serious enough you could be arrested, even if the threats were made in anger.

➤ You have the option of mirroring people's obnoxious verbiage back to them or to really let them have it verbally. Sometimes the only thing they will respond to is a loud angry tone peppered with curse words.

Chapter 13

Enough Is Enough! Knowing When to Retreat

In This Chapter

➤ Know when to get out

➤ No more excuses for being verbally tormented

➤ The "Three Strike" law

➤ Knowing when it's finally over

➤ No looking back

➤ How to heal

When is the verbal war over? How do you know if you were the winner or the loser? The answer is simple. If you have used up *all* of the verbal defense strategies in the last two chapters, and nothing has worked, it's time to retreat. This means "unplug." Get away from the extremely toxic verbal abuser. Run. Run as fast as you can! Run for your life.

Some individuals are similar to drug addicts on PCP. It's very difficult, if not impossible, to quell their bizarre and often violent and intensely destructive behavior (like running naked down the street). They develop the strength of ten men, to the point that in many cases they are impermeable. They are literally like "Supermen" who can't be defeated by the usual methods. They are physically resistant to pain, perhaps because the alteration in their biochemistry doesn't register the sensation of pain.

Because individuals on PCP are usually a danger to themselves and to society, great efforts are made to capture them and lock them up. Several law enforcement officers report that such individuals are so strong that it can take up to twelve officers to subdue them. Additional reports claim that they easily burst open their handcuffs and chains and can even bend the bars of their jail cells.

Similarly, if none of your verbal strategies worked to subdue the verbal bully, you need to cut your losses and move on; otherwise, like people on PCP, they can annihilate you.

If you have done everything, from giving them love and kindness to giving them hell and yelling a them, and if none of the techniques could soften or change the verbal bully's behavior, you have absolutely no other recourse than to run for your life!

Three Strikes and You're Out!

People stay in horrible relationships way too long with the hopes of "working things out." More often than not, things never work out! The time to get out of a verbally abusive relationship is NOW! In baseball there is a rule that after three strikes, you are out. And in some states across America there is a "three strikes" law.

Bon Mots

The "three strikes, you're out" rule means that if you commit three crimes, there is no parole for you—you're in prison forever, without possibility of parole! This rule applies to your relationships as well.

Therefore, I believe as well in the "three-strike rule" when it comes to being verbally abused. The first time a person verbally abuses you, even though it's awful, can be written off to "having a bad day," "not feeling well," "having PMS," or "testing you to see how far they can go"—pushing their limits with you.

The second time it happens is horrible, but it can be attributed to "a life crisis" (such as job problems, problems with children or with family members excluding you, health issues involving anything from a cold to impotence, menopause, or a life threatening illness).

But the third time it happens, there are no more excuses. You're out! Leave!

Yes, But...

Don't "yes, but..." me. Don't "yes, but..." yourself. Verbal abuse is verbal abuse! That's it! If someone is saying to you any of the things mentioned in Chapter 2, guess what? You are the victim of a verbal crime, and the verbal criminals need to be out—for life! Out of *your* life for the rest of *their* lives!

Many of you will think that this statement is too harsh, but there's nothing harsh about telling you that you are shortening and diminishing the quality of the most precious gift that has been given to you—your life! I'm telling you this because I really care about you. I care so much that I am willing to dedicate my life to helping people in the same situation you find yourself in. So please open your mind. See and hear what I am trying to tell you. The longer you stay in a verbally abusive relationship, the longer you will feel bad about yourself. You are in a losing battle and you will never win the verbal war.

If you have truly done *everything* I've discussed in this book thus far, using every single verbal defense strategy correctly and following the steps in the book to a "t," but your results are to no avail, then there are no more "yeah, buts..." to hear.

I Say "Yes," You Say "No"

You may have some good reasons (at least they seem good in your mind) for staying in a verbally abusive relationship. Well, I have even better reasons for you leaving that horrific situation, a situation where your self-esteem is eroding every day you are in the verbal perpetrator's presence.

The following list gives explanations of why I keep saying "no" to your "yes." There are no more excuses, so pay close attention to my answers.

1. Your "yes!": I don't want to upset my comfortable lifestyle.

   Dr. Glass's "No!": How comfortable is your lifestyle when you are living with someone who uses you as a verbal punching bag? No matter what the two of you do together—no matter how many yachts you sail on, privates jets you fly in, designer clothes you wear, exotic places you visit, and beautifully decorated homes you have—nothing is worth the emotional torment that verbal abuse brings. All of your material goods mean zero when you are in a hospital bed dying of cancer, a stroke, or heart attack because you let the abuse fester and fester until it erupted in devastating illness.

2. Your "Yes!": I'm staying for financial reasons.

   Dr. Glass's "No!": Sure, it's going to be hard at first, but millions of people are the breadwinners without a spouse, partner, or roommate. It is better to live on bread and water than eat in a home with a verbal abuser.

3. Your "Yes": I can't leave for the sake of the kids.

   Dr. Glass's "No": I say that you *should* leave for the sake of the kids! Who in their right minds would want their child to grow up hearing their parent get verbally beaten up on a daily basis? Children do grow up, and they grow up learning that they can speak to others in a verbally abusive way or that others can speak to them in a verbally abusive way.

4. Your "Yes!": But, I'm In Love With Him/Her!

   Dr. Glass's "No": First of all, you need to redefine what you mean by "love." Great sex is not love—it is just great sex! Sex may be an expression of love for

continues

continued

some people, but if that love is not expressed outside of the sexual liaison, then it's not love! IT'S JUST SEX! Love is having respect and admiration for someone. If someone doesn't respect and admire you enough to speak to you with civility, guess what? (I hate to be the one to break it to you, but this book is about honesty, so here's the bottom line.) They may not really love you in the true sense of the word.

5. Your "Yes!": What will everyone think?

    Dr. Glass's "No!": Who cares? They are going to think whatever they want to think. They aren't the ones living your life—you are! So live it through your eyes, not through anyone else's eyes! Besides, anyone worthwhile will respect you for getting out of an abusive relationship.

6. Your "Yes!": They didn't really mean it. They were just under a lot of pressure at work, with the family and everything else going on in their life.

    Dr. Glass's "No!": As fast as your legs can carry you, go to an AlAnon meeting so you can see what enabling is all about and what an enabler you are. If they had Verbal Abusers Anonymous (VAA) or VerbAnon, I'd insist that you go to their meetings, but since they don't (at least not yet), go to the next best thing. Go *now!*

7. Your "Yes!": With me in their life, maybe they'll change.

    Dr. Glass's "No!": And maybe green pigs will dance in the trees! I don't think so! Get this through your head: "What you see is what you get!" "What is, is what is!" People don't change their ways unless they really want to. There is sufficient evidence that people don't change their behavior unless they are retrained with extensive therapy. Even then, they still might not change unless their positive behaviors are continuously reinforced!

It's similar to leopards. We've all heard the expression that "leopards don't change their spots"—unless of course you paint some additional spots on them. When the paint eventually wears off, they are back to looking like they did before, with the same old spots. Unless you continuously keep painting new ones on, the old spots will remain the same.

If a leopard doesn't want you to change its original spots, but you insist on changing the leopard by painting new spots on its fur anyway, be prepared to become its lunch! It will destroy you, chew you up, and swallow you. If it's had enough of you, it'll spit you out!

The same is true for a person whom you think you can tame or change. Like the leopard, he too will eat you for lunch. He will destroy you, chew you up, and swallow you, and when he's had enough of you, he'll spit you out!

You Finally Got the Message!

Some people, usually ones who are a bit masochistic due to self-worth issues, take a much longer time to get the message. Those who have really worked on themselves psychologically to rid themselves of any mental demons take less time to see the light. They kick the verbal vulture to the curb. After three strikes maximum, they are history!

You finally get it! Yeah! After trying each and every way to rationalize and convince yourself of ways it could work out, you now realize that there is no hope. You simply can't have this person destroying your identity and your life. You have resigned yourself to the fact that you cannot fool yourself any longer.

Now you are so excited—free at last. You feel as though a ton has been lifted from your shoulders. You can't believe how good you feel. You are smiling all the time. People tell you how great you look. You feel that you have a new lease on life. People actually like being around you now, because you're not always depressed and talking their ear off about your troubles. You are invited to more places and you are having more fun than ever. You are open to new things. You even get a new hairstyle, and shed the 10 pounds you gained in the toxic relationship, which literally "weighed you down!" You look great! You feel great! Everyone around you now is great! Life is great!

Talk Back Tips

You have now discovered, beyond a shadow of a doubt, that my "no!" answers make perfect sense. Congratulations! You have passed one of the most important hurdles in your life—you have become brutally honest with yourself. Now mark this page so you can look back on it the minute you start to doubt yourself.

Noooooo! Don't Do It!

Then one evening, things are quiet. The phone isn't ringing and you have no plans. After partying like mad to celebrate your newfound freedom, you are beginning to come back down to earth as you realize that the party's over. Now you have to start a new life with new people who are not verbally toxic.

It's tough. You think, "How am I going to meet someone to start a new verbally healthy relationship?" "Where do I go?" "What do I do?" "Oh no!," you think to yourself, "What if they don't find me attractive? What if they don't like me? What if I am alone? What if I never find a relationship again? What if nobody wants to sleep with me? What if everyone who meets me rejects me? What will happen to me? What if I get so depressed because of all of this and don't want to go on living? What if I decide to kill myself?"

Now that you have worked yourself over mentally and looked at your newfound freedom as a scary and horrific nightmare, instead of an exciting and thrilling adventure, you are paralyzed with fear! You feel so naked, so exposed, so vulnerable—as though you are so completely naked that you aren't even wearing your skin, let alone your clothes!

So, what does your first instinct tell you? Why, of course, reach for the phone and call that familiar person—your verbal abuser. It's safe. He might be abusive, you reason to yourself, but at least he was yours. He'll make it all better! You won't be feeling as naked and insecure if you go back with him, you think. So, you reach for the phone to call the "Him." Just when we all thought you were doing so well, you are now back for more. The saga continues, and now we definitely don't want to hear about it. We're sick of hearing about the abuser, and by now we're sick of you.

Help!!! Emergency!!!

Before you reach for the phone, call your family members, close friends, clergy, and the person you desperately need the most—a psychotherapist. If you don't know any, call the local mental health association in your area. Call a university or a medical center in your area. Call your friends. Ask them if they know of one or if any of their friends know of a good therapist. Call your doctor. Call the health department. Call the American Psychological Association in Washington, DC.

Talk Back Tips

Insurance might also pay for mental health treatment. Check your policy. If it doesn't cover treatment, ask your therapist if you can work out a financial arrangement. She may be able to give you a reduced rate by spending less time with you per week, or simply out of the goodness of her own heart.

If you think you can't afford professional help, stop thinking that right now! Often your community has a low-cost mental health program. The Department of Social Services in your city, county, or state can also help you. University programs often have clinical counseling available at a low cost. Your clergy can also help you—that's what they are there for. Their inspirational guidance just might be the mental medicine you need. Maybe they can at least comfort you during your time of great emotional distress, until you can actually see a mental health professional who is trained to deal with your specific issues.

I have given you all kinds of options, so there is no excuse! *Get help!*

Do it now!

Throwaways

What happens when the verbal abusers are the ones who pull the verbal plug? No matter how difficult, even impossible, the communication was between both of you, nobody likes to be tossed away like a dead raccoon.

Just know that you are probably feeling worse than they are right now. The rejected always feels worse than the rejecter.

Along with everyone else, I can sit here and give you words of sympathy. Even though we try to say sympathetic words and phrases in our attempts to comfort you, you'll think we don't know what we're talking about. You'll wish we'd just shut up, listen to your sob story, dry your tears, and wear a shirt, blouse, or sweater that feels soft, so that when you cry on our shoulder your face will feel more comfortable and less scratchy.

The following "Talk Back!" section lists some phrases of comfort usually said to a rejectee, and what the rejectee really thinks about your stupid advice.

Talk Back

Comforter says: "I know just how you feel."

Rejectee thinks: "No, you don't know how I feel! I'm the only one who can feel what I feel! How do you know what's going on in my body? I'm the one who feels like I've been run over by a truck. Have you been run over by a truck? Nooooo!"

Comforter says: "That awful person! You are better off without her."

Rejectee thinks: "She wasn't all that awful! No, I'm not better off without her! Who's gonna go to the movies with me? Who's gonna go to 7-11 with me at 2 A.M. just because I want a fudgecicle?"

Comforter says: "Don't worry, it will be fine."

Rejectee thinks: "Are you out of your mind? I can't sleep. I feel like vomiting all the time. My head hurts. I can't stop crying. I can't eat. I want to drink a whole fifth of whisky and keep drinking and never come out of my drunken stupor! It will not be fine!"

Comforter says: "You'll find someone else."

Rejectee thinks: "It took me ten years just to find this guy! When will I find someone else? When I'm 90?"

Comforter says: "There are plenty of fish in the sea."

Rejectee thinks: "Yeah, but what sea do you catch them in? Where are they? How come all the good fish are taken? If there are so many fish in the sea, how come I only attract sharks?"

None of these words help you feel better. Instead, they make you feel worse! Just know, you will feel bad, very bad, *horribly* bad for a while. But then, after you are able to hold some food down, sleep, stop crying and have an occasional smile on your face—when you have spent time away from the rejecter—you will see something you never saw before! He did you a favor.

If he left you and you were a verbal tormentor, you learned something very valuable. Don't mess with people's self-respect. Talk to them like human beings with the dignity they deserve, or you won't be talking to anybody!

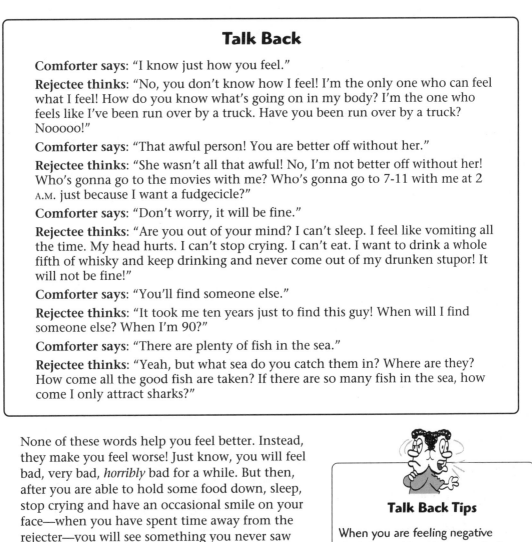

Talk Back Tips

When you are feeling negative thoughts and hostility towards the verbal perpetrator, keep repeating the mantra "What goes around comes around." It will make you feel so much better.

If, on the other hand, he left you and he was the verbal tormentor, he probably left you for a number of reasons that most likely have nothing to do with you! Here are some of the reasons that tormentors might leave you:

Talk Back Tips

Remember that if the verbal abuser left you, good riddance to good rubbish! He did you a huge favor by making you examine your masochistic tendencies and tolerance for verbal abuse.

1. They felt shame, embarrassment, and guilt over how they treated you.

2. They didn't feel that they were worthy of you.

3. They didn't get the reaction they wanted out of you. They either wanted you to fight back, and you didn't, or they wanted you to take their abuse, and you fought back instead.

4. They were tired of you. You were a verbal toy. They were done playing with you, so they threw you away.

5. They needed more people to abuse, to feed their sick souls. They were like verbal vampires, who need to suck the lifeblood out of their verbal prey and quickly move on to the next innocent victim.

No Stalkers or Fatal Attractions Allowed!

If someone leaves you, sure you can try to work it out, but if it doesn't work after three attempts, don't go back for more verbal hell. It is not worth it!

It's also not worth the legal hassles that would await you. Instead, listen to the song "Got the Message" on my *Love Healing—Music for the Heart* cassette or CD (ordering information is in the back of the book). I'm not just being a self-promoter here; I am trying to help you through music. I have received letters and phone calls from people all over the country telling me that this album has helped them tremendously in getting over some of the most difficult moments in their lives.

Mourning and Waking Up Renewed in the Morning

Certainly you will go through a roller coaster of emotions, and grieving the relationship, no matter how verbally toxic it was. The key here is to hurry up and grieve, so that you can get on with a brand-new, healthy, and positive perspective on life. A therapist or great friends can help you with this grieving process by allowing you to verbally vent. The best way to get over this difficult period is to make a list of all the verbally toxic things your opponent ever said to you. It doesn't matter if you don't remember the exact words. Just write down the specific circumstances or the different times it occurred.

Whenever you are feeling down and wishing you could go back to the relationship, just pull out your list. That will cure you and speed up your emotional recovery period!

When You're on the Verbal Merry-Go-Round

After you have finished mourning, you will from time to time have negative thoughts about the verbal tormentor. Do the "Stop the Thought" Technique mentioned earlier in this book. It will help you a lot!

Also, find solace in the fact that what goes around comes around. You might not see the immediate results, but rest assured they will suffer the consequences of their actions. If they are treating you with verbal disrespect, chances are they are doing the same with others. As I said earlier in this chapter, leopards don't change their spots.

Never forget what they did to cause you such pain! And yes, no matter what the self-proclaimed gurus tell you, you do not cause yourself pain, others cause you pain.

Forgiving Yourself Right Now!

Look, you didn't purposely seek out this verbal abuse. Chances are that you were attracted to this individual, no matter what area of your life he was in, and you found out what a verbal jerk he was! It's not your fault! You did nothing wrong, trust me! The only thing you need to examine is if there is a pattern here. If you find that your life has been filled with too much verbal abuse, you may want to look at why this is so. Perhaps there was something familiar about their behavior, something that you were conditioned by early on in life. If that is the case, you have to be conscious of this and watch yourself so that you are not drawn to another similar type of person.

Later on in the book, I share with you the various types of verbal abusers. Examine these types carefully. Once again, you might see even more of a specific pattern developing with regard to the person you're attracted to.

And yes, as a counseling psychologist, I am strongly promoting the value of my profession. Go see one! Earlier I told you how to find one, so do yourself a huge favor and see one as soon as possible.

> **Talk Back Tips**
>
> One of the most profound statements by the founding father of psychoanalysis, Sigmund Freud, is "What we don't resolve, we repeat!"

Make Yourself Feel Reeeeal Good!

This is the time you have for yourself!

As I said earlier, the best thing you can do is get professional help of some kind. The next thing you can do is to heal yourself.

Next, pamper yourself! And I mean major pampering! Don't feel guilty. This is money well spent! Pretend you are a prince, princess, sheik, king, or queen, and take one day off to book yourself solid in order to do things with the sole purpose of making yourself feel not only good but *great!*

Whatever it is, do it and enjoy! Here is a list to give you some ideas for having this great day just for you.

➤ Go to the theater or a live sporting event (no matter how expensive it is).

➤ Go somewhere or do something you always wanted to, although you never had the time or the energy.

➤ Go dancing or to a club.

➤ (Unless you have an alcohol problem) Go to a bar (even a cigar bar) and have all the drinks you want, providing that you do not drive home in a drunken state (you don't want to make it your last day!).

➤ Go shopping and splurging on whatever you want, forgetting about the money and knowing that you will somehow pay it off in time.

➤ Get a manicure, pedicure, facial, haircut and style; get waxed (if you are a woman or a man for that matter), get a shave at the barber's (if you are a man), and top it all off with a warm and relaxing bubble bath, followed by a full body massage.

➤ Have many of these pampering specialists in your home to carry out your regimen of being pampered.

➤ Lie in bed all day sleeping.

➤ Have an eating marathon, not caring about diets and calories, but eating your favorite food, perhaps in your favorite restaurants, even going to a different restaurant for coffee, breakfast, lunch, tea, dinner, and drinks.

➤ Have a book marathon, reading everything you ever wanted to read.

➤ Participate in a sport you love or take lessons in a sport you always wanted to try—for example, snowskiing, waterskiing, in-line skating, hanggliding, horseback riding, skeet shooting, and polo.

➤ Have a video marathon, watching every video you've ever wanted to see.

➤ Spend the day having a sex marathon with a loved one.

No matter what it is that you do, you have one sole purpose, and that is to make YOU feel good. No calls! No meetings! No problems! This is your day and your day only, so take advantage of it, cherish it, and don't feel guilty about it!

This pampering can also help prevent you from going back to the verbal abuser or heal the emotional pain and distress she caused you! Whenever you think of her or see another one coming your way, think of this marvelous day, and it will help you get through the difficult days.

Talk Back Tips

Trust me: This one day can be the best vacation you ever had in your life! I know—I've done it many times. You will feel so fresh and renewed, ready to take on the world and knowing that your sole purpose to make yourself feel like a worthy human being, always deserving to be treated well!

The Least You Need to Know

➤ Get out from under the clutches of the verbal abuser only after all the other techniques mentioned earlier in this book have failed.

➤ You can't make excuses anymore. You've got to face the fact that this verbally toxic person can ruin your life.

➤ Give them a chance using the "three strikes" rule—three verbally toxic deeds and they are OUT!

➤ To heal from the reeling experience of dealing with a verbal tormentor, you've got to pamper yourself in the most spectacular way. Live out your fantasies without guilt!

Part 4
Verbal Warfare with Specific People in Your Life

We have been brought up to believe that all people are created equal and need to be treated the same. In reality, people are not all created equal. They are created quite differently. Some people are pushier, nastier, quieter, sneakier, friendlier, happier, and sadder than others. Now we know that there is not only a biochemical component to these behaviors, but also a very strong environmental influence.

At this point, it doesn't matter how or where the toxic verbal behavior began. The only thing that matters is the fact that these adversaries don't make you feel good whenever they are in your presence or whenever you think of them.

These verbally toxic people seem to crop up in just about every area of your life! They might appear in your own family, at work, when you need to deal with a professional, or when you're minding your own business, going about your daily life. These verbal abusers, who will be discussed in Chapters 17, 18, and 19, are everywhere!

In this part you learn how to actually deal with these people, depending who they are in your life, and what your relationship is to them. You'll learn to apply appropriate techniques, depending not only on who that person is, but upon what "verbal crimes" they've committed against you.

Chapter 14

Gaining the Winning Verbal Edge Between the Sexes

In This Chapter

➤ Being bilingual in male/female communication

➤ Seeing how upbringing influences the way we communicate

➤ What males mean by what they say

➤ What females mean by what they say

➤ What men need to do to be understood

➤ What women need to do to be understood

No more male bashing! No more female bashing! No more lectures about how different men and women are! No more hearing how "men are from Mars and women are from Venus!" Trust me, we get it! We don't need to be beaten over the head with the same information. In this chapter, you learn less commonly shared information that strictly concerns how men and women speak to one another. I will discuss specific body, facial, and head positions, vocal patterns, pronunciation of sounds, words, phrases, and content of speech that are specifically indigenous to men or to women. This chapter is not designed to make you feel bad or guilty for how you speak to members of the opposite sex. Instead, it is designed to teach you the language of the opposite sex, so that you will know what the other truly means by what he or she says.

Because today's litigious society demands respect and equality, you have no choice but to put the information you learn in this chapter into action. If you do, you'll never experience the pain and frustration that comes from miscommunication.

What's the Real Deal?

What is the number one reason for divorce? What is the number one reason for marital affairs among couples? With the exception of medical problems, what is the major reason for sexual dysfunction among couples? What is one of the main reasons women are not advancing up the corporate ladder as rapidly as they should?

Aside from a few unsavory individuals whose main concern is financial gain, why are there so many sexual harassment suits bombarding our courtrooms today? The common denominator of all of these questions is "lack of communication." This lack of communication between the sexes is a serious issue, so serious that it can determine not only the quality of your professional life, but your personal life as well. It can even affect the seemingly benign things you do on a daily basis and your interactions with people you encounter throughout the day.

Listen Up!

Lack of communication can affect your sex life—your intimate relationship with your loved ones and even your sexual performance.

Not knowing how to effectively speak and understand employers, employees, and co-workers of the opposite sex can make the time you spend at work "hell on earth."

Learning to Be Bilingual

Perhaps the people who have the best opportunities in life are those who know another language. I know this first-hand. Understanding and speaking languages other than English has proven to be invaluable to me in my personal and professional life. Even understanding certain dialects and slang words and expressions among young people has helped me, as I mentioned earlier in this book (see "Bingo! You Got the Lingo!" in Chapter 9).

What has been the advantage of knowing these different languages, aside from allowing me to order a meal, get appropriate hotel service, and understand spoken direction (so I don't get lost) in another country? Knowledge of these languages has helped people to relate to me more quickly and to have immediate affection for me, unless of course I'm yelling at someone who has been totally mean and obnoxious to me. Similarly, when women learn to speak "man talk" and men learn to speak "woman talk," suddenly there is more affection, camaraderie, communications, friendships, and more exciting intimate relations.

Throughout the rest of the chapter you learn how to speak one another's language and decode the signals, so that you never again have to worry about being misunderstood.

Once Upon a Time There Was an Infant Boy and Girl

Men are raised differently than women are—yes, even in this day and age when we are supposed to be more sophisticated and aware. We clearly see this difference in people as early as infancy. For example, in a study at an Ivy League university, men and women were put into a room with infant boys and girls. Before entering the room, the men and women were told that the infants were all little girls. As they entered and stayed in the room, both men and women spoke in a soft voice, making delicate cooing sounds and saying comments to the infants such as "You're so pretty." "Look at how beautiful you are." "You are a little princess." There was hardly any physical contact.

Next, these same men and women were lead into another infant nursery, where—they were told—all the babies were little boys. Upon entering the room and subsequently spending some time there, the behavior of the adults changed greatly. The decibel level rose. The infants were actually taken out of their cribs and held under their arms as they kicked the air beneath them. The adults used phrases such as "What a big strong boy," "You're gonna grow up to be a football player," and "Hey, you little pumpkin head."

More often than not, a parent will tolerate a boy's impoliteness—"Gimme that"—over a girl's impoliteness, insisting that "little girls don't talk that way and have to say 'please' and 'thank you.'"

Listen Up!

When a toddler boy bites someone, the parent doesn't get especially mad. After all, they say, "he's just being a boy." But when a little girl bites, the parent shrinks back in horror. "Oh no! Hurry let's call a child psychologist. She might grow up to be who knows what...even a lawyer!"

There's Only One Brain!

Now of course I have to bring in the other element—not nurture, but the biology of how little boys and girls are wired neurologically and hormonally. Unlike little boys, little girls have an initial growth spurt in the left hemisphere of the brain. As a result of this difference in neurological development, they tend to become more fluent and develop a greater repertoire of speech and language skills than boys. Little boys take about four years to catch up with this growth spurt. In the meantime, some serious environmental stimulation has taken place, and little girls get more parental verbal attention because they are more responsive, due to the advanced growth of their neuroanatomy.

In this case, the behavior of parents corresponds to real physiological characteristics. This is not true in the case of parents conditioning their sons to be more mechanically and mathematically inclined. The right hemispheres of boys' brains do not grow more rapidly than those of little girls; the difference is purely environmental. In fact, I, along with many other specialists in the field, believe that if little girls were equally encouraged in mechanical and cognitive abilities, we would observe little or no differences between the sexes in this area.

Verbal Vignette

I want to clear up the dangerous misconception perpetuated in uninformed self-help books on male/female communication. **There is no right brain and left brain, no male and female brain.** There is a speech and language center located in the left hemisphere of that one brain; the right hemisphere is responsible for processing analytical, mathematical, and conceptual information. However, *both* hemispheres work in harmony due to a series of neural connections between the various anatomical parts of the brain.

What Shall We Talk About?

A major study by Dr. Adelaide Haas at the State University of New York department of Speech Communication found that the conversation topics most likely discussed among men and women vary greatly. The following list shows the topics in order, based on gender:

Women	Men
1. Men	1. Women
2. Food	2. News events
3. Family relations	3. Sports
4. Clothing	4. Arts
5. News events	5. Sex
6. Work-related issues	6. Work-related issues

Men tend to discuss things and what they did, while women tend to discuss their feelings about what they did as well as their feelings about other people.

What does all of this mean? It means a lot! It means that when you are around the opposite sex, you will be more confident in bringing up these topics, as you will establish a communication bond more quickly.

He Says—She Thinks! She Says—He Thinks!

Because there is such confusion in the way men and women speak to one another, a man might innocently say something to a woman that causes her to fly off the handle. In turn, she might say something that aggravates him. Both of these people have no clue why the other has gotten so mad at what they said. The man often thinks the woman might just be going through PMS. The woman, on the other hand, thinks that the guy is just being a jerk. "Who is right? Who is wrong? What is going on here? First of all, nobody is right! And nobody is wrong! In fact, they are both right! The man is just talking "male," while the woman is understanding what he says in "female." Conversely, the woman speaks "female" while the man hears in "male." It's as simple as that! If the man understood her "female" language and the woman understood his "male" language, I wouldn't be using them as an example in this book.

Here are five common examples of conversations that are misinterpreted merely because one person doesn't really understand the other's language. I'm sure that at one point or another, every one of us has experienced at least one of these situations.

No-No Scenario 1

John (in the living room while Mary is in the kitchen): Hey, Mary, get me a beer!

Mary: Get you what?

John (thinking she didn't hear him, he yells even louder): GET ME A BEER!

Mary: Get it yourself! Who do think I am, your maid?

John (shocked): What is wrong with you? All I asked you was for a lousy can of beer and here you go and chop my head off!

Mary: Well, I don't appreciate being ordered around like some slave!

John: Who is ordering around? What is this? Do you have PMS or something?

No-No Scenario 2

Ann (wearing a brand new outfit, hair perfectly coifed, and looking stunning): So, how do I look?

Bob: You look nice.

Ann: Nice, what do you mean?

Bob: I mean, nice.

Ann: Well, if you don't like how I look, why don't you just tell me!

Bob: I am telling you. You look nice.

Ann: Look, if you want me to change my outfit I will.

Bob: What are you talking about? What's wrong with you?

Talk Back Tips

As we'll discuss later, try to use specific language, not generic words such as "nice," when responding to people.

No-No Scenario 3

Dave (seeing Debra sulking and looking sad): What's wrong?

Debra: Nothing!

Dave: Are you sure?

Debra: Yes. I said nothing's wrong.

Dave: Well, then, how come you are sulking?

Debra: You should know!

Dave: No, I don't know! Tell me!

Debra: Well, if you don't know, I'm not going to tell you.

Dave: If I knew then I wouldn't be asking you.

No-No Scenario 4

Fred: I can't believe the day I had. Everything went wrong—from getting a ticket, to getting reprimanded at work, to losing an account, to hearing that my cousin John is in the hospital.

Jill: I had an awful day too. I saw so many clients today. I overdrew money in my account...

Fred (cutting her off): Why do you always do this to me?

Jill: Do what to you?

Fred: Compete with me?

Jill: Compete with you? What are you talking about.

Fred: What you said just now, you're competing with me—your day was worse than mine.

Jill: I'm just trying to relate to you and comfort you.

Fred: Well, you're not!

No-No Scenario 5

Tina: You never call!

Jack: Yes, I do.

Tina: No, you don't, and you never surprise me with flowers or any gifts!

Jack: What did I do for your birthday?

Tina: That was a year ago! Two years ago you got me a junky bracelet. You didn't even bother to get me anything on Valentine's day four years ago. You never even remembered my birthday!

Jack: That was in the past. Why do you always have to bring up the past?

Do any of these scenarios sound familiar to you? If they do, you are definitely not alone. These scenarios typify the common miscommunication between men and women. Either sex might think they are being kind or neutral, but in reality they are perceived as mean, bitchy, unreasonable, and insulting. The following section gives a translation of what was really meant to be conveyed in each of the scenarios.

Talk Back Tips

Remember that bad feelings result from broken communication only because each sex is ignorant of how the other speaks.

He Says—He Means! She Says—She Means!

In Scenario 1, when John says "Get me a beer," Mary interprets that as being ordered around, feeling that John is insensitive to the fact that she too just came home from a hard day's work. When he repeats it again, in an even louder voice, Mary is furious and lets him have it by telling him to get it himself while using a huffy and upset voice. John is totally confused about what happened here. His only explanation is that Mary must be tense due to pre-menstrual syndrome. Unknowingly, John created this situation, which results in both parties being upset.

Scenario 1 Shoulda Said

Had he said "Honey, would you mind please getting me a beer since you're at the refrigerator? I'd really appreciate it," none of this would have happened.

Bottom line solution: Don't talk in command terms!

Scenario 2 Shoulda Said

In Scenario 2, when Bob answers Ann's question about how she looks with the bland and benign word "nice," Mary thinks that he doesn't like what she's wearing or how she looks. His one-word response with this vague word really didn't satisfy her insecurities and, more important, her desire to have Bob think she looks beautiful and sexy.

Had Bob said "Honey, you look [phenomenal, gorgeous, beautiful, sexy, fantastic]" (take your pick), Ann would have felt great, thereby boosting her confidence, especially her confidence about how Bob saw her. She would have felt wonderful because she was able to provide Bob with something pleasing to his eyes. Had he gone on to explain in more detail why she looked so gorgeous (for instance, "Your hair looks so shiny and silky and that color brings out the green in your eyes"), she would have felt even better.

Bottom line solution: Use more descriptive adjectives. Never use average or bland words.

Scenario 3 Shoulda Said

Had Debra honestly opened up and told Dave what was the matter, he would not have become so frustrated with her. He felt hopeless and confused, emotions that subsequently turned into anger.

Bottom line solution: Don't think that the other person is a mind reader. Open up and say what's on your mind.

Scenario 4 Shoulda Said

Had Jill not told him about her day, immediately after Fred poured his heart out to her, he would not have become irritated with her. Innocently, Jill was just trying to make him feel better by sharing with him that he wasn't alone and that she too had a bad day. She was trying to be empathetic; Fred interpreted this as her being competitive with him, being insensitive to his distress, ignoring his feelings, and not providing him with the sensitivity and nurturing he needed.

After Fred verbally unloaded his burden, Jill needed to say something like "Oh, I'm so sorry, you must feel awful. What happened when you got the ticket?" She could have asked him to give her more detail about anything else that upset him about his day. That way, he would think that she really cared and was greatly concerned about him.

Bottom line solution: Listen to a problem. Be sympathetic and ask questions (in kind tones) to further explore the person's problem so that he or she can vent further. Never talk about what's bothering you and your problem until after you have completely addressed his.

Scenario 5 Shoulda Said

Had Tina not started out the conversation accusing Jack, he might have been less defensive and less closed off to her plight. To top it off, she brings up things from the past that have nothing to do with what's going on in the present. Because of her accusations and whining, he probably never feels like getting her a gift, or for that matter, even seeing her.

Listen Up!

Remember to try *never* to impose the past onto the present. You cannot be effective in communication until you clear your mind and observe the person before whom you stand.

Tina needed to start the conversation saying something to the effect of "It really hurts my feelings" or "It really makes me sad when I don't get a gift from you as a token of how you feel about me." Jack probably would have answered with "Oh, I am so sorry, you know I love you. It's just hard for me to pick out gifts. I wasn't raised with gift giving, so it's not important to me. But since it means a lot to you, I'll be more conscious of it." Later that day or the next day, Tina might indeed be surprised by his token of affection. Instead, Tina put him on the defensive. And she added insult to injury by bringing up his misdeeds of the past. This further alienated him and made him feel more defensive and angry. Now he felt like really never wanting to get her anything.

Bottom line solution: Don't accuse. Instead, tell how the situation makes you feel. Secondly, don't bring up the past.

Oh! So That's What You Meant!

The next two sections explain how to speak "male language" and "female language." Included are some of the most common body signals, facial signals, words, phrases, and conversations that are indigenous to each of the sexes. As was discussed earlier, this has a lot to do with our social conditioning!

Not all males do these typical behaviors, nor do all females exhibit the typical female behavior patterns. What I discuss in this section is general information, where the psychosocial research done on these areas reflects the norm—the typical communication pattern used by the general population of males and the general population of females.

Don't be surprised if you recognize yourself as you read some of the points that are common to a specific sex. You might see how you have misinterpreted the actions of the opposite sex, thereby causing yourself unnecessary emotional pain, frustration, and aggravation. On the other hand, perhaps there are several behaviors you don't do—this indicates that you either were raised with a better understanding of how to communicate with the opposite sex, or learned by experience. Now is your opportunity to learn everything you didn't know before about the main points indigenous to the communication skills of the opposite sex.

Basic Male 101

This section lists typical male communication patterns—some of the key things men communicate and how they may be misinterpreted. A woman's knowledge of these patterns will help her to realize that men's seemingly rude, distant, or obnoxious behavior is not that at all. In their innocence, men are just speaking "male."

Body Language:

1. Taking up more space. Perception: they are hogging space and trying to take over.

2. Sitting further away. Perception: they don't like the woman.

3. Gesturing with their fingers, often pointing their finger. Perception: they are admonishing you.

4. Fidgeting and shifting their bodies more than women do. Perception: they are not interested or are anxious to leave the situation.

Talk Back Tips

Remember this list is "typical" behavior. There are some men who don't do these things because they were raised or conditioned in the ways of properly communicating with the opposite sex.

5. Assuming a more reclined position when sitting or leaning back when listening. Perception: they are being judgmental.

Facial Language:

1. Cocking their head to the side and looking at the person at an angle while listening to them. Perception: they are being judgmental or disinterested.

2. Frowning and squinting when listening. Perception: disapproval.

3. Using little eye contact in positive interaction. Perception: they are disinterested and distant.

4. Providing fewer facial expressions and fewer reactions than women when listening. Perception: disagreement or disapproval.

5. Avoiding eye contact and not looking directly at the other person. Perception: disinterest or dislike.

Speech and Voice Patterns:

1. Interrupting and allowing fewer interruptions from others. Perception: they regard the other person as unimportant or not knowledgeable.

2. Using less intonation or vocal inflection. Perception: disinterest, disapproval, apathy, and dislike for the other person.

3. Allowing more silence during conversation lulls. Perception: they have nothing more to say and want to end the conversation.

4. Giving more command terms. Perception: they are acting with hostility.

5. Using fewer emotional state verbs (such as "I feel," "I hope," "I love"). Perception: they don't care and are insensitive.

Communication:

1. Teasing more, playing practical jokes, and using sarcasm as humor (often making a joke out of "sensitive" issues). Perception: acting in a hostile way and not liking the woman.

Listen Up!

When you don't disclose much about yourself, others might think that you are being deliberately secretive and trying to hide something.

2. Apologizing less often after an argument. Perception: being stubborn and uncaring.

3. Liking to hear accolades about themselves and talking more about their accomplishments. Perception: they are being egomaniacal.

4. Confronting issues less. Perception: being uncaring and disinterested and purposely hurting the woman.

5. Disclosing less personal information. Perception: they are hiding something, being dishonest (possibly cheating).

6. Invading one's personal space more than women do. Perception: being obnoxious and trying to be intimidating.

Basic Female 101

Before a man thinks that the woman is driving him nuts or just having PMS, here are some common communication actions that typify women's communication patterns. Knowing about them can save the male a lot of unnecessary grief and nurture a more positive and upbeat—and in turn, healthy—relationship.

Body Language:

1. Assuming a more forward position than men when sitting or listening, and leaning forward. Perception: caring a lot about what is said; extreme interest.

2. Having a weaker handshake. Perception: being weak and powerless.

3. Sitting closer to men. Perception: the woman really likes the man.

4. Taking up less physical space, and sitting with arms and legs towards the body. Perception: being inhibited and submissive.

5. Sitting directly in front of a man, and having forward face-to-face contact. Perception: being extremely interested in the man or being forward. It can also be misconstrued as an uncomfortably confrontational act.

Face Language:

1. Nodding head "yes" even when not in agreement. Perception: Wanting to be liked and accepted.

2. Lowering their head during every negative confrontation. Perception: being weak and submissive.

3. Providing more animated facial expressions during conversation. Perception: being overly emotional.

4. Eyes facing the person directly when speaking. Perception: being forward or even invasive.

Speech and Voice Patterns:

1. Allowing more interruptions. Perception: being weak.

2. Ending sentences with a rising pitch, adding a tag ending to a declarative statement, or asking a question when it calls for making a statement (for example, "It's a nice day?" or "It's a nice day, isn't it?"). Perception: being uncertain, weak, not powerful, and not in control.

3. Using more intensifiers such as "very," "really," and "much." Perception: being overly effusive and exaggerating, and being more emotional.

4. Saying more words per sentence or thought. Getting very detailed and taking a long time to get to the point. Perception: being unprofessional, wasting time, being thoughtless, scattered, and frivolous (this usually creates the reaction of impatience).

5. Often having voices that are too high, breathy, and little girl-sounding. Perception: being a lightweight, less bright.

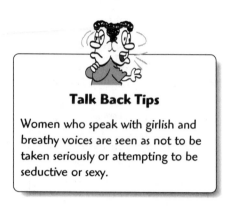

Talk Back Tips

Women who speak with girlish and breathy voices are seen as not to be taken seriously or attempting to be seductive or sexy.

Communication Patterns:

1. Tending to take rejection more personally. Perception: being overly sensitive.

2. Not laughing at or responding favorably to practical joke and cutting sarcastic humor. Perception: having no sense of humor.

3. Trying to match troubles by relating similar experiences. Perception: competing with the man or trying to top him, and not listening to or caring about what he says.

4. Confronting issues and situations more than a man would. Perception: being nagging or harping on the past (this often makes the man feel angry and defensive).

5. Censoring thoughts less than men and communicating more through stream-of-consciousness. Perception: being ditsy, spacey, or flighty.

See What I Mean?

In looking at the differences in the preceding section, it is no wonder that men and women are always at one another's throats. Little wonder that these misinterpretations of the male and female language result in explosions of tempers and devastation of feelings. It is sad and, when you think about it, also rather amusing. If we had the key to unlock the box of mysteries about how the opposite sex communicates, there would be less divorce, fewer sexual harassment suits, and much less ill will between one another. Now you have some of the tools right at your fingertips.

The next section lists several easy steps men can take to immediately improve their relationships with women, and women with men. I have chosen only some points for each sex, since they represent the differences leading to the most common misunderstandings.

Note than I am not trying to turn men into women and women into men! I am just giving you some things to do if you want to modify your communication patterns when you deem it necessary, in order to get along much better. Of course, these are only suggestions, but rest assured that if you do employ them, you might see some amazing and instant results.

What Men Need to Do

1. Stop making commands. Make requests instead.

2. Always use the words "please" and "thank you" whenever making a request. Use terms of politeness as often as possible.

3. Use more psychological state verbs to express how you are feeling.

4. Don't be embarrassed to ask for help as soon as possible.

5. Don't use sarcastic or cutting humor.

6. Don't interrupt.

7. Don't take up so much room physically.

8. Have more enthusiasm in your voice. Don't wear your emotions on your sleeve. Instead, wear them on your vocal tones.

9. Don't lecture someone—have a dialogue and not a monologue.

10. Look at a person face to face when speaking.

11. Use more descriptive adjectives.

12. Don't frown when listening.

13. Show more emotional reaction in your face when you speak and listen.

14. Open up more—don't use one-word responses to answer questions.

15. Don't keep changing topics midstream in a conversation a woman brings up.

16. Stop fidgeting and rocking back and forth.

17. Disclose more personal information about yourself.

18. Don't point your finger at people when talking to them, especially when you want to express a point.

19. Apologize immediately if you have done something wrong.

Talk Back Tips

For more information on the 105 differences between men's and women's communication techniques, as well as to learn exactly what to do and say in social settings, at work, and even during moments of intimacy, read *He Says She Says— Closing the Communication Gap Between the Sexes* (Putnam, 1992) by Lillian Glass, Ph.D.

What Women Need to Do

1. Get to the point—stop beating around the bush.

2. Never cry in a work situation when frustrated, no matter what.

3. Never use tag endings or make a statement as though it sounds like a question.

4. Never match experiences or tragedies. Listen and sympathize instead.

5. Lower the pitch of your voice and talk louder.

6. Don't hold grudges.

7. Don't apologize if you haven't done anything wrong.

8. Don't accuse or you'll always lose! Ask instead!

9. Think about what you are going to say and are saying. Edit and don't say everything that comes into your mind.

10. Don't shake your head "yes" (indicating agreement) just to be polite, when you really disagree or aren't interested.

11. Take up more physical space and move around more when you speak.

12. Stay in the present. Don't bring up the past when arguing about an issue at hand.

13. Speak up in terms of what's bothering you. After all, the other person is not a "mind reader." You have to clearly state what's bothering you and stop playing the guessing game with him.

14. Disclose less personal information about yourself.

15. Be more open to "male humor." Even if you can't relate to it, don't dismiss it or chastise men for using it.

Talk Back Tips

When you try to show empathy to match experiences with someone else, he is likely to hear it as an attempt to be competitive. Listen instead.

16. Bring up more male-oriented topics.

17. Make fewer tentative statements that indicate "I'm not sure" or "maybe."

18. As impossible as a task might seem, try not to take criticism and rejection personally, in a way that affects your self-esteem, security, and subsequent performance.

19. Speak in more modulated tones, so that you don't give the illusion of being out of control emotionally.

20. Try not to giggle or laugh all the time, especially when you are feeling nervous and uncomfortable.

Saving You a Lot of Grief!

Incorporating the majority of these points, where appropriate, may help you in all aspects in your life where you need to communicate effectively with the opposite sex—from the boardroom to the bedroom. Sometimes, when you are fully aware of these differences, you no longer get upset, irritated, hurt, or confused by what the other said. Instead, you now know that it's just "male talk" or "female talk." You have the option of doing something about it or doing nothing.

The basic message of this chapter is that just being aware of these differences can make you laugh, chuckle, smile knowingly, or shake your head. Now you know for sure that what is being said by the opposite sex is not intended negatively or meant to irritate you, intimidate you, or hurt your feelings.

Therefore, you won't get angry, cry, feel sad and depressed, or jump to conclusions that have no basis whatsoever! If you take advantage of everything in this chapter pertaining to your new-found understanding of the opposite sex, you'll save yourself an enormous amount of grief!

Verbal Vignette

According to a recent Gallup poll of 911 adults, only 20 percent of the women responded that their best friend was a man, while 18 percent of the men said that their best friend was a woman. Perhaps after reading this chapter and having better understanding of and communication with the opposite sex, these statistics will increase.

The Least You Need to Know

➤ There is a genetic as well as environmental component to how little boys and little girls develop their communication skills.

➤ Even today, we have stereotypical expectations for how little boys and little girls should behave.

➤ There is no male brain and female brain. There is only one brain, consisting of two hemispheres. The left one focuses primarily on various aspects of communication while the right is more concerned with analysis and mechanical functions. The difference between the two hemispheres is not sex-related.

➤ Much miscommunication between the sexes could be avoided if we understood one another's language—male language and female language.

➤ In general, male language is more direct, to the point, and mostly devoid of communication that focuses on emotions and detailed descriptions.

➤ Female language is more indirect and filled with more emotional state words and extensive descriptions of places, events, and people.

Chapter 15

Blood Is Not Always Thicker Than Water!

In This Chapter

➤ Verbal defense tactics with a verbally abusive parent

➤ How to deal with verbally abusive brothers and sisters

➤ How to speak to and verbally respond to teenagers

➤ How to help children develop communication skills that are not verbally offensive

➤ How to communicate with infants, toddlers, and young children

Just because people are related to you doesn't mean you have to take their verbal abuse. You might say, "Well, after all, it's my mother (or father); it's my flesh and blood." Although this is true, there are some family members who can make your flesh crawl and make your blood boil. Even if someone happens to be a family member, you still need to protect yourself against his verbal venom, which, as we discussed earlier in the book, could even be life-threatening. Now you have choices! You can use different techniques on different family members—whichever is most likely to work. The purpose of the general technique is to get you the results that you need to establish a harmonious and peaceful relationship with people to whom you are related.

Defense Against Verbally Abusive Parents

When your parents verbally abuse you, your first instinct is to say or do something to stop them, but then you might hold yourself back, reasoning that after all, they are still your parents.

While all religious teachings encourage honoring your father and mother, clearly some parents have no business becoming parents. Such parents physically, mentally, and emotionally abuse their children to the point that they inflict painful, severe, and irreparable damage on their offspring. This verbal abuse doesn't occur only in childhood—it is carried on into teen and adult years.

Listen Up!

I have seen clients in their 70s, 80s, and 90s still unable to shed the emotional harm that they suffered during youth from the mouths of their verbally abusive parents. This is living proof of what I said earlier in this book: "Words stick."

Long-Lasting Effects

This damage is so lasting that I have seen the devastating results in my own private practice. In fairness to the parents, most do not mean to become verbal terrorists. Often a continuous legacy of verbal abuse exists: They learned it from their parents, who in turn learned it from their parents, and so forth. Sometimes parents will make fun of their child without even realizing the comments' devastating and lasting impact on their children's psyches.

Your Best Bet!

Parents' most common crime is to be the accusing critic or cut down their child constantly, even to point where they are unaware of it, and it becomes second nature.

If this has been done to you, you should use the Direct Confrontation technique discussed in Chapter 11 to help heal your emotional wound. Your parents need to be told directly and bluntly that what they are saying is very hurtful to you and that you would appreciate if they did not "get on your case" all the time.

Most parents react well to this approach, which needs to be repeated on a number of occasions. In essence, you have to recondition them. Old habits and ways of talking are hard to break. So when your parents do the same thing again and again, don't just get angry—continue to use direct confrontation. The more often you set limits with them, the more your request will be ingrained into their minds.

The reason most parents nag you is not because they mean to hurt you. In fact, they want the best for you and only have your interests at heart. But many parents don't know how to express this. It takes time and patience to establish boundaries and new ground rules for any relationship. Therefore, in addition to the Direct Confrontation Technique, try using the Tension Blowout Technique to help you to become more non-reactive. The Tension Blow-out Technique is when you breathe in through the mouth as you think of a tension producing situation or a verbally abusive or toxic person. You hold the breath in for five seconds and then with all your might, BLOW out the air as forcefully as you can while thinking of that person. Your goal is to not allow your parents to "push your buttons," which causes you to react in your usual manner of either harshly lashing back or holding it in so much that you suffer.

If after reading this section you realize that you are a verbally abusive parent, stop this behavior immediately. Use the breathing technique you learned about earlier. Breathe in, hold it, and then speak. This technique allows you to have more control over what you say to your child and how you say it.

This technique is merely the one you start with. Depending on what type of verbal abuser your parent is, however (which you will learn about in the next two chapters), your parent might require additional approaches. For example, if your parent refuses to listen, verbally abuses you, and even physically abuses you, in such a harsh and continuous fashion, you may have no choice but to use the Unplug Technique.

Sometimes it is effective for a little while. Your total unplugging from them can be so painful for them that for the first time they might actually hear your pain and stop contributing to it. In other cases, the scars are so deep and the abuse is so bad that you will need to let go forever!

Defense Against Verbally Abusive Siblings

Brothers and sisters probably cause one another more emotional pain and agony than anyone else. This is the result of the competitive element common between siblings.

Verbal Vignette

According to research, siblings are more likely to compete with one another the closer in age they are. They may compete in order to gain an edge over the other on such things as parental love and the material things they get. There may be competition over activities, friends they possess, and even athletic and academic performance.

Too Close for Comfort

Why are siblings so competitive? Perhaps they are living proof of the old adage that "familiarity breeds contempt." Each sibling thinks he or she knows the other quite well, and, consequently, they often assume that their own values and wants are the same as their sibling's. This is the main reason brothers and sisters get on one another's nerves. They inevitably do things differently, and one sibling might lose respect for another, thinking the other is doing it wrong. Therefore, a fight ensues; one constantly puts the other down, creating an uncomfortable and hostile environment.

Your Best Bet!

Perhaps the best technique to use with your verbally toxic siblings is humor. This might take the edge off of things and allow them to see the light. If humor doesn't work, the Love and Kindness approach can be very effective. In this approach, you confront them directly, letting them know how much their words and actions hurt your feelings and how much you care about them and don't want anything to come between the two of you.

If the verbal fighting won't stop and gets so intense that it leads to blows and physical fighting, you need to "unplug," usually for an extended period of time. Siblings often desperately need time apart in order to regroup. In some cases, they come to see how empty their lives are without one another, and they reunite with a newfound mutual respect. But it can take days, months, or even years of separation for siblings to overcome the emotional hurt and pain created by verbal and even concomitant physical abuse.

More rarely, the damage is irreparable and there is no hope. Even siblings who have applied all of the techniques mentioned in Chapters 10 and 11, and have "unplugged" for a while might still resume their same behavior when they come back together. For the sake of the mental (and physical) health of both parties, they need to go their separate ways permanently.

Listen Up!

When dealing with your children, respond to and discourage inappropriate behavior *immediately*. Don't give it time to become an ingrained habit.

Verbal Defense with Teens

It is not uncommon today to hear teens freely mouthing off at their parents, or at anyone else for that matter—teachers, service workers, anyone who stands in the way of them doing whatever they want to do. When they are restricted from doing what they want to do, they usually rebel.

In the "Talk Back!" section that follows, you will see a conversation that has occurred in most households. What are parents to do when their teen speaks to them so abusively? The answer is simple: Don't ever allow them to. The first time you hear your teen talking this way to you should be the last time. You need to nip it in the bud and be consistent as a parent.

Talk Back

Mom: Tom, I want you to clean your room. It's a mess.

Tom: I don't wanna.

Mom: Okay, then you aren't leaving this house until you do.

Tom: But I have to meet everyone at two o'clock for a ballgame.

Mom: Too bad. Until I see a clean room, you're not going anywhere.

Tom (extremely angry): *&^$@ #&%!!!!!!

Mom: No way will you ever use that language in this home, ever! [Said using the Give 'Em Hell and Yell Technique.]

Do you understand? Never talk to me like that. Show some respect! Do you know how it makes me feel when you talk to me like that? [Direct Confront Technique.]

It hurts me so deeply. I have tried my best for you in every way and I have enough self-respect that I cannot allow you to speak this way, to me under any circumstances! How would it make you feel if I spoke like that to you, especially in front of your friends? How would you feel if I constantly talked trash to you and treated you like dirt—as though you were worthless and unimportant to me? [Calm Questioning Technique.]

I love you so much and want you to grow up to be as wonderful as you really are inside. I asked you to straighten up your room, not to be mean or unreasonable. I want you to live in a pleasant environment, with order and no chaos, so that you can find things and enjoy where you live. I want you to develop good habits that you can carry with you in college and as an adult. Please don't disappoint me and hurt me by talking to me like that when I am trying my best to give you everything I can as a parent. [Love and Kindness Technique, said in a soft and loving tone.]

This dialogue illustrates the combination of verbal self-defense techniques, including Give 'Em Hell and Yell, Direct Confrontation, Calm Questioning, and Love and Kindness. One or more of them can be used to get your point across. Chances are that if you use these techniques, your teen will hear what you are saying. One of these ways will be the key to unlocking communication with them. They have to know that you will not tolerate them throwing verbal trash at you!

Trash Talkin' Teens

Just listen to some of the music teens listen to. Listen to a phone conversation or a face-to-face conversation they are having with their friends. You'll be quite shocked—things aren't the same as when you were growing up! In the past few years, teens have heard so many obscene words in songs and films that the words have no effect on them at all. They speak in curses as though they are saying something as benign as "how are you doing?" For instance, the "f" word, which we used to regard as extremely vulgar and offensive, is now used in a number of ways. Sometimes it is used as a noun, for something pleasant ("Did you hear their new CD? Those f—ers were great!") or unpleasant ("I'm gonna get that little f—er"). Similarly, as an adjective, it can also be used either negatively ("Get your f—ing car out of here") or positively ("Your f—ing car is awesome").

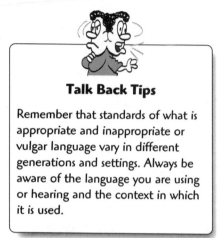

Talk Back Tips

Remember that standards of what is appropriate and inappropriate or vulgar language vary in different generations and settings. Always be aware of the language you are using or hearing and the context in which it is used.

Whether a teenager uses the term in positive or negative way among his or her teenage peers, however, the term is socially unacceptable to others. In fact, consistently using this term outside of their own little world can create such a negative image that it affects their potential employment and social interaction.

The bottom line is that teenagers mustn't use this kind of talk in your home. They need to be conditioned to this fact the very first time you hear them use obscenities. If they have already gotten in the habit of cursing and you failed to condition them initially, you need to start doing so right away. Of course, it might take a little longer to get the message through to them, but if you maintain your consistency, it will eventually sink in.

Expect to Hear This from Your Teen

Following is a list of common teenage concerns that parents have to learn to address effectively. Don't freak out and get mad or flabbergasted—handle it! Be in control! You now have choices to make concerning which verbal defense strategy you plan to employ.

I can't tell you exactly what to say, because for all I know you might say "Go ahead take the car" or "Here's $1,000, go have a ball!" or "What kind of liquor can I get you?" If you need to contest their request, however, your best bet is to use the Direct Confrontation, Calm Questioning, or Love and Kindness techniques.

➤ I want to drive.

➤ I want to date.

➤ I want to stay out late.

➤ I want to hang out with my friends.

➤ I need money.

➤ I need the latest style clothes.

➤ I need more computer stuff.

➤ I need stereo equipment.

➤ I want the right gym shoes, and I don't care about the price.

➤ I want to sleep over at a friend's house.

➤ I don't want to study.

➤ I want to see that movie—I don't care about the rating.

➤ I got wasted (drunk).

➤ I like doing drugs.

➤ I am ugly.

➤ Everyone hates me.

➤ You're always picking on me.

➤ Nobody asked me out.

➤ Everyone I asked out said "No!"

➤ I hate school.

➤ I hate YOU!

Talk Back Tips

Remember that when you verbally respect your children, nine times out of ten they will verbally respect you in return.

Verbal Defense with School-Aged Kids

Children often become obnoxious as they try to push the envelope to see how much they can get away with. They may become verbally belligerent, speak in "street" (verbally incorrect and accented) language, or curse in order to fit in.

Best Bet: Set Limits Immediately!

If you don't set limits at this crucial age, you might never have the chance to do so again! This bad verbal behavior can become so ingrained in them that it will become difficult to control. The techniques used with teenagers are also effective with school-age children. Their reasoning powers may not be as highly developed, however, so you might want to communicate with them so that they can really "hear" you. They need to be corrected (not in a negative way but in a positive and upbeat way), reinforced, and encouraged to repeat the correct form of speech after you. Even if they don't repeat the word, they will still be learning the correct usage by hearing you say it over and over; you will subconsciously ingrain positive verbal habits in them.

Parental Verbal Control

While it is good to have verbal control by repeating the correct form of the word—correct grammatical form or pronunciation—don't overdo it!

Every child stutters or stammers while developing speech and language, so don't go nuts if your child does this. It has long been said that "stuttering

Talk Back Tips

School-age children have more numerous influences. Their peers and people in the media (including MTV) speak in street slang, which is filled with improper grammar, incorrect pronunciation of words, and filler words such as "like" and "you know."

begins in the parent's ears." In other words, don't make children nervous when they talk or ever tell them to shut up or to "slow down." Instead, let it go by and repeat correctly what they were going to say.

Sometimes in frustration, when a parent is angry, he or she tells children how stupid they are or that they are no good. No matter how angry you get as a parent, be aware that if you say these horrible words, the consequences of your actions will be serious. As I said earlier, "words stick."

You are doing your child a huge disservice. In essence, you are robbing your child's self-esteem and contributing to the destruction of her self-worth. If you are using this method as a way of controlling your child, find another way. You are playing with fire. It can be extremely dangerous!

Best Bets: Ask Your Child If She Wants to Go Somewhere with You

Respect them. Don't drag them along! If they don't want to go, let them know that it would mean a lot to you if they came, and that you enjoy their company. Just showing them this bit of respect changes their entire outlook. They no longer see it as an obligation, but as being needed, wanted, and important. If they really don't want to go, you'll save both of you a lot of grief by letting them stay at a friend's house or hiring a baby-sitter. Often the word "baby-sitter" cures their attitude, and suddenly they want to come along!

Talk Back Tips

Never hesitate to apologize to your children if you have done something unfair or wrong. Saying that you're sorry and why you are sorry can literally save your children a hefty bill from a psychologist when they grow up.

People hunger their entire lives for the words "I'm sorry" from a parent who wronged them. A common wish for many patients who consult with health care professionals is the following statement: "If only they (one or both parents) would have apologized for what they did. That would have made all the difference."

Verbal Defense with Pre-Schoolers

This section explains how to communicate with pre-babies, infants, toddlers, and young children. You learn what to say to them and how to say it, factors that are crucial during their period of speech and language development. You even learn how to effectively respond to their sometimes-aversive communication patterns.

Verbal Defense in Utero

I firmly believe that verbal stimulation of the fetus in the third trimester (months 7, 8, and 9) is crucial to pre-infants developing communication skills.

Verbal Vignette

Studies have shown that when certain music is played and headphones are placed on the mother's belly, the fetus reacts physically. There is more fetal activity (kicking, and so on) when loud rock music is played and less activity when Mozart is played. Studies of babies' facial expressions, verbalizations, and head and body movements have also shown that when the baby emerges from the womb, it can recognize the music it heard in utero.

The same holds true for voices. When a father speaks to an infant by placing his mouth near the mother's belly and talking, the infant is able to recognize the father's voice as distinguished from other voices. Considering all the new information continuing to come to light, I recommend that you play it safe and talk to the developing person in your womb. Speak in soft, well-modulated tones. The infant might experience greater calmness as it enters the world. Who knows? Perhaps by doing this, you are creating a calmer and less stressed person.

Verbal Defense with Infants and Toddlers

Don't talk to your infants as though they are idiots. Their receptive skills have the potential to grow exponentially, but this depends on how much you communicate with them and thus verbally stimulate them.

Not doing so can retard their speech and language development. That doesn't mean sounding like a rocket scientist or teaching them quantum physics. It does mean speaking to them in complete sentences that are appropriate to the situation.

For example, if your baby is eating, say "I'm putting your food on a spoon. Good baby. You ate all your food. Here is some milk." Even though babies can't answer you in complete sentences, you will be surprised at how much they will understand. And with you and your family's constant verbal stimulation, their vocabulary and their ability to communicate will increase. The more able they are to communicate, the more interaction they will have with the people and the world around them. The results? A happier and less frustrated little person.

Terrible Twos Are Verbally Terrific!

Two-year-olds say "no" all the time, and this usually makes parents crazy. Despite the phrase "terrible twos," however, this time is not terrible when it comes to verbal development—it's a great time. Instead of getting frustrated when they say "no," get happy. For the first time, children are asserting themselves and making decisions. Encourage them with affection and kind words. If you really want them to do something and they strongly resist, this could be the opportune time to teach them about rejection and not getting everything they want. In calm tones, explain why they can't do something.

Talk Back Tips

No matter how much your two-year-olds scream and fuss, don't Give 'Em Hell and Yell. Even though you think they may not understand your calm explanations, they often already do or will quickly learn.

Listen Up!

Watch how you talk to children who act out verbally. The words you say to them are more important than you can imagine. If you say "be quiet," "shut up," and "you are headed for big trouble," *you* are the one headed for big trouble. You are eroding your child's self-worth and helping create a sad, angry little person who often will grow up into a sad, angry big person.

Respect them! Correct them! But don't do it in harsh tones. As they become more verbal and understand more, repeat what they said correctly. Reinforce the good and correct the bad with love and kindness as you ask them to repeat correctly.

Talking to Children Who Act Out Verbally

Children usually act out when they are angry at something that just happened or continues to happen, harboring emotional pain. They also act out to test the limits of what you will and will not tolerate in their behavior.

Like when communicating with teens, with children you need to set limits immediately. They have to know right away that you are in control. Unlike teens, however, many children are too young to follow a reasoning process. What might work best, therefore, is a combination of Direct Confrontation and Love and Kindness. These techniques often produce guilt feelings in the child, as they begin to distinguish right from wrong and learn what they can and cannot say to you.

Children need to learn early on in life that there is a cause and effect for everything they do or say. They will learn that hurtful or nasty things they say can evoke negative reactions and consequences. Either they will hurt someone's feelings or be unable to do certain things or participate in certain activities, or they will have the chance to do certain things they enjoy and get certain things they want. Usually Calm Questioning, asking them a series of yes and no questions, is highly effective in getting children to understand that what they said was inappropriate and possibly hurtful.

Your Best Bet: Children of This Age Crave Respect

Young children want to know that their opinion and feedback mean something. Parents make the biggest mistake at this stage as they pay no attention to a child's opinion. Even parents who regard themselves as hip and with the times often perpetuate the idea passed from parent to child from time immemorial, that children should be seen but not heard. Many parents don't even realize they are communicating this idea. If you are, be conscious every time you do it and stop it! Children have to be both seen and heard if they are to have any sense of self-worth. Their opinion has to matter. Ask them what they think about various issues, from what clothes they prefer to what they think of certain movies or news events appropriate for the child of their age. Get their opinion. Get them involved. Respect their opinion. Teach them that what they say matters.

Verbal Vignette

According to researchers, the first five years of a child's life are the most important years psychologically. How you speak to them during that time, and how they respond, can determine the course of their life.

Cursing Kids

Children are great imitators. When they hear what you say and how you say it, they often parrot it back to you. If you use ugly words and tones, make sure you don't use them around children, or chances are you will hear them again—this time, "out of the mouths of babes."

Many children start to learn curse words around the ages of $3^1/_2$ to 4, so watch what you say in front of little ears.

Remember the experiment where the ducklings followed a man around, thinking he was their mother? The reason for this strange behavior was that he successfully imprinted this in their minds. The same process occurs with children when it comes to learning words and speech. They too—both good words and bad words—are imprinted in a child's mind. So when a child hears you tell someone to "go to hell" or to "f— off," don't be surprised if you hear these curses echoed back to you by a little mouth.

Kids also pick up these words from their older siblings and peers, or from TV shows or song lyrics. Best Bet: set limits and be consistent. Let them know right away that these are bad words that make them look bad when they say them. If you as the parent or caretaker are the cursing culprit, you need to apologize to them for your mistake. Tell them that you were wrong for saying those bad words and that it made you look bad, just as it makes them look bad.

The key is to R-E-S-P-E-C-T your child and your teen. That is the best bet for parental verbal self-defense.

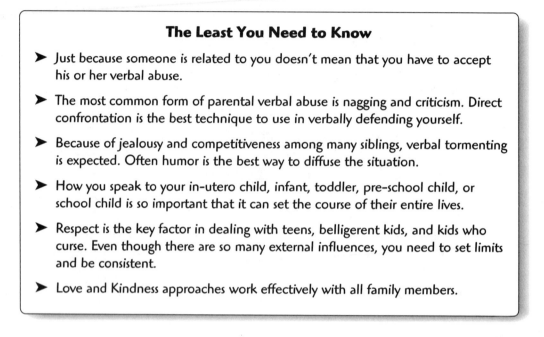

The Least You Need to Know

➤ Just because someone is related to you doesn't mean that you have to accept his or her verbal abuse.

➤ The most common form of parental verbal abuse is nagging and criticism. Direct confrontation is the best technique to use in verbally defending yourself.

➤ Because of jealousy and competitiveness among many siblings, verbal tormenting is expected. Often humor is the best way to diffuse the situation.

➤ How you speak to your in-utero child, infant, toddler, pre-school child, or school child is so important that it can set the course of their entire lives.

➤ Respect is the key factor in dealing with teens, belligerent kids, and kids who curse. Even though there are so many external influences, you need to set limits and be consistent.

➤ Love and Kindness approaches work effectively with all family members.

Chapter 16

Verbal Warfare with Specific People in Your Life

In This Chapter

➤ Talking back to rude strangers

➤ Handling friends and enemies

➤ Dealing with verbally venomous salespeople and service people

➤ Being more sensitive to those who don't speak your language

➤ Handling verbally toxic professionals and authority figures

---

Besides your family, there are other people in your life you wish weren't there. Unfortunately, they are there to stay, so you have to deal with them. You have no choice.

They come across your path and enter your life unexpectedly. They appear out of nowhere. Even if you never step out of the house, you can still run into them.

They are there when you pick up your phone or call someone to help you with something. They are there when you buy gas, go to a restaurant, go to the grocery store, or go shopping for clothes. They are there when you drive or when you see a physician or dentist. They are even there when you get a haircut or a manicure. They are everywhere! You can't escape them!

Verbal Self-Defense Techniques for Various Groups

If you don't plan to stay in bed for the rest of your life with the covers drawn over your head, you will need to learn how to deal with these verbally abusive toxins who infiltrate your life. This chapter gives you pointers concerning what verbal defense strategies are most effective with particular people in your life.

Invasive Strangers

One of the best ways to meet people is to spontaneously come up to a perfect stranger and start talking to her. Likewise, if strangers are attracted to you and want to meet you, they do the same thing. That is what makes the world go around. When you share pleasantries with a stranger, it is a wonderful feeling. It makes you smile and feel good all over. It makes you feel important, as though you matter.

On the other hand, perfect strangers can say things to you that can make you feel not so wonderful—things that make you unhappy, angry, or hurt. Their words make you doubt yourself and feel insecure.

As I mentioned in the scenario in the beginning of this book, who wants to wake up, walk the dog, and hear a dead dog story or a tragic tale about someone's animal? Who wants to hear how strange they look, how overweight they are, how weird their hair looks or anything else negative about them? People can be rude—unknowingly or knowingly.

When you encounter verbally toxic strangers, effective techniques include directly confronting them or calmly questioning them or mirroring back their own obnoxiousness. These techniques are best done in the form of snappy comebacks. Some of the best snappy comebacks include saying things like, "Do I know you?" or "Have you ever tried manners?" Be sure you use these types of comebacks only with someone who has been equally obnoxious to you, strangers who are either unconsciously or purposely invasive. Using comebacks as part of your verbal repertoire usually helps you feel a lot better. It prevents you from that "If I had only said..." Syndrome, where you lie awake at 3 A.M. thinking about what you "woulda" or "shoulda" said to that obnoxious interloper.

Listen Up!

There is nothing worse than finding out that someone you have trusted with valuable information about you and others has spilled the beans and ruined you or someone else. There is nothing more despicable than being betrayed by someone you once loved and trusted.

"Friends"

"With friends like you, who needs enemies?" Saying this to them lets them know that you are onto their ways. It represents the Direct Confrontation Technique and opens the door for further dialogue. By making this rather bold statement, you can see how your "friends" handle it. If they get defensive and begin to blame you, well, you obviously know where you stand. On the other hand, if they try to explain or plead with you, they are showing that there might have been some type of miscommunication, or they are trying to express remorse.

How do you ever forgive being betrayed? How can you ever trust someone again?

While it is true that everyone makes mistakes, in most cases you can't ever trust a verbal betrayer again! Thus, you have to use the Unplug Technique. To do otherwise is to take a big risk. How can you be sure that they won't do it again? By doing and saying what they did, you perhaps have seen a glimpse of their character—a glimpse that will protect you from seeing a more horrible sight!

Enemies

An old expression recommends that you keep your friends close, but keep your enemies even closer. The reason is that you can always keep tabs on what your enemies are doing and what they might plan to do to you. This doesn't mean that you have to like them, but it does mean that you have to know their whereabouts and what they might be up to. After all, this is what happens in full-scale wars.

Intelligence officers infiltrate the enemy camp or even a neutral party to find out what's going on and tell the other side. It works the same in verbal warfare. It is best to have a neutral party who lets your side know what the other side is up to if you ask. So, ask!

It's obvious when two people don't like one another. This happens for a multitude of reasons, from betrayal to fear of destruction to jealousy and so forth. It's normal and to be expected on this planet as a form of human nature. Even though we strive to "love everyone," to "love our neighbor," it doesn't always work out that way. Some of our neighbors are just plain unlovable.

To keep your enemies from totally destroying you, use the Stop the Thought Technique: Silently shout "Stop the thought!" in your head whenever you think of the person. The Tension Blowouts help you get the people out of your system when you are or have been in their presence.

I do not recommend directly confronting them, questioning them, or using the Give 'Em Hell and Yell Technique. This can inflame tempers, create stronger verbal ammunition to be used, and maim or even annihilate the opponent. It's not worth the emotional hassle. Avoid it.

I do recommend the Love and Kindness Technique with your verbal enemies, no matter how difficult it seems. Before you tune me out or even want to throw this book at me, just read a little further. This technique helps you to keep your enemy close by, so that you can keep tabs on him. It also takes away the constant stress and useless energy that hating someone creates. And finally, you might be shocked to learn that repeated positive energy and kind and loving words can often turn your worst enemy into your best friend.

There is mighty power in verbal love. Try it! You might be surprised at the results!

Customer Service Representatives

Imagine the following scenario. You innocently call up someone from a credit card company to talk about a problem with a bill on which you were charged twice for the same item. You explain your problem in a calm and collected manner, only to hear a robot on the other end of the line. I'm not talking about the mechanical, taped message telling you which buttons to push in order to be connected to the appropriate department. No, I'm talking about a very unhelpful, monotonous, condescending sadist on the other end of the line. Your voice reflects your annoyance at her, to which she robotically replies, "I'm sorry you feel that way."

Most people can relate to this scenario. Your best alternative is to give the person on the receiving end a little of the Give 'Em Hell and Yell Technique. Unfortunately, it's too easy for them just to hang upon you. Now you have other options that will be effective. The best is the Calm Questioning Technique, peppered by a friendly Love and Kindness approach, as you slowly do the Tension Blowout Technique. While using this technique to get further up the customer service food chain, calmly and pleasantly ask to speak to a customer service representative.

People Entrusted with Yourself or Your Property

You go to the dry cleaner and pay lots of money for your clothes to look and smell good. Upon careful inspection of your garments the next day, you find that they neither look good (ironed improperly, with creases on the sleeves of your jackets) or smell good (the smell of your "ironed" perspiration almost knocked you over). You politely ask him to re-clean some of the garments. Angrily, he accuses *you* of ironing and creasing the sleeves of the jackets yourself! Quite an impossible task, since you haven't held an iron in your hand since you were forced to in your junior high school home economics class. To top it off, he accuses you of dirtying and smelling up your own pants and jackets.

You feel like punching the man in the face. Instead, you punch the computerized cash register, hoping you broke it! Then you run as fast as you can before he calls the police on you or before your temper gets so out of control that you do the dry cleaner some bodily harm.

Whether you have to entrust your clothes, swimming pool, home repair, or hair to another person, serious repercussions can result from them not performing their jobs up to par! A floor being ruined, clothes destroyed beyond repair, and hair damaged to the point that you are embarrassed to be seen in public are not only costly because you have to have these things redone at further expense to you, but emotionally devastating!

Some mishaps with service people are the result of you not properly explaining to them what to do. Most often, mishaps result from them being overwhelmed by excessive business or just plain incompetence. In these cases, you have no other choice than to Give 'Em Hell and Yell. This not only helps you to get it out of your

Listen Up!

When these unfortunate things happen to you, they make you paranoid, afraid to trust anyone ever again with your things, your home, or anything attached to your body. If it happens to you repeatedly, it becomes difficult for you to function without being downright rude to others.

system, but it gives you the satisfaction of embarrassing them in cases where there are other customers in their establishment—they might think twice about doing further business with them.

Then you must obviously Unplug and never do business with them again. If they make you furious, whenever you think of them do the Vicarious Fantasy Technique. Seeing their head under the steam press can give you a little sadistic chuckle and release a lot of your own steam.

If the mishap is your fault because you didn't explain it right, admit it. Be a mensch. You know what that means! You learned it in Chapter 9 in the section on "Bingo! You Got the Lingo!" In case you forgot, it means a decent person.

To help prevent this misunderstanding from happening again, speak slowly, have them repeat the instructions, and, if appropriate, write them down!

Salespeople, Store Clerks, and Realtors

Whether they are selling a car, house, suit, or apple, nobody has the right to be rude and obnoxious to you, just as you have no right to be rude and obnoxious to them.

We have all encountered unexpected hell from someone who ended up putting us in a horrible mood, even though we started out being excited. If we were kids, we would literally be jumping up and down to show how thrilled we were and that we couldn't contain ourselves because we were getting a bigger and better house, the car we always wanted, or a new designer outfit.

Then all of a sudden, our smiles turned into frowns as the happiness and eager anticipation was sucked out of our veins by this evil sales vampire. He was cold, abrupt, curt, nasty, rude, condescending, acted as though he was doing us a favor just by waiting on us, gave us attitude, and took his sweet time, making us wait until things were convenient for him.

Why Did They Do It?

Many sales vampires don't mean to suck out your happiness and enthusiasm. They just can't help themselves. As a result, they make your life miserable, and theirs as well. Ironically, they aren't accomplishing what they are there to do in the first place—make a sale and earn some money so that they, too, can have the opportunity to have the things you are buying from them.

Bon Mots

Even though they are paid to serve potential buyers, *sales vampires* are people who suck the joy out of new purchases with their arrogance and rudeness.

Talk Back Tips

Remember that quite often when salespeople are rude to you, it has nothing to do with *you*. They may simply be very unhappy people looking to direct their hostility at anyone who crosses their path.

There are many reasons why a salesperson might be rude to you, although there is still no excuse for their behavior. Perhaps seeing it from their point of view might give you a little more empathy and compassion towards them. Maybe their previous customer was rude to them, maybe they don't like their boss, or maybe they are exhausted after a long day.

Whatever the reason for a salesperson's rudeness, try killing them with kindness. You might just be the one to turn their entire day, and their mood or attitude around.

What Else You Can Do!

Sometimes no compassion and understanding in the world will change the attitude of a salesperson, or douse the fire burning inside of you as you experience the wrath of the salesperson from the world below. You don't care what the reason is. It's not your problem. You came there for a reason—to purchase something—and you weren't helped.

All you know is that you are mad as hell and you are not gonna take it anymore. Who can blame you? You need to express your disdain. But do it in a way that is both fire- and anger-releasing and productive, so that you can get the results you want.

The best of all worlds is to Unplug and get a new salesperson. Let them know you don't want to deal with them, using whatever strategy strikes your fancy at the time. If you choose, Give 'Em Hell and Yell. If you want to be more civil, directly confront. In any case, the message is clear—you won't take it and you are "outta there." "Outta there" means either going to a new place to do business or going to a new sales representative to do business.

People Who Serve You

It's time to eat, so you go into an impressive restaurant with two important clients who finally arrived in town. You need desperately to impress them because a lot is riding on this deal. If they like and trust you, you are in! You are ready to order when you notice the waiter from hell standing directly in front of you. This verbally hostile creature with a huge frown, lifeless eyes, and a lifeless voice asks for your order in the tone of voice that says "You disgust me and I'm doing you a favor to even talk to you." You and your colleagues take a little extra time, as you can't decide between the chicken or the lamb dishes. The waiter looks at all three of you like you are suffering from a rare infectious disease. When you all finally make up your minds, the waiter snatches the menus away from you. The others give you a quizzical look and you give a sheepish smile. You don't want to make any waves. You want to ignore this unpleasant moment—too much good is about to happen.

Finally, your food comes. The vegetables are undercooked and the lamb is raw. When you notice that one of your guests is having difficulty cutting into the rubbery chicken, you politely summon the waiter and tell him what the problem is. Treating you as though you have committed a felony, he blames you for choosing that particular dish: "That's the way it comes, and I can't do anything about it." By now you are ready to take the plate and shove it in his face, but you don't dare because of your important clients. They insist that everything is fine, that their meal is fine.

Even though you feel nauseous, you smile weakly and pretend nothing happened. Your clients like you, and so you ultimately get the account—but not without the expense of a severe migraine, neck and shoulder pain, and diarrhea.

There is nothing more upsetting than a rude serviceperson who causes you stress and frustration when all you want to do is have a good time, close a business deal, make a good impression, or woo someone in whom you are interested. You get so mad you are ready to spit nails. But often, as in the preceding scenario, you can't do anything about it because you are with a person who is very significant or important to you. You can't yell or even say anything, for fear your companion will think you are pushy or overly aggressive. Thus, you keep it in and simmer.

Listen Up!

If you work in a service industry, remember that your rudeness can cause others a great deal of frustration and misery. If in your unhappiness you are unable to be attentive to people's needs, it's time for you to change your attitude—or change your profession.

There's No Excuse!

The restaurant scenario is maddening. How dare someone treat you with less than respect when you have come into their establishment to relax, be entertained or to entertain someone, eat well, or just to be among people?

There really is no good reason why a person in a business that is supposed to help you ends up hindering you! The main reasons they act this way have to do with jealousy, insecurity, or feelings of superiority. In reality, of course, they reflect their inner inferiority through their toxic verbiage. Perhaps they "cop an attitude" because they hate what they are doing. They might feel that the job is beneath them or that they are just biding time until the work day is over. They want their paycheck and they want to go home immediately! Many are envious of their customers and patrons because they want to be in their shoes, with someone waiting on or serving them.

Here is a list of seven types of verbally toxic service people you have most likely encountered:

1. The Fighting Rudee: These are people with a hostile attitude who usually instigate a confrontation with the patron. They have a chip on their shoulder and have no idea what the saying "the customer is always right" means. They only know what "always looking for a fight" means.

2. The Prejudiced One: These ignorant and backward people have a preconceived notion about a certain sex or ethnic group and treat all members of that group with hostility and disdain. They are abrupt, unhelpful, and uncooperative.

3. Abruptees: They are curt and will either interrupt you or not let you speak in the first place. They are impatient and can't seem to get you to leave fast enough.

4. Sourpusses: They are so upset about where they are—their plight in life or their present situation—that they can't help but wear their expression on their face. They have a squinched and bitten facial appearance with a perpetual look of disgust, anger, and frustration. Their faces tell you that they don't like what they are doing, they don't like you, and they don't want to be there. Because their energy is so toxic and they are so hard to be around, you don't want them there either.

5. Power for the Hour: these are people who act as though they are better than you by taking the power they have (such as letting you into a club or seating you at a restaurant) and throwing it around. These people are obviously insecure and have to push others around to feel important. Such people are more to be pitied and laughed at than to be angry at.

6. Robots: These unhelpful, monotonous, droning repeaters of the company's doctrine live in great fear. They are afraid to think for themselves and to say what is really on their minds. There is no getting through to them, because they are set in their ways. They are condescending, will never see your point of view, and will always minimize what you say, unless it happens to fit into their programmed script.

7. Extreme Incompetents: These types always screw up! They'll end up costing you money because of their frequent mistakes. They are the type that forgets a charge off your bill or always does the opposite of whatever you tell them.

When You Can't Afford to Make a Scene

You don't ever need to let your blood boil again! Suppose you happen to be in a situation similar to the one presented earlier, where it is difficult for you to speak your mind because of the company you were trying to impress. In such a situation, breathe, breathe, breathe! In this case, as in most cases, the Tension Blowout Technique is a lifesaver—no question about it!

The "Stop the Thought!" Technique is also effective. Use it so that you never have to go back there, even in your mind! You'll get the verbal toxins out of your system for good.

When You Can Afford to Make a Scene

The Direct Confront Technique is usually the most effective way to deal with verbally toxic servers. You need to immediately bust them on what they are doing and what they are saying to you.

Talk Back Tips

If you can't afford to speak out or directly confront someone without the possibility of causing a scene, then use the Tension Blowout Technique: let the tension go as you exhale, and then leave the situation.

Another excellent choice is the Mirroring Technique, in which you have to talk to them exactly as they are talking to you. Use the same tone and similar words. This usually shocks them into place. They see that you are on to them and so they usually will turn their behavior right around. You can also use the Calm Questioning Technique, where you calmly ask them why they are treating you so rudely. You might also ask them if they are having a bad day. They might admit they are, and immediately apologize and change their actions, tone of voice, and what they say to you.

If these three techniques don't work, don't ignore them—Unplug them! You don't have to sit at a table where you are being treated poorly. You don't have to patronize an establishment where you are not being accommodated. You can leave a restaurant immediately! You do not have to take it! You do not have to be punished. You pay—they play! There is often someone above the unhelpful person and someone above that person and someone above *that* person who can help you solve your problem and address your concerns. Seek them out. You'll not only save your own esteem, but you'll prevent others from experiencing the nastiness you just went through.

Even after you have unplugged and sought and perhaps even received justice, you might still be steaming over how they spoke to you and what they said. To release built-up tension, I suggest you use the Vicarious Fantasy Technique; fantasize what you would love to do to them or what you would love to see happen to them. Once again, I repeat for the umpteenth time, *fantasize*—you don't actually want to do bodily harm to another person.

Listen Up!

Don't reward people for disrespecting you: never ever tip any service person who treats you rudely. By the same token, don't disrespect others. If someone is especially good to you, tip them extra. And always treat maids, housekeepers, and other service people with the respect and dignity they deserve. They are not your slaves!

People Who Don't Speak Your Language

These days it is pretty common to meet someone who does not speak English at all, or at least very well. It is important when trying to communicate with someone in this situation, that whatever you do, *don't yell at them! They aren't deaf!* Don't get upset with them! Instead, be patient. Think of what it would be like if you were in their shoes. Show a little compassion. Speak softly and take some time. Gesture or make signs to get points across; point, draw, write. You will eventually be able to communicate.

If you are speaking with someone who has an accent that you don't understand, ask them to speak slowly and don't be afraid to ask them to repeat. Only do it in pleasant manner, not angrily or impatiently. Also try to listen to others speaking English in a similar accent in order to familiarize yourself with sounds and tonal qualities indigenous to the accent.

For example, some people from Japan confuse their *l* and *r* ("led" for "red") sounds, and some Swedes do not say *z* sound ("pleass" for "pleaz"). Some Latinos say *ee* for *ih* sounds ("sheep" for "ship"), and some Russians say *d* sounds for *th* sounds ("dis" for "this"). Chinese people who speak Cantonese sometimes sound as though they are angry at you and yelling at you when speaking English to you. They are not: this is just the way they adapt the tonal qualities in their language to our language.

You can see how easy it is to get the wrong message conveyed. The sounds and tones people use in their native language might represent something entirely different in our language.

Professionals and Authority Figures

Unfortunately, some abusers might literally "hold your life in their hands"—an employer, doctor, attorney, police officer, or teacher.

Just because they have a long list of degrees or hold the reins to your financial status does not give them the right to speak to you in a condescending or hostile way. Like the service person, these professionals exist to guide and assist you, to take care of you, not to verbally assault you.

But sadly, they do assault you too many times.

You can use numerous verbal self-defense techniques with such abusers. But note, the more harsh and severe the techniques you choose, the more likely it is you will alienate these people in power. The good news is that you will feel a lot better. You will have defended yourself and stuck up for your rights, protecting your dignity. The bad news is that you might have gotten into more trouble than you bargained for—getting arrested, being kicked out of places, or being fired.

Listen Up!

All too often, authority figures speak badly to you just because they feel that they can get away with it. Perhaps doing so makes them feel more powerful. In reality, of course, anyone who has to talk rudely, condescendingly, or with hostility to you is not powerful at all. She is insecure and pathetic!

Talk Back Tips

Whatever response you choose, do *something*, so that your health doesn't deteriorate as a result of carrying all your emotional pain caused by this verbally toxic employer. Breathe. Fantasize! It will not only help keep you sane, it will keep you from getting into trouble.

Verbally Toxic Employers

Sometimes you have the good fortune to have an employer or teacher who is a gem. They are supportive, caring, understanding, open, and respectful. They value your opinion and what you have to say. They reward you for your efforts in praise or in a raise. They are appreciative of your efforts and consistently let you know how much they value your work.

But more often than not, there are the Toxic Employers who are here to make your life miserable. Your employer might be a bully, a wimp, a mental case, a liar, a silent-but-deadly erupting volcano—any of the 30 types of "toxic terrors" mentioned in my book *Toxic People—10 Ways to Handle People Who Make Your Life Miserable*. The verbal strategy you use to defend yourself depends largely upon what type of verbal terrorist they are and how much you want or need your present job. Milder strategies work better if you need your job. If you don't really care, go for it—Give 'Em Hell and Yell, Confront, and loudly Unplug.

Verbal Medical and Dental Disasters

You decide that it's about time to go to the dentist. You have finally gotten up enough nerve to tolerate the shots you know your gums will be receiving. You make that call, and a rude-sounding person abruptly tells you the fee, saying that they don't take dental insurance and that you have to arrive exactly on time or the doctor won't see you. To top it off, she massacres your name as she asks you to spell it three times and still pronounces it wrong. If you didn't need to have that root canal, you'd have hung up on her long ago.

You show up at the scheduled appointment, and the hostile and rude assistant gives you an attitude. You tell her to cool it—reminding her that you're a well-paying customer about to pay a significant amount of money. She goes into the dentist's office, probably to fill him in on how difficult you are being. You're already scared and nervous, and now you are in front of the dentist. He speaks abruptly and has a cold tone. You know that this is not his normal tone as you heard him talking on the phone a few moments earlier, where he was warm and animated. You're scared of him. He sounds mean! He doesn't like you, but it's too late—his fingers are already in your mouth.

Many times you have to hold back your tongue, because these people can make your life completely miserable if you don't. For example, giving a police officer hell and yelling might land you in jail. Mirroring a bullying boss or teacher (giving them a taste of their own verbal medicine) can get you fired or kicked out of class. Even if your questioning is cool and calm, many verbally toxic physicians and attorneys might misconstrue your questions as a form of interrogation. This automatically places them on the defensive, and more often than not, they verbally attack back! Professionalism and Hippocratic Oaths aside, they are still human, and if they don't like you, there is a chance this will be reflected in their work.

If you don't really care whether you lose your job, have to get a new physician or attorney, get kicked out of class, or get thrown in jail, you can use a more aggressive approach like Give 'Em Hell and Yell, Mirroring, Questioning, or Unplugging—getting these people out of your life!

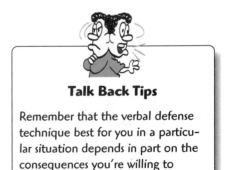

Talk Back Tips

Remember that the verbal defense technique best for you in a particular situation depends in part on the consequences you're willing to accept.

On the other hand, if you choose to keep your job or your status in a company, not land yourself in jail, and not upset the status quo, you might want to employ some techniques you learned about in Chapters 10 and 11: Tension Blowouts, Love and Kindness, Direct Confrontation, and Vicarious Fantasy. These less aggressive approaches can even be the catalyst to turn around the attitudes of these "professionals" and authority figures. Sometimes these people say mean things to you unwillingly, because they are under an inordinate amount of pressure, which stimulates their short verbal fuse. Sometimes a kind word and compassion is all it takes to turn their toxic words around.

The Least You Need to Know

➤ Vicarious Fantasy and Unplugging are best to use with uncooperative people with whom you have entrusted yourself and your personal items.

➤ Try to be empathetic with service people and be kind but direct. Let them know you won't stand for their verbal abuse before you Unplug (your last resort).

➤ Learn the pointers of how to talk to people who speak your language poorly or not at all.

➤ Think twice before letting an authority figure have it. A more benign approach to handling their verbal abuse might save you a lot of grief. But if you don't care, let them have it verbally!

Part 5

Verbal Combat Against Verbal Abusers

Throughout the next three chapters, I refer to verbal abusers, and sometimes painful verbal abusers, because of the emotional and sometimes physical pain these people can cause. Verbal abusers don't always do that much harm. They are simply annoying. Others are rather revolting and disgusting, and still others are downright dangerous and can do tremendous damage.

Chapters 17–19 discuss each of these categories of verbal abusers and how to handle them. You will learn how to defend yourself against them and to either control their invasion or exterminate them from your life. You will begin by learning about the most benign vermin, the annoying ones, then graduate to learning about those vermin who disgust and revolt you, making your life so uncomfortable that they make you paranoid and suspicious of everyone around you. Finally, you will learn about the worst kind of verbal abuser, those who can destroy you by gnawing at your insides. You will learn how to extinguish them from your lives by using effective verbal weapons to annihilate them forever.

Chapter 17

Verbal Combat Against Annoying Verbal Abusers

> **In This Chapter**
>
> ➤ Coping with speakers who annoy you because you don't understand them
>
> ➤ Talking to people who turn you off by what they say
>
> ➤ Coping with people whose voice drives you nuts
>
> ➤ Learning foolproof strategies to deal with those you find verbally obnoxious

These types of verbal abusers won't hurt you; they are just uncomfortable to be around. If they are around for a short period of time, you can live with it, but if they are around for prolonged periods of time—watch out! They will eventually get on your nerves, just like an infestation of ants. Just remember that if you are not careful with which defensive technique you use you might cause them major emotional damage. These Verbal Annoyers come in 13 different types. In this section, you will learn characteristics of each of them and the best techniques to handle them.

Mumble Jumble

According to a Gallup poll, people who mumble are so off-putting that 80 percent of those questioned found mumbling to be one of the most annoying speech habits. The reason is obvious. You can't understand a word they say! You have no idea what they are talking about, so you ask them to repeat. They do. You understand them and then they mumble again. You end up asking them to repeat what they said after everything they said, which is frustrating for both of you. They are mad at you for not understanding, and you are mad at them for not speaking up!

To avoid the two of you wanting never to speak to one another again, you need to be open and directly confront the mumbler, but you must do it with a Love and Kindness Strategy. You might also want to help them by giving them some pointers on how to stop mumbling, but be very careful. Do it in a diplomatic way so that they won't be offended. Since most mumblers tend to suffer from fragile self-esteem—they often feel they aren't worthy of being heard—be gentle with them!

Here's what you might want to say to a mumbler: "I am so sorry, I don't mean to be disrespectful, but I am having trouble understanding everything that you are saying. Since it's important for me to hear everything [or "since I'd like to hear everything"], don't be offended if I ask you to repeat something."

If you feel comfortable doing this, you might want to say the following: "You know, I was reading this book on verbal self-defense the other day, and it said that people need to spend about one second on each vowel when they speak. I tried it, and it really helped me. It really worked. Once again, I don't mean to be offensive, but perhaps if you can try this technique and draw out each vowel for a second, I can understand you a lot better." Then smile. A smile diffuses the intensity of the situation and presents it in more casual light. If they still mumble and you really need to listen to what they said, do the best you can. Block out all other stimuli and concentrate like mad. If the person is not very instrumental in your life, unplug—leave! It's not worth being tortured.

Sonic Boomers!

Ouch! These people are not only embarrassing to be around, they can actually hurt your eardrums or shock your nervous system every time they speak. According to a Gallup poll examining the most annoying speaking habits, close to 75 percent of the respondents found a loud voice to be annoying.

People tend to speak too loudly for several reasons. First of all, they might have a type of hearing loss due to an obstruction in their ears.

Talk Back Tips

Loud speakers sometimes come from a large family, where they had to speak loudly in order to be heard and to get attention. Unfortunately, their loud voice often carries over outside their family circle and into all their interactions with others.

A second and more common reason people speak so loudly is that they need attention. They suffer from such insecurity that they think only of themselves and their need to be noticed. This usually makes them unconscious of the world around them. They don't care if they are in a doctor's office, on an airplane, or in a library. No place matters, and nothing they say matters. They could be telling you the most intimate detail of their life or of someone else's life. It makes no difference: everyone within 100 miles of them will hear their sonic-booming voice.

Once again, you have to be a diplomat. Smile and use the Calm Questioning Technique, saying "I don't mean to be rude, but do you think you can perhaps lower your voice? My ears are really sensitive to certain tones." You aren't lying. Your ears certainly are sensitive to certain tones—their tones!

The key is to couch your words with politeness and sensitivity, since you need to have empathy for the possible understandable contributing factors to their loudness. If they can't reduce their decibel level, you can reduce yours, by either walking away from them (if you don't have to be around them) or by wearing earplugs (if you do have to be around them).

You might also want to use the specific Direct Confrontation Technique that I talk about later in this chapter. This approach encourages you to direct them to see a physician or a speech pathologist who can possibly help them lower their booming voice. A person who speaks in such a loud voice often has related problems, such as hoarseness of the voice, vocal nodes (growths on the top portion of the vocal cords), vocal ulcers, or ear problems. On the other hand, they might just have bad speaking habits. Whatever the problem is, you might be doing them a huge favor.

Meek, Weak, and Squeak

Like the Mumble Jumblers, these people frustrate you because you have so much trouble hearing them. Like the Sonic Boomer, the sound of their high-pitched voice can also hurt your ears. Over 60 percent of the people surveyed feel the same way you do. They don't respond well to people who sound like this and don't know why.

The reason is that they are registering that these people are psychologically passive-aggressive. They are sickeningly sweet-sounding. But beware! They can blow their top on you any minute!

If you experience the wrath of a meek squeaker, run for your life! Unplug from them as rapidly as you can! They are dangerous and can cause you lots of trouble. If for reasons you can't control, you can't unplug, do the Tension Breathing Technique and know before whom you stand. Keep checking in with them and confronting them so that there are no surprises. Keep asking them questions, so that you know where they are or have an idea about what is on their mind most of the time. Obviously they won't be open and forthright, but they might slip up from time to time, so keep asking.

Listen Up!

Although squeakers sound so sweet, their volcano is bubbling deep inside, just waiting to erupt with the most venomous of verbiage.

Baby-Voiced and Cutsie-Wootsie

The worst part about these people is that they actually think they sound great, that they are getting points for sounding like a bimbo. They might be cute during intimate moments in the bedroom with their lover, or while talking to babies or small animals.

But when people talk like this in public, others cringe. You cringe. You might cringe so badly that you feel the hair standing up on the back of your neck whenever you hear them speak. That voice might even stop you in your tracks.

If you are the one cringing, it is rather awkward to tell them to cool it and to grow up, unless you are very close to them or related to them and, thus, used to speaking boldly and bluntly to them.

Short of telling them to grow up or to shut up, you might just want to Breathe Them Out and Unplug. If you don't have to be around them, don't be. Try to get away from them every chance possible, before you say something you might regret or something that will probably make them cry. Since those who possess this voice quality are often exaggerations or cartoonish caricatures of stereotypic female roles, this expression of emotional behavior might occur.

Your best bet is to breathe them out! If you keep hearing their miserable tones resonating in your heads at a later date or time throughout the day, employ the "Stop the Thought!" Technique immediately! Both tactics will reduce your blood pressure and calm you down.

Listen Up!

If you are a lisper, keep in mind that what's cute at six years old is not cute at 26 or 36. If you want people to take you seriously in life you need to speak like an adult, not a child.

On the other hand, if you have nothing to lose and you don't care whether you will alienate them, perhaps for good, go ahead and use the Mirroring Technique, where you actually imitate or mirror back the way they are coming across. In essence, you are mocking them. Sometimes, they might be good-natured about it and laugh as they know that they sound that way. They like that they sound that way and they want to keep sounding that way. On the other hand, they might still be laughing with you, but crying inside. They might have always been made fun of and your cut is deep. You might have really hurt them and caused them more emotional damage.

Other times, they might become serious and say that they hate the sound of their voice. Since you do too, and assume that others do as well, do them a favor and suggest that they see someone to help them improve their voice.

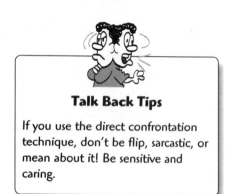

Talk Back Tips

If you use the direct confrontation technique, don't be flip, sarcastic, or mean about it! Be sensitive and caring.

Besides the Mirror Technique, you might just want to directly shoot from the hip and use the Direct Confrontation Technique. The following "Talk Back!" section gives you an example of how to tell them they need help with their voice.

Talk Back

Gary: I don't mean to offend you in any way, but I think that it might be in your best interest to improve the sound of your voice.

Sherry: I hate my voice. Some people tell me it's cute, but I can't stand it.

Gary: I know that you can get help with it from a licensed speech pathologist who specializes in helping you with your voice.

Sherry: Really? Where do I find one?

Gary: Look in the Yellow Pages or ask an ear, nose, and throat doctor, but it's important to see only a speech pathologist who specializes in treating the voice. I'll even see if I can get you some names.

Where to Direct a Person with an Annoying Voice

What I am about to say is extremely important, so read carefully! Specifically, do *not* recommend that they see a singing teacher, but rather that they see a licensed and qualified speech pathologist. And it is not enough for them to see just any speech pathologist. They must see *only* a speech pathologist who specializes in and has extensive and ongoing experience with patients who have voice problems. Otherwise, you are opening yourself up to possible further problems, or no improvement at all, by treatment from someone who might not be very well educated or trained. If your therapist is competent, you should see results in three months. If you don't, quit immediately!

In order to find such a speech pathologist, consult with a qualified otolaryngologist. You might want them to examine your vocal cords to see whether any medical problems exist. If so, your private health insurance or HMO can often cover the speech therapy treatment program, depending on your policy. If the doctor finds nothing wrong with you, see the speech pathologist anyway. Tell the pathologist that your health insurance won't cover treatment because the doctor found no medical condition, and that you would appreciate their working with you financially and, perhaps, providing you with a lower rate. Any decent therapist (or human being, for that matter) will usually accommodate you, since treatment is often costly.

Another way to find a speech pathologist who specializes in voice disorders is to look in the phone book! It's a great place. And whether you look in the phone book, get a name from a physician, or a friend refers you, ask questions!

Talk Back Tips

Although the American Speech Language and Hearing Association keeps a record of who is and is not licensed, it does not always have other information you need, such as how to find a speech pathologist in your area, or how to find a pathologist with a lot of experience in treating voice disorders.

Ask these questions before seeing any speech pathologist:

1. What kind of patients do you mostly see in your practice?
2. What is the largest percentage of people you see with that condition?
3. How many speech and voice patients have you seen over the past year?
4. How do people usually find out about you?
5. What is the average length of time you treat a patient?
6. What kinds of techniques do you normally use?
7. Where were you trained? What degree do you have? Are you licensed?
8. Do you take insurance if a doctor refers me due to a medical problem?

The Monotonous Drone

You, along with 75 percent of the population, can't stomach listening to someone who puts you to sleep when you are not sleepy. This monotonous voice is the number one killer of interpersonal relationships between men and women. So much of the meaning of what the person wants to communicate is lost in the communication when there is a lack of vocal excitement. They are so confusing because you really never know where you stand with them. You don't know whether they like you, whether you have done something wrong, or whether they are pleased or angry about something.

People who sound boring and monotonous usually don't mean to be. Often, they live in fear. They are emotionally repressed. They might have come from a family where it was considered bad to express themselves with unbridled emotion, and so they were conditioned to act in a more controlled manner. Unfortunately, the results of their upbringing turned out to be deleterious to their communicative abilities with others. It ruined many intimate relationships by helping to create misunderstandings. It both confused and frustrated the person with whom they were having the relationship, which often resulted in a sad ending.

Listen Up!

The Monotonous Drone's "poker voice" can be most confusing, causing you to read them wrongly and thereby make a big mistake in interpreting what they are trying to say. Be sure to ask questions.

You need to keep checking in with the Monotonous Drone. Keep asking them questions to see where they are coming from—how they are thinking and what they are feeling. Don't be afraid to ask them about their feelings. Use the direct confrontation to share your feelings with them. If you're doing business with them, also check in with how they are feeling about a particular issue.

Unless you are super close to them—you've been intimate, are best friends, or are close family—you might want to suggest that they get into either a speech or regular counseling program to help them express themselves. Let them know you are not criticizing them.

Gingerly, speak to them in a loving and delicate manner. After all, they are sensitive, and they do tend to keep a lot inside. Make it safe and comfortable for them. Let them know that you are in no way judging them, nor do you think less of them.

The Fast Talker

These people are also very frustrating to be around; they placed in the top ten of the Gallup poll's most annoying people. Like the Sonic Boomers, they often don't even realize they talk so fast. Like the Mumblers, they become quite frustrated because they are constantly asked to repeat things over and over again.

The Fast Talkers are often angry and frightened people. They, like the mumbler, suffer from a lowered sense of self-worth. They apparently don't feel worthy enough to have the other person take the time to listen to them, so they hurry up and get it over with. They might also be highly neurotic people or suffer from bipolar disorder that makes them always in a hurry and on the go. Because they usually don't even realize what they are doing, don't ever abruptly tell a Fast Talker to "slow down" in an agitated manner. Because of their often lowered sense of self, they are likely to get defensive and shut down. They might even begin to resent you. Unless you use the Love and Kindness approach with them, you can forget about ever understanding them again. They will continue to speed through sentences, leaving you in their wake, and not caring whether you understand them or not. The Fast Talker is more hostile than the Mumbler, who is more concerned about whether you understand him.

You can try to keep up with the fast talker by listening intently. But this is sometimes nearly impossible to do. Therefore, consider using the polite Love and Kindness approach used with the Mumbler, but use more of it, since they are more hostile. Put the blame on yourself. Don't blame them. Let them know that you are having a hard time concentrating today and that they can really help you out if could talk a little slower. If they are a more receptive type of Fast Talker, you might want to use the identical approach that you used on the Mumbler. Let them know that you have no intention of offending and that you read a book (this one) that suggested that for people to better understand others, it is best that the speaker draw out each vowel for approximately one second. This usually works, especially if it is said diplomatically and respectfully.

Name-Dropper

How annoying it is to sit through a conversation and hear about this person and that person and what they said to do and what they did to you. The people don't necessarily have to be top celebrities. They can also be prominent people within your community. Name-dropping also includes always bringing up family members (such as, "My wife said this," "My son did this," "My husband said that."). Who the heck cares what they said and think? We care about what *you* said and think. Are you brainless? Do you always need other people's opinions or words to function?

Certainly, once in a while it is good to hear a comment from someone else as it pertains to a particular topic being discussed, but a steady diet of it is beyond annoying—it is obnoxious. People find this so odious that they will turn against you at the drop of a hat.

Verbal Vignette

Many celebrities and talk show hosts get ridiculed for name-dropping too much. Whether it is a husband, wife, child, or celebrity friends, no one wants to hear too much information about people they don't know or don't care about.

Many people name drop because they have nothing going for them on their own, so they have to ride on someone else's coattails in order to feel important! Even if they seem to be important by other people's standards, they might not feel so important deep down inside. Therefore, they have to resort to such annoying behavior.

Because they are insecure, you might just want to Breathe Them Out and let them get their jollies dropping all the names they want all over the place. Even though you and everyone else thinks they are obnoxious, let them feel that they are important.

Try to look at the situation as amusing and entertaining rather than getting mad and annoyed. They might think they are being snobby or trying to come across better than you by letting you know all the important people they know, but in reality, they are screaming out how very insecure and empty they are. So have pity. Be compassionate. Give them love and kindness, and remember to breathe out any tension they might still cause you, despite your efforts to be compassionate.

Talk Back Tips

Research has shown that, outside of the social milieu where cursing is the norm, over 85 percent of the population surveyed does not tolerate the use of curse words as a regular and accepted part of conversation.

The Know-It-All

The Know-It-All is very much like the Name-Dropper: both have a great need to show off and feel important. They both need an audience and need others to think that they are in some way superior. Instead of trying to impress you with the important people they know, they try to impress you with the important information they know. In reality, they are feeling inferior and insecure about themselves. They might indeed know a lot and have a great deal of information at their disposal.

However, there is certainly one thing they don't know about, and that is how to deal with other people. They tend to talk at you, not with you.

Blow and let them go. They need the attention more than you need to be right, so let them impress themselves with how much they know. In essence, let them talk to themselves. Don't take what they say to heart. Just use the Tension Blowout Technique to let out any of your excess frustration. Often, similar to the case of the Name-Dropper, the more they feel attended to and appreciated, the less they will have to prove themselves and the less reason they will have to show off.

Therefore, the Love and Kindness Technique might put a stop to their annoying actions quicker than ever.

SlangGangers

While, as we discussed earlier in this book, it might be appropriate to use slang or even four-letter words in some social circles, it is most annoying when used out of context. It is met with a great deal of disdain when used away from the group where it is accepted as the norm.

Besides cursing, the SlangGanger's speech is consistently peppered with "like," "um," "ya know," "know what I mean," and "man." It also contains poor grammar, mis-pronounced words, and a whole host of made-up words constituting an entirely new language.

If you are on SlangGanger's turf, if you don't know what certain words mean, ask them. Better yet, as soon as you know that you will be around them, try to find out from someone who is familiar with their slang and way of speaking what certain words mean. Like speaking in a true second language, you will relate to them much better if you incorporate some of their terminology into your own speech pattern. Take care, however, that you don't use the words in the wrong context. Doing so will only embarrass you.

Don't correct their poor grammar or their use of filler words, since this is part of the accepted lingo.

On the other hand, if they are on your territory, it becomes a different matter. You have the right to establish communication ground rules on your turf, just as they did in theirs. It's the old concept of "when in Rome, do as the Romans do." Be strongly advised, however, that you must never embarrass the SlangGanger, especially in front of others. This is demeaning and puts them on the defensive. They might rebel, clam up, or lash out at you verbally, and in certain cases even physically. They will become extremely angry at you, and from their perspective rightfully so. You have insulted who they are. You have disrespected them! When you have a private moment with the SlangGanger, let him know, in a calm and collected, unemotional manner, while smiling, that you would prefer it if he would modify his words in front of you. In essence, you are using the Direct Approach in a calm manner. You might also want to incorporate the Humor Technique and make light of the situation in order to help him get the message.

Conversation Hogs

The Conversation Hog or Interrupter types of verbal abusers are absolutely, without a doubt, the number-one most annoying type of person. According to a Gallup Poll, close to 90 percent of respondents could not stand a person who interrupted them. They tolerate this offensive behavior less than any other. If someone interrupts you, they're keeping you from finishing your thoughts, which will undoubtedly frustrate you and cause you to either clam up or lash out. Perhaps some of the biggest arguments you had were when you were put on the defensive because you kept being interrupted. Someone who constantly interrupts you is a major control freak. They are so insecure that they always have to have the floor. They always have to have the attention.

Talk Back Tips

Conversation Hogs are often belligerent bullies who have some resentment or ax to grind; usually, this has nothing to do with you. They are poor listeners and usually cross over into the Know-It-All category.

A sub-category of the Conversation Hogs are the Topic-Changers, who will not hesitate to change the topic of the conversation midstream. They disrupt both your and their own train of thought. Both types of verbal abusers are into controlling others and situations.

Be direct! They might not hear you because they are often so self-absorbed! You might have to tap them or have light physical contact so you get their attention.

Tell them that you are not finished talking yet. First, do it politely with a smile. If it doesn't work, do it louder. Give 'Em Hell and Yell! You also have the option of Mirroring them as you talk over their interruptions. Whatever the case, it is not only frustrating, but exhausting. Be careful knowing "before whom you stand" before you do the last three techniques. If you want to maintain your dignity, Unplug for the moment and interrupt them by calmly excusing yourself. This way, they will have nobody to interrupt! Let them know that they cannot take over the reins and always be in verbal control.

Repeat, Repeating, Repeaters

In this case, I am not talking about people with speech impediments who stutter, have a neurological condition, or have Alzheimer's. Instead, I am talking about people who seem to enjoy hearing themselves talk. They say the same thing over and over again. They not only tell you the same story or joke, they tell everyone else, too! Often they repeat the same story because they want more feedback from you or they want to vent their emotions, or they want to relive the situation. No matter what the reason, it is annoying and you feel like running away!

Since these people are usually quite insecure or emotionally distraught, or perhaps they suffer from some form of brain damage, have some compassion! If you are feeling impatient with them, use the Breathing Technique to calm yourself down. Primarily give them Love and Kindness. If you find that they have really overstepped their bounds and overstayed their welcome, politely and kindly tell them that you heard the story before. Unplug for the moment by either changing the topic or by physically leaving the present environment. By leaving to go to the bathroom and returning, you might get them off the repetition tract.

Wordy Ones

Like the Know-It-All, the Wordy Ones are out to impress. They try to use big words to show off and are extremely verbose. They say a mouthful when they can just say a biteful. In their insecurity, they attempt to reflect a "better than you" or a "snobby" attitude, when in reality they are screaming out in emotional pain. They hunger for social acceptance and want to appear smart. They have the illusion that people perceive them as being smart, and that they will therefore be treated with more respect.

Just as you would do with the Slangmaster, if you don't know what a word means, Ask! If they are too wordy, you might want to stop them and use the Calm Questioning Technique. Ask "What's the bottom line?" If they keep being wordy throughout the conversation, keep asking what the bottom line is. Without their knowledge, you are conditioning them. Remember the experiment in Psychology 101 about Pavlov's dog? It's the same thing! When you ask them the bottom line, do it with Love and Kindness because of their need to be accepted, even though it might not seem like it at the time.

Bon Mots

Conditioning occurs when you train someone to associate one event with another. For example, if you repeatedly ask the Wordy One what the bottom line is as he rambles, he will come to expect your response and will begin to rein in his rambling even without you having to intervene.

The Whiner

Unless it's actress Fran Drescher (my ex-client and dear friend), star of *The Nanny* who makes tons of money because of her nasal voice, people will cringe around those who sound nasal. Nearly 70 percent of those questioned in a Gallup poll said that they were turned off by the sound of this type of voice. Other research shows that when someone sounds nasal, they aren't taken as seriously and aren't considered to be as attractive and intelligent as those with non-nasal sounding tones.

I'm not talking about people who sound nasal because of a neurological condition or birth defect.

Talk Back Tips

Regional variations can cause nasal speech; in some parts of the country, such as Texas, Oklahoma, and New York, it is the norm to speak nasally. But nasal speech can also be caused by sloppy speech.

Instead, I am talking about those who sound nasal because they have sloppy speech and don't open their mouths when they speak. In that way, they are similar to the Mumbler. They don't realize how their poor speaking habits negatively affect those who listen to them.

If you're one of those unlucky souls who is forced to listen to a Whiner , especially for a long time, it is best to use the Direct Confrontation Technique coupled with the Calm Questioning Technique. Do this as gently and politely as you can, while incorporating the Love and Kindness Technique, as difficult as that might seem. You might want to start out by saying to them that their voice sounds rather nasal. Then ask them the question, "Do you have a cold?" If they say no, which they probably will, ask whether they have allergies. If they say no, go back to the Direct Confront Technique and say that you don't mean to be offensive but their voice really sounds nasal. Say this in a polite tone, as gently as possible.

Now don't just leave them standing there. Give them something to help them. If you've criticized them, offer them a solution. Tell them that you read in a book (this one) that when people have nasal sounding voices (which many people have) your back teeth should never touch when you speak. This helps you keep your mouth more open, so you won't sound as nasal. Tell them you tried it and it worked! If they tell you they too hate the sound of their nasal sound, refer them to a speech pathologist using the method I taught you earlier in this chapter.

The Least You Need to Know

➤ There are people who annoy you by what they say, but more who annoy you by how they say it.

➤ People who mumble, talk fast, sound timid, use a lot of slang, or are loud talkers are frustrating because you can't understand what they are saying.

➤ Those who drop names, interrupt, know it all, or constantly repeat are terribly insecure.

➤ Never embarrass people by confronting them in front of others. Do it privately, or the repercussions could be disastrous.

➤ When you face annoying vermin, your options include Confronting, Questioning, Tension Blowouts, and, infrequently, Unplugging.

Chapter 18

Verbal Combat Against Painful Verbal Abusers

In This Chapter

➤ Dealing with those whose words can make you feel ill

➤ Dealing with the unresponsive and the too-responsive

➤ Coping with flatterers or liars

➤ Talking to braggarts and complainers

➤ Talking to those who think their word is gospel, those who underestimate you, or those who tune you out

---

In this chapter, you learn how to use a variety of the most effective strategies against the eight types of painful verbal abusers who may infest your life. You learn about the weapons that best deflect their repulsive verbal goo. The verbal abuser may often require somewhat stronger approaches than those you used in Chapter 17.

Verbal Abuse Can Actually Make You Nauseous!

Unlike the annoying verbal vermin, who mostly irritate you, the painful verbal abusers mostly anger you and cause you extreme emotional upset. Different degrees of emotional upset can bring out the worst in you and cause you to react in ways alien to your normal behavior. Although you are usually not pushed over the edge—to the point of no return—the verbal abuser could be the one to finally push you there!

Their abuse can embarrass you. It can frustrate you. It can confuse you. These people can make you feel suspicious and untrusting of others. In essence, they can make you feel sick to your stomach. They can even cause you to feel nauseous and on the verge of throwing up!

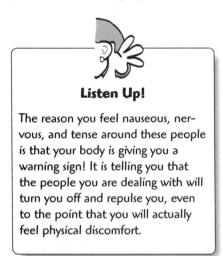

Listen Up!

The reason you feel nauseous, nervous, and tense around these people is that your body is giving you a warning sign! It is telling you that the people you are dealing with will turn you off and repulse you, even to the point that you will actually feel physical discomfort.

Although they are definitely toxic, they are usually not toxic enough to cause havoc in your life, hurt you, or attempt to destroy you like the dangerous verbal abusers will. In the Chapter 19, we will learn what ammunition to use to protect ourselves against those verbal enemies. For now, let's focus on the opponent at hand—the painful verbal abuser.

The Verbally Dead

They are verbally cold and secretive. They rarely if ever divulge information about themselves. They just gather information. They don't give you any vocal reaction one way or the other, so you find them very difficult to read. You don't know how they really feel about something— if they really like something or can't stand it. Their reaction is the same in either case.

Initially, one might be attracted to them. Women in particular might fall prey to the stereotypic "strong but silent type" of man—the John Wayne type, the man of few words. What they fail to realize and soon come to discover is that you can't have an open and meaningful relationship with anyone who doesn't talk to you. It's not going to cut it with someone whose conversations consists of "yep," "nope," "I don't know," "maybe," "I guess," or "I don't care." This is not the case for men only. There are women who are The Verbally Dead as well. No matter what their sex, they always keep you off guard.

They may not be indifferent, and they may really care, deep down inside. The fact that they are so inexpressive, however, makes you think they don't like you, that they are judging you and being critical of you. It makes you think that they are indifferent about you. They don't care if you live or die.

Some of The Verbally Dead use their silence to try to manipulate you or even intimidate you. They derive a great deal of pleasure out of watching you behaving uncomfortably and squirming around their silence. In essence they are using their "iced state" as sort of a power trip to see how long you can actually "chill out." When they become more talkative and share their thoughts and feelings, then they begin to feel uncomfortable. The reason is that they feel out of control—as though they have lost their power over you! Their perceived power lies in keeping you guessing and wondering what is going on inside of them.

The bottom line with these of The Verbally Dead is that you can never change them and force them to open up. They have to want to open up on their own.

The one thing you cannot do is to demand that they show some emotion in their voice and sound more animated. Doing this will make them clam up even more. Though you feel like choking them and screaming your head off at them, neither physical violence nor using the "Give 'Em Hell and Yell" strategy will make a difference.

Two tactics seem to work best with the Verbal Refrigerator. No matter how angry or frustrated you feel at them, force yourself to use the Love and Kindness Technique. They desperately hunger for it. Most of The Verbally Dead are that way because of some deep-rooted psychological problem. Most of these psychological problems developed in childhood, where the people might have been so emotionally scarred or traumatized that they clammed up! They may have done this as a psychological survival mechanism. Unfortunately, they may have carried this now-unnecessary protective gear into their adult years, which makes for some huge complications in human relationships. Therefore, accepting them through this technique makes them feel safer and more apt to trust you and thereby open up to you.

The Calm Questioning Technique also works very well, but you have to know when to back off. You can't fire a series of machine gun-like questions at the Verbally Dead. You have to ask them slowly and wait for an answer. Be quiet. Be silent! Wait for them to talk! Consciously or not, they may be using this as a ploy to test you. Let them talk. Ask open-ended questions about what they think about a topic or issue. Ask questions that do not require a "yes," "no," or one-word answer. Use the Elaboration Technique you learned about earlier in this book when learning how to develop you own conversational skills. Just keep asking them questions, and make sure that you ask in calm, warm, soothing tones.

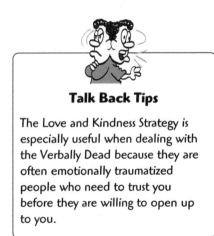

Talk Back Tips

The Love and Kindness Strategy is especially useful when dealing with the Verbally Dead because they are often emotionally traumatized people who need to trust you before they are willing to open up to you.

Verbal Vomiters

People in this category are not fully aware of what they are saying to you. In fact, they speak in a free-flowing stream of consciousness that often makes little or no sense. They are often thoughtless and rarely think before they speak. They tell all! And I mean ALL!!! While it may be amusing and even titillating and interesting at first, after a while they end up telling you things you really don't want to know. The information is all too often inappropriate and way too personal. People who reveal too much information not only tell you their intimacies and problems, they tell everyone else with whom they come in contact—from their bosses to their colleagues to anyone who will listen. They don't discriminate. They won't think twice about telling a perfect stranger their life story. They have no boundaries. Anyone and everything is fair game. They also have an incredibly difficult time keeping secrets.

As long as someone will listen, they will talk—often non-stop. These chatterboxes are so hungry for attention they will say just about anything to get it.

If there were a TA (Talkaholics Anonymous) group, the first thing I would recommend would be to encourage them to attend meetings on a regular basis. However, since it does not exist yet, the following techniques can be as helpful to you as they have been to so many others who have been exposed to verbal abusers.

You must never tell these people anything you wouldn't want anyone else to know. Therefore, think before you speak to them. As talkaholics, they need material to talk about. What better material than that which someone else told them? It doesn't matter if that "someone else" is you and you swore them to secrecy. Chances are that they were so self-absorbed, they didn't remember that you told them not to tell anyone what you just divulged. So, don't be as unconscious as they are. Know before whom you are talking.

Talk Back Tips

You can think of people who give too much information as children who haven't been taught that there are things they can and cannot say in public or to strangers.

Listen Up!

Not everyone who flatters you should be held in suspicion. Only those who are overly effusive to you (and to everyone else) should be examined a little more carefully! Chances are, they need you more than you need them. The relationship rarely works both ways!

If you can somehow get their attention, the Direct Confrontation strategy can be most effective when it is coupled with the Love and Kindness tactic. Tell them how much you care about them (if you do) and that you are not there to criticize them, but you want to tell them something that can perhaps help them. Point out to them that sometimes they might talk a bit too much and say things that are rather inappropriate; that maybe they should monitor what they say better.

If they ignore your efforts and continue on their merry chatty way, in order to keep your sanity, just use the Tension Blowout Strategy so that listening to their stupid unconscious verbal diarrhea won't make you want to rip your own hair out.

Sugary Sweet Phonies

These people tend to be so phony that they can make you sick. These sneaky brown-nosers will stab you in the back every time. They manipulate and flatter to death just to get their way.

They may sing your praises and lavish you with all kinds of verbal gifts—sweet words and compliments. When you attempt to assuage their flattery or shrug it off, they will have none of it. They keep insisting that they mean what they say. That you really are "all that." They won't let up until they see that smile across your face staying there. They got you! They got you hooked! Congratulations! You have been manipulated. They are either after something you have, something that you can give them (even the prestige of being associated with you), or even a contact you may have who could somehow help them. Watch what happens when they don't get what they want! Suddenly the sweet words either stop or turn sour.

Humor is the best strategy to use with these verbal candies. This lets you know that you are onto them and that you aren't buying their manipulative ways. Another approach is the Direct Confrontation approach, but always in a lighthearted way, in which you let them know that you appreciate their kind words, but you aren't buying it. For example, you can say "Okay, now that you've buttered me up, what is it that you really want?" With this approach as with the humor tactic, they will usually realize that you are onto them and back off. Keep smiling. Laugh it off. They'll get the message.

Talk Back

Here are some light-hearted things you can say to sugary sweet phony people to let them know you are on to them.

"You know, I could probably go into insulin shock if you keep that up!"

"Watch it! If you say anymore of those sweet words, there will be an army of ants marching all over me."

Poor–Poor Me

These people are so difficult to be around because their often-sad words, sounds, and phrases bring you down. Their favorite party is a pity party. They love others to "poor poor" them to death. It is like marrow to their bones, fuel to their system. This makes them feel worthy, alive, that someone cares about them. They are so needy for attention and affection that they use depression and illness as a means of getting it.

If their verbal sadness is issue-related or happens at certain times, there is no problem. But if it happens a lot, you are dealing with someone who may have a serious mental condition—an acute depression, bipolar disorder, or borderline personality disorder.

One of the things you can't do is cheer them up. Deep inside, they get off on spreading gloom and doom. Because they do it for effect, in order to get a reaction out of people, they obviously need attention and affection. The best approach is to use the Love and Kindness approach; acknowledge that they are hurting or are upset and let them know that you hear them and understand what they are saying—that you empathize how they must be feeling.

Talk Back Tips

Remember that you cannot make everything better for these who think Poor-Poor-Me by giving advice, no matter how useful it is. They will always find a way to shoot it down. Give them an ear, but no advice, and no pity.

They do not want you to solve their problem. They do not want to hear a list of your brilliant ideas. The fact that you said you can understand that they feel bad is what they need to hear. If you offer advice, they will "yeah but" you to death. So, the key here is to give them no reaction—especially no pity.

If their verbal sadness is sporadic or situationally related, then you can stick around and do the Tension Blowouts so that their negative energy doesn't glom on to you. On the other hand, since they require so much work and are so draining, being around them for long periods of time may be debilitating. You might have to Unplug from them, no matter who they are in your life. If you can't unplug physically, you might want to do it mentally.

"Fibbers"

Sometimes these "Fibbers" are so caught up in their own lies or stories that they themselves lose track of whether they are telling the truth. They are the ultimate verbal manipulators and usually lie to protect themselves so that they can either get out of something or into something. Sometimes liars are blatant about it and exaggerate highly. Other times, they are subtle. Sometimes their manipulative stories are harmful, not only to themselves but to others. But the majority of the time, their stories are meant to enhance their poor image, persona, and self-esteem. No matter what they do, their self-worth has a huge hole in it.

Listen Up!

Do Tension Blowouts to control yourself, no matter how upset you get, so that you can open the lines of communication between you and the liars. If you don't, and instead use hostile and harsh accusatory tones, they will often take offense, and World War III will start.

The story they have told and how you perceive it decides what strategy you should use. Depending on who they are in your life, you may want to use the Direct Confront Technique or the Calm Questioning Technique to let them know that you are no dummy, that you know they have been lying, and that perhaps they have an explanation. This technique allows for open channels in communication. It is essential for you to remember, however, that you must always keep your cool. Breathe, breathe, breathe.

You might want to consider using Tension Blowouts. Use humor, even if it's only funny to you. Let it blow and let it go!

*%#&@ Cussers!

Some people don't mind others who curse—in fact, they may like it a lot, as they may feel a closer bond to the person, especially if they too curse. In many instances, some curse words don't have the same negative or shocking charge as they once did. In fact, they are commonplace. However, in most aspects of society, people don't approve of cursing. That is why there are movie ratings available for parents who may not want their children to hear films with verbal vulgarities. A Gallup poll showed that out of 10 annoying speech habits, using curse words was the second most annoying habit.

Often people who curse want to sound tough or appear "cool," "hip," and "with it." They are not necessarily bad people. They are just desperate for acceptance and want to portray a certain image. As mentioned earlier in the book, sometimes that image works in one area of society and not in others. If a "cusser" is in your area of society and you don't like it, here's what you can do!

If the cusser is related to you, you have more of an opportunity to use the Direct Approach Technique. If the cusser is your child, you have even more leeway, because you have access to the "Give 'Em Hell and Yell" Technique. This of course is a technique of last resort, used when your child doesn't get the message through Love and Kindness, Direct Confrontation, Calm Questioning, or Humor. Then and only then would it be recommended to Give 'Em Hell and Yell as a final option.

If the person is not related to you but is close, use the Direct Approach Technique. However, it is imperative to let them know in a lighthearted, matter-of-fact manner that you don't like cursing. Don't chastise them like a schoolteacher or reprimand them. That will definitely drive a wedge into your friendship. Let them know in non-threatening, non-judging, easy language that it sounds better to you when they don't curse.

You see, since they mostly curse in order to appear cool and to be accepted as part of the group or scene, help them feel part of the scene through a Love and Kindness tactic. Let them know that they are "way cool" in your scene when they don't curse.

After all, they are the ones who need the most acceptance, so accept them with Love and Kindness by saying "You really sound better" or "you have a better image" or "you come across cooler" when you don't talk like that. You know what I mean?" And then smile. You may even want to put your arm around them or hug them for assurance, depending on how close they are to you. The one thing to remember is not to talk down to them or reprimand them for cursing. Do it using the suggestions I just listed, so that they will actually listen to you.

Listen Up!

When addressing cussers, don't say "It makes me feel uncomfortable when you curse." That will immediately put them on the defensive. They don't care how you feel; they care about how they feel.

Me, Me, Me

I am not talking about the "me me me" that a singer sings when doing vocal warm-up exercises. Instead, I am talking about the self-consumed narcissistic person who can't see past the mirror. These poor souls are so insecure, they need constant approval from the mirror, and from everyone around them, including YOU! They are always seeking someone to say how great they are. They always talk about their favorite subject—themselves. Heaven forbid you try to bring up another topic—they will somehow manipulate the topic so that it applies to them. And voilà, you are now back discussing the only thing they can relate to—themselves! Even if you are discussing a world crisis, somehow they will manage to manipulate the conversation to bring it back to them.

The me me me crowd will go for hours and hours talking about themselves without even considering you or asking you any questions about what your thoughts are on a particular matter. They are self-consumed in every way.

Even though you may not realize it, these tortured souls suffer greatly. They are not self-absorbed because they want to be; they are self-absorbed because they have to be.

Even though their self-absorption may test your patience, you need to have compassion for them. The most effective technique to start with is the Tension Blowout Technique, where you let go of any tension you feel when you are around them. Next, give them a dose of Love and Kindness, followed by Directly Confronting them in a calm yet controlled tone. Never accuse them, because this puts them on the defensive.

Talk Back Tips

The me me me folks are really not malicious people and are often worth having in your life. If you can be patient and learn to speak their language, you will eventually have more of an opportunity to establish a greater mutual give–and–take relationship with them.

In talking to this narcissistic type of person, you need to say something like "You can make me feel a lot more welcome in the conversation if you ask me some questions about myself." In addition, you can ask them what they think of your opinion. Since everything pertains to them and since they hear things only in terms of what effect they have on others, they will most likely accommodate you and heed your request, and thereby change their behavior. Why? Because you have given them the power—power they require so badly as part of their self-worth, to help you. You have spoken to them in their language—THEM!

The Anointed One Has Spoken!

These verbal abusers tend to underestimate others or blow off and tune out what anyone else says. They consider it irrelevant. What is relevant is only what they say! They are know-it–alls who often use their knowledge as a defense mechanism to overcome their insecurity. They feel that they have spoken, and so be it! Even if they have little or no knowledge about a subject, it doesn't matter. They have convinced themselves that they know anyway. They have a false sense of self-aggrandizement, which they mask by their rigidity, judgment, and verbal arrogance. The basis for this is usually fear.

This is why they are so adamant that they should be heard and that their point of view is the only point of view. Usually, they say things that indicate that they are extremely self-righteous or use a holier-than-thou tone. In reality, it is quite the opposite.

They are making such a fuss because they are trying to justify their hypocrisy. They feel guilty about their misdeeds. They know that deep inside, what they have said is nonsense. They know that they aren't "talking the talk." Therefore, they have to scream louder, not only so that they can convince you, but so they can convince themselves.

As we have seen time after time, especially from our experiences, those who constantly banter about how things should be, how moral and righteous they are and how bad others are for not accepting their ways of thinking, often don't practice what they preach! Those who claim self-righteous purity are often not as pure in thought and deed as they portray themselves. Perhaps they subconsciously believe that the more they pontificate, the more their verbal demons will disappear, so that what they say will be true after all.

Listen Up!

Always heed, but don't always believe

Those insisting they are always pure in deed.

These people should know that they need to get off their pedestal—that others too have valid opinions. Usually the Calm Questioning Approach isn't as effective as the Direct Approach combined with the Give 'Em Hell and Yell (if necessary).

When I am talking about giving them hell and yelling, I actually mean talking louder than they do. As they robotically cite their doctrine, cite yours over theirs. Since they think that they are so anointed, they will usually be so shocked by your audacity to speak over them that they will stop. When they stop speaking, continue to speak in a confident, audible, and resonant tone so that they can hear what you are saying to them, in hopes that at least a few points that you are trying to make will permeate their suit of "superior" armor.

If that doesn't work, depending who they are in your life, you may want to use the Tension Blowout Technique to blow out your anger toward them. If nothing works, blow them out of your life for good—Unplug them! It is way too exhausting and debilitating to try to communicate with someone who tunes you out, underestimates you, and believes their doctrine or point of view is the only one. It is a no-win situation to try to communicate with someone who has no respect for whatever you say or who says to you "It's my way or the highway." You need to retort with "Hit the road, Jack!"

The Least You Need to Know

➤ You don't make *yourself* sick, *other people* do—by what they say to you!

➤ If people are unresponsive to you, keep asking them open-ended questions to which they can't give simple "yes" or "no" answers.

➤ Pointing out that someone talks too much and divulges too many intimate details may do them a huge favor. But do it in a gentle and caring manner, because they are quite insecure to begin with.

➤ Be aware of Flatterers, who usually are after something you have or someone you know. Watch out for the Gloomsters. Their negative energy can rub off on you.

➤ Those who always talk about themselves are insecure. Try to be sympathetic and not angry. Asking their opinions of your opinions is one of the first steps towards a more mutual interaction.

➤ Let the Anointed Ones know that they are not so anointed. Let them know up front that they cannot get away with disrespecting or dismissing what you have to say. You are important too!

Chapter 19

Verbal Combat Against Dangerous Verbal Abusers

In This Chapter

➤ How to deal with the most dangerous of verbal abusers

➤ Handling people who misrepresent themselves

➤ Dealing with those who are always down or are mentally disturbed

➤ Dealing with those who are envious, controlling, cutting, mean, and manipulative

---

The information in this chapter can literally save your life! The verbal abusers you'll read about here are scary. They are the most toxic people, and the ones who have to be most closely watched. Whenever you are around them, you not only have to look in front of you to know that they are there (which is obvious). You also have to look to the right, to the left, and in back of you. They can come out of nowhere. You must be on your toes at all times.

These people can make you the sickest—mentally, emotionally, and even physically. They represent everything bad. They make you feel absolutely horrible about yourself. They are the ones to cause you so much grief that your life is always in turmoil. Should you be so unfortunate that you happen to be around them for any length of time, realize that they can erode your self-confidence to the point where psychologically you feel lower than a snake's belly.

PROCEED WITH EXTREME CAUTION!

As I discussed earlier in the book, when you ask most people what they would do if they were in the presence of a severely verbally toxic person, many naively say they would walk away. You can't simply walk away. If you do so, you will be walking away with hurt and pain. You will still need to cope with the havoc that they cause or else you will be carrying their verbal wrath for years to come. In this chapter, you first learn specific characteristics of these dangerous people. Then you will learn the most effective strategies to use with the most severe types to shield yourself from their verbal poisons. You will learn what to say and how to say it.

You have a number of choices for verbally responding to these dangerous people. In many instances, you will be given some snappy comebacks from which to choose, if the situation warrants it. No matter which strategy you use with a particular person, choose carefully. Just trust your instincts—you are almost always right!

Lambs to Lions

These are the most passive-aggressive and the most dangerous of all the verbal abusers because you really never know where they are coming from. They are meek and delicate sounding, often using high-pitched voices when they do communicate. But most often, they are non-communicative. They harbor extreme inner rage and are often jealous—even though they may smile and act as though they are supportive.

Talk Back Tips

Play the devil's advocate with the lambs-to-lions. Say what you guess they may be thinking or feeling. This may get them to react non-verbally, so watch their body and facial expressions. If they loosen up their body stance and posture, most likely they're in sync with what you just said. If not, they may be feeling the opposite.

They are walking time bombs, because you never know when they are going to blow up at you. They harbor resentment and swallow perceived hurt feelings, slights, verbal cuts, and injustices they feel are done to themselves or to others. And then one day, BOOM! A volcano of verbal violence explodes, often complete with yelling, insults, and blaming. Needless to say, this is not only shocking, it is frightening as well, because you don't know what they are going to do next.

Always keep abreast of what is going on with them. Constantly check in when they are in conversation with you. Do this only if you have no choice and must have them in your life due to business- or family-related matters. Use the Calm Questioning Technique, requiring more than just a yes or no answer.

However, the ideal situation is to run for your life! If you ever experience the wrath of a Lamb to Lion, never experience it again! It is best to Unplug forever!

Control Freaks

These people have to control others because they are so out-of-control themselves. They are abusive and hostile and often walk around with a chip on their shoulder, especially if they don't get their way. The other extreme is that they will lose interest and do nothing if they don't get their way. They are invasive, tenacious, stubborn, not team players, and have difficulty delegating responsibility. They also have difficulty with authority figures. They feel that they must orchestrate every move, instead of letting things happen.

They force issues and often drive former allies away from them. When things do not go their way, they get more manipulative and angry, because they are so out of control. They are the type of person who punches holes in walls when they don't get their way.

Parents who are control freaks can ruin their children's lives, making them spend a lot of time on the psychiatrist's couch in their adult years.

Humor is often a great antidote because if you didn't laugh, you would surely cry. You may use humor to "call their bluff." The following "Talk Back!" section has some good snappy comebacks to use with a Control Freak. Keep in mind, however, that there is a 50/50 chance that they can become even more violent if you say these things to them. So if you can give it a try and you are willing to take a chance, go for it!

Listen Up!

These people often have a profoundly negative effect on other people's lives because of their noisy, vocal, and intense characteristics. They end up giving people ulcers and making them physically ill.

You may want to Directly Confront them by letting them know that they overstepped their bounds and that they simply cannot control you in the manner that they are presently exhibiting. You need to let them know in a calm manner how you prefer to be treated and that you need to be respected. You need to tell them that your opinions matter and that they cannot speak to you or treat you the way they have been doing.

As I said earlier, Control Freaks often back down after they get a taste of their own medicine. Therefore, the Mirror Technique may work wonders. However, once again, depending upon who they are in your life and how instrumental they are to your livelihood (such as a boss), you may have to think twice about using this strategy.

If nothing works, you have no choice but to Unplug, especially if their actions are affecting your health. It may not be worth the money or the aggravation to you! Your mental and physical state are more important than anything else in the world!

Backstabbing Enviers

First and foremost, know that "jealousy is the root of all evil." It causes people to have bad feelings, and to say and feel bad things towards others. If the jealousy continues, it turns to envy, which is a more severe form of jealousy. Envy seeks to destroy. It causes one to do extremely harmful things to others—always in a manipulative manner, behind the person's back.

Like the Lamb to Lion, these people are among the scariest, because they act one way and really are another way. Usually fawners, they are overly effusive and overly complimentary about you; they have "sugar on their lips" but "salt in their eyes."

They are sneaky, clandestine, and incredibly passive-aggressive. They do whatever they can to get ahead. They don't care whose toes they step on, but they do it gingerly, carefully, and unobtrusively. When you find out that the person who sang your praises to your face was definitely not singing your praises behind your back, you are often in shock.

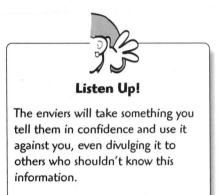

Listen Up!

The enviers will take something you tell them in confidence and use it against you, even divulging it to others who shouldn't know this information.

So how do you recognize these sneaky plotters? First, watch what they say about others. If they are friendly to others and then trash them, rest assured that you are next. Secondly, if they are overly effusive with you and with everyone else, *watch out!*

A rather effective approach is to use the Direct Confrontation Approach combined with a little humor. This way, you let them know that you are onto their backstabbing ways; this will often shock them back! The following "Talk Back!" section lists some examples of what you can say in order to "bust them" so that they get the message.

Talk Back

Snappy Comebacks for Backstabbing Enviers!

You can start with a common phrase you have heard many times before: "With friends like you, who needs enemies?"

"Wow! You certainly rolled out the carpet for me one day, and then pulled it out from under me the next."

If you caught them in the act and they committed a rather serious crime that really ruined you, your reputation, or your livelihood don't hesitate to Give 'Em Hell and Yell. That will definitely shock them as they usually won't expect it! *Let your anger out!* Go for it! Just remember what I keep drilling into your head throughout this book. The only way to truly get back at someone is through verbal self-defense. Avoid at any cost using physical means to express your anger.

Hitting-Below-the-Belt Abusers

Like the Backstabbing Envier, these people will not hesitate to tell people what you have told them in confidence. However, unlike the Backstabbing Envier, these dangerous Hitting-below-the-Belt Abusers will bring up these most intimate confidences right back in your face. What they say will shock you. It will feel as though a stun gun just shot you or a swarm of bees stung you. All the blood seems to drain from you as you become numb. Your ears cannot believe what they just said!

You may have told them something that you were embarrassed about, like being a bedwetter as a child, or something that you were sensitive about, such as your weight, only to hear it back in either direct-aggressive form (especially after a disagreement), or in passive-aggressive form: "I was only kidding." No matter what the form, it is definitely "verbal murder," which I discussed at the beginning of this book.

Here is where your facial cues can be your best weapon. Look at the person with disgust, narrowing your eyes and staring them right in the face. Be silent! Say nothing! Here is where silence truly is golden. Do the Tension Blowout Strategy! Take the breath in, hold it, and then slowly let it out! You will gain control, and the silence will often make them fumble and bumble. They will feel extremely uncomfortable.

The ideal way of retorting to someone who drops the shocking verbal bomb is to use the Calm Questioning Technique by asking them questions such as those listed in the following "Talk Back!" section.

Listen Up!

Whatever the form of being hit below the belt, the fact remains that the verbal abuser betrayed your confidence. This is unconscionable! No one should ever excuse this kind of behavior.

Talk Back

Snappy Comebacks for Hitting-below-the-Belt Abusers

"Are you really so low that you would have to resort to throwing back to me something I told you in my deepest confidence?"

"How do you think it makes me feel when I trusted you with my heart and soul?"

"Are you willing to win an argument or be right at all cost—even at the risk of destroying another person?"

"Do you feel better now that you deeply hurt me?"

"That stings"!"

"You won!"

How can a person ever trust another person who betrayed her in such a verbally poisonous way? It is very hard to do. Even though you both may shake hands and bury the hatchet, the relationship can never be the same. You can never trust him again! So beware and be aware!

Verbal Interrogators

Like the Control Freak, these interrogators need to be in control!

They try to gain that control and "trip you up" by bombarding you with questions! No matter how stable you think you are, you usually find yourself thrown off-center. You find yourself answering questions that you never had any intention of answering!

These Verbal Interrogators have a way of getting things out of you by asking such rapid-fire questions. Often, the questions are so intimate and invasive that they shock you to the point that your guard is down. They do this to establish their power in their attempts to intimidate you. When you finally accommodate them with answers, they feel tremendous power over you.

Listen Up!

When you answer the interrogators, they feel that they have succeeded in intimidating you to tell them what they need to know. You are caught in a momentary vulnerability where you did or said something, even though you didn't want to. So when you are being interrogated, pause to regain your footing.

The first thing you have to do is to get yourself back on strong footing. You have to regain control of yourself. You can only do this by slowing down. Don't allow them to make your head spin! Immediately do the Tension Blowout strategy. Immediately stop! Take a breath in, and as you breathe out say to yourself "No, I'm not gonna answer" or "I'm in control" or "No, no, no!"

Now use the Direct approach, smiling all the while. Ignore their loud voice and barrage of questions. Just keep breathing and keep talking over them! You can combine the Direct Confronting approach with some humor, but make sure that you take control! Don't get caught up in the frenzy of their tones and verbal bullets. You will find in the "Talk Back!" section some actual things you can say to the Verbal Interrogator that are designed to put them back in their place and let them know that you will not fall prey to their verbally bullying tactics.

Talk Back: Snappy Comebacks for Verbal Interrogators

(Smile as you say) "I feel like I'm on the spot here!"

"Let me digest one question at a time before you ask me another."

"You are going too fast for me."

"That's way too personal a question for me to answer."

"I don't feel like answering that."

"Why do you want to know that?"

"I feel like I am being interrogated."

Another technique to use is the Mirror Technique. Interrogate them back. Ask them the same questions they ask you in a rapid-fire motion. Usually, they will get the message!

Fanatics and Zealots

I'm not talking about a Star Wars fanatic or a person obsessed with a certain product or event! I'm talking about someone who is so obsessed with another person or with a point of view—a belief system—that he is a real danger to others. Any extreme in any group is dangerous, whether it be religious, political, or social. They are scary because they see only one thing. They have a *Cyclops* view of the world: anyone who disagrees is the enemy. Often, the fanatic is out of his or her mind. They may be mentally or emotionally disturbed, so you must not take them lightly. There is no convincing them. There is no having a dialogue with them! It is their way or no way! They are very similar to the Control Freak in this regard.

Since there is usually no way with these people unless you agree with them, you are in a losing battle. If you are forced to work with them because your livelihood depends upon it, do the Tension Blowouts combined with the Fantasy strategy. Imagine them tongueless or locked away in a padded cell for life—anywhere, just as long as it is away from you! If you have a choice in the matter, UNPLUG! Leave! Adios! Goodbye! Sayonara! Go—and don't look back!

If they continue to verbally harass you, a court system can help put a stop to it via restraining orders. If they continue to verbally harass you, tape record their calls on your answering machine, since in many states you may use this for evidence against them. They may be facing jail time if they persist! You may even want a legal representative to make them aware of this if appropriate.

Bon Mots

The **Cyclops,** as you might remember, was a creature in Greek myth with only one eye. Someone with a Cyclops view of the world can tolerate only one perspective: his or her own.

Yes-Yes Do-Nothings

These passive-aggressive people may seem benign, like they wouldn't hurt you, but often no action is as horrible as destructive action. Often, just like the Backstabbing Enviers, they may harbor a lot of hidden resentment or anger towards you. That anger is shown in the form of their saying "yes" to your face but doing nothing about it!

If this behavior seems to be the norm, trust will be nonexistent. The only thing you can trust about them is that they will do nothing because they either can't decide what to do, or they just don't want to do it. However, in both cases, they will lead you to believe that they will do it. Don't be fooled.

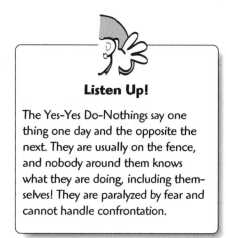

Listen Up!

The Yes-Yes Do-Nothings say one thing one day and the opposite the next. They are usually on the fence, and nobody around them knows what they are doing, including themselves! They are paralyzed by fear and cannot handle confrontation.

The most important thing when dealing with this type of dangerous person is to let them know that you are on to them! They are so upsetting. They can mess up your plans. They can destroy your emotions. They can devastate your hopes and dreams.

They may have led you on with "yes" after "yes" so that you think that you are going in one direction. You make plans for that direction, when that wasn't the direction they planned at all. As a result, you are left "holding the bag"—basically fooled! When they say "yes-yes," you need to use the Direct Confrontation Techniques with them. You need to let them know that, based on your past experiences with them, they said "yes," you depended on them to do something, but they never carried it out. If it happened on several occasions, let them know that you find it difficult to trust them.

Verbal Vignette

As I have seen time and again in my practice, the Yes-Yessers carry over their dangerous behavior even into your health crises or other important life events where you most need someone. Since such people rarely come through for you, you should seriously think about not dealing with them at all.

Now you may want to employ the Calm Questioning Technique by asking them if there is any way you can help them arrive at a decision. Ask them if you can help them do something to make it easier on them. Get some specifics from them, some time deadlines! Ask direct questions concerning when they think it will be done or what will be happening. Then check up and see if it is done as you approach the specified deadline. This is done so that you can be assured it will be done on time.

Talk Back

Snappy Comebacks for Yes-Yes Do-Nothings

"When will it be done?"

"When can we expect this to be completed?"

"Are you sure this is going to happen?"

"I would really like to know one way or the other."

"Do you need my help on anything?"

"Perhaps I may be sounding pushy, but I really want to make sure...."

"The uncertainty of the situation is making me feel uncomfortable."

"Is there anything I can do to make sure it will happen?"

"Does 'yes' really mean 'yes' or does it mean 'maybe' or 'no?'"

"Does 'yes' mean 'no, I'm not gonna do anything?'"

"I would be more focused and productive if you could give me a definite answer."

If you don't get an answer one way or another, it is way too frustrating to do business with this person. Even if you are related to them or they are a friend, it is impossible to be around them, for the simple reason that you can't depend on them.

If you have tried the snappy comebacks or a direct confrontation with a yes-yesser and they still aren't following through for you, it might be time to unplug.

The Mentally/Verbally Disturbed

This is the most difficult group. On one level you feel sorry for them, because they can't help it; on the other hand, if you are around them long enough and don't know how to communicate with them, they will drive you insane. They should never be underestimated in terms of their intelligence. Mentally or emotionally challenged individuals are often smarter and more aware than they are given credit for.

The problem with them often lies with the biochemistry in their brain functions. Biological components, coupled with psychological and environmental dynamics, affect what type of socially unacceptable behavior may occur. Being around them is extremely draining, and unless they are under medical supervision, life with them can be a living hell.

They may be suffering from depression ranging from chronic to acute. They may always seem gloomy, which is very taxing to be around. Like others who suffer from mental and emotional dysfunction, they many need to be treated medically.

Others may be self-destructive or have alcohol- or drug-related problems. Some may have bipolar disorder mood swings or something more severe, such that they cannot relate to people at all (such as borderline personality disorder), or they may be completely out of touch with reality (suffering from a condition such as schizophrenia).

With all of the individuals who have mental-verbal disturbances, you need to use the Direct Confront Technique coupled with a lot of Love and Kindness! Because they are usually so emotionally tender, fragile, and even raw, they need to be handled with the utmost sensitivity, caring, and empathy. It is imperative that you encourage them and even help them to get into some type of program that can help them.

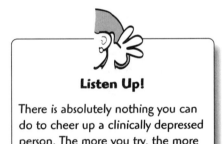

Listen Up!

There is absolutely nothing you can do to cheer up a clinically depressed person. The more you try, the more depressed you become because, as research has shown, his or her depression can be contagious.

If the person has drug, alcohol, or gambling problems that require outside help, whether in the form of AA, a rehabilitation program, a therapist, or a combination of all three, you must use loving and encouraging tones. Sometimes you may have to employ more of a "tough love" technique with harsher and more severe tones so that they will hear you. Whatever the case, you need to be direct and loving.

The same holds true for those with the other mental or emotional conditions that I just referred to. Kind and gentle tones with love, combined with direct honesty, help to create a more secure environment, which allows for effective healing and faster progress. One thing to remember is that people with mental conditions need not be kept at bay, shunned, ostracized, or treated differently. In this day and age, with all the wonderful medications available, psychopharmacologists, and psychotherapists, they can live a rich and fulfilling life just like anyone else. Therefore, if they happen to open up to you about their condition, never hold it against them.

Never scrutinize them for the slightest waiver in their behavior or make them feel guilty or embarrassed just because they have this life challenge.

Racist, Sexist, Verbal Xenophobes

Truly they are among the most revolting and evil of the dangerous verbal abusers. Their aim is to promote that they are better than everyone—that everyone else around them is less than they are. They make others feel badly.

If they take their xenophobic views to the limit, they destroy! If they can destroy with the spoken and written word, who is to say they can't destroy physically?

There are various reasons why they hate others so much or they have targeted a specific group to hate. First, they hate themselves, so they project their own self-hatred onto others. Secondly, they are usually envious of the object of their hate (remember "envy seeks to destroy"). Even if you put a gun to their head and they vehemently deny it, the fact is that they are indeed envious. They may not even be conscious of the fact that they are being envious! Maybe deep down they are envious of the group's power, love among one another, closeness, unique and strong culture, and their perceived ability to get ahead, to have more, get away with a lot, or be in a more controlling position than they are in.

Verbal Vignette

Some of these haters hate out of ignorance. They don't even know why they don't like a particular group. They only know that others around them don't like the group, so they follow suit. They may have also had one or two experiences where a bad apple in their hate-targeted group offended them, and now they have generalized their dislike to the entire population.

Racism, sexism, and xenophobia should not be tolerated in any shape or form. Direct Confrontation and Direct Questioning are musts; so is Unplugging. While Giving 'Em Hell and Yelling is probably justified and can release your anger, it can also get you killed. So if you decide to Hell and Yell it, just know that there is a 50/50 chance you may end up getting hurt or hurting someone physically.

Vicarious Fantasy, Tension Blowouts, and Unplugging work best with this type of person! Sometimes you have no choice but to be around these miserable creatures. Your best bet is to Unplug anytime you can—leave, let go, and never look back!

Talk Back Tips

One effective way to rid ourselves of the haters' poison is to "re-educate" them about other cultures or groups. Knowledge often eliminates their once hateful feelings towards other groups.

Verbal Lumberjacks

Verbal Lumberjacks spend a good part of their time cutting others down. They may even be humorous, but they are not so funny when they are cutting you down. It is degrading and demoralizing. These people are arrogant, mean, and highly disrespectful. They seem to always find fault with everyone. Nothing is sacred. If they do give a compliment (a very rare occurrence), it will definitely be back-handed.

The basis for these Verbal Lumberjacks' barbs is their insecurity. They are so full of self-loathing and are so afraid about what others think about them that they try to beat them to the punch—cut the other person down first.

Humor is one of the best ways to call the Verbal Lumberjack's bluff. Sometimes they will laugh with you, but most of the time they won't. They can readily dish it out, but because they are so insecure, they have a hard time taking it. When you do dish it back to them in the form of the Mirror Technique coupled with humor, however, they will definitely get the message. It will come as a big surprise if they still continue their cutting ways in front of you.

The Calm Questioning Technique may also be a good strategy to use. As soon as they make a cutting remark about another person, don't laugh, chuckle, or in any way indicate that you agree with them. Instead, ask them a serious question about what they said and keep asking questions to their every negative response until they get so frustrated and finally get the point you are trying to make. See the example in the "Talk Back!" section that follows. In essence, you are cross-examining them, and when they see how illogical their words are, they will usually keep their mouths shut (at least in your presence for the time being)!

Talk Back Tips

The Calm Questioning Technique helps other people see the logic of their position—that is, the illogic of their position.

Talk Back

Verbal Lumberjack (VL): "Look at that fat girl over there!"

You: "Why do you call her fat?"

VL: "Look at her! She looks like a pig!"

You: "Why does it bother you to look at her?"

VL: "Cuz she makes me sick! Women aren't supposed to look like that."

You: "Don't you look beyond her weight to see if she's good person inside?"

VL: "No! I wouldn't want to know a person who had no self-control. She's probably a mess!"

You: "So, you find all overweight people looking like pigs and messes?"

VL: "That's about right!"

You: "So, since your mother is overweight and even you have that little tummy, would you say that you and your mom look like pigs and are messes?"

VL: (MOUTH OPEN, S-I-L-E-N-C-E!!!)

When the Verbal Lumberjack cuts you down, it is either because you have something they want or represent something that they cannot face. In any event, they feel inadequate around you. Therefore, having this added knowledge may allow you to be more sensitive towards their plight and perhaps sprinkle them with a little of the old Love and Kindness Technique.

Nosybodies

These people can destroy your life forever. They can spread rumors about you that can damage your character and destroy your reputation, and you may never be able to recover from the repercussions. The consequences of their verbal damage may resonate and travel over great distances over long periods of time, thus potentially ruining your life forever!

They usually have so little going on in their own lives that they have to get involved in other people's lives to stir up some action. This enables them to entertain themselves at the other person's expense!

First of all, let them know that you are onto them and that you won't take their butting in anymore. Directly Confronting them is your best move. You can also Calmly Question them using a combination of these two tactics along with humor.

Sometimes they will not hear you, so you have to Give 'Em Hell and Yell. You have to talk very loud so they

Listen Up!

One of the gossips' dirty little tricks to get you to open up to them is to tell you a little gossip about themselves in order to break down the barriers. They think you will feel obligated to divulge a little in return. And guess what—when you do, everyone will know about it!

finally get it! Just let it go! They will think twice about bringing your name up again. If they do, at least they will take extra precautions to make sure that the dirt doesn't get back to you!

You cannot Unplug without letting them know that they are jerks for what they did and for what they said about you! Only after you let them know that you're onto their little game can you feel free to Unplug from them!

The Least You Need to Know

➤ Those who try to control others, cut others down, meddle in people's lives, interrogate, or instigate things are usually very insecure.

➤ Although most of these people need Love and Kindness, you need to set clear limits and let them know that you will not tolerate their shenanigans.

➤ Those who are envious or hit below the belt by divulging a confidence are cruel; they seek to destroy the other person. Those who gossip, meddle, instigate, or talk about you should be confronted and then unplugged from your life for good! They are dangerous!

➤ Insincere people, fawners, yes-people, and those who are too quiet should be watched like a hawk.

➤ It's best to stay out of the way of fanatics and xenophobes.

Part 6

Dodging Verbal Bullets in Specific Battlefields

Now you know how to identify your verbal enemy, arm yourself verbally, and use all the possible strategies with which to defend yourself. You understand which tactics to use against specific people you may confront throughout your life, and the specific verbal defense tactics to implement against different types of verbal vermin.

In this part of the book you learn how to verbally handle yourself in any situation that may come your way. You will learn what to say in any situation, from the most benign to the hairiest.

After reading this part, you will never again be at a loss for words! No situation will ever leave you with your tongue hanging out of your mouth or your brain spinning. You will never be mute, whether on the phone, in a business meeting, or in the bedroom.

You will know exactly what to say, whether you are breaking bad news or receiving it. You will learn how the words you use in specific situations can actually save your life. Finally, you will learn what to say in the most important situations in your life—when you are talking about YOU!

Chapter 20

Verbal Defense over the Telephone

In This Chapter

➤ How to deal with telephone salespeople

➤ Avoid being talked into buying something you don't really want

➤ Get an unhelpful person to help you

➤ Diplomatically get someone to speak softer, louder, slower, faster, or to stop mumbling

➤ Leave the right phone message, so you don't embarrass yourself

➤ Express your concerns to people with rude telephone habits

The telephone can be your best friend. It can be a great source of pleasure as it helps you accomplish things like making money, enhancing business contacts, exploring career opportunities, purchasing things you need, and connecting with friends, family, and loved ones.

But there are times when the telephone can be your worst enemy. It can be a source of tension and unhappiness!

In this chapter you learn exactly what to say in just about any situation you will face over the telephone. Some of the scenarios you'll read about will ring close to home. You, along with just about everyone else who has a telephone, have experienced these things at one time or another.

The unique aspect of this chapter is that not only do I discuss the specific telephone scenario with which you can identify and then share with you all of your viable verbal defense options, but I tell you *exactly* what to say. Nine times out of ten it will work for you, so go for it!

Pesky Persistent Telephone Sales Calls

You're home from a long day's work at the office. You throw off your shoes, plop down on the sofa, and smile with relief. All of a sudden, the phone rings. Since you're not expecting any phone calls you wonder who it could be: your mom, your best friend, your girlfriends, your guy friends! In any event, you still have a smile on your face as you say "hello" in your bouncy, upbeat tone. Suddenly your smile turns upside down. It is a salesperson, and she won't stop talking! She is reciting her obviously rehearsed pitch for you to change to her telephone service. You try to get a word in edgewise to tell her you're not interested, but you can't! She just keeps talking and talking and talking and talking!

Before I tell you what to say to pesky sales people, I need to point out that not all salespeople are pesky. Telephone solicitation is not necessarily a bad thing. In fact, it may be a wonderful thing! It may be a wonderful way of doing business! It is wonderful to have someone call you up and tell you about a product or a seminar that you were thinking about or that you thought sounded interesting after hearing their pitch. There is nothing more wonderful than to have purchased or to have signed up for a product that positively enhanced your life in some way.

Listen Up!

Never buy anything over the phone unless you do the following things:

➤ Carefully read the literature you have asked the company to send you that explains the product or service.

➤ Discuss it with knowledgeable people unconnected to the product.

➤ Take time to mull it over and think about it on your own time.

Never allow anyone to make you feel pressured to buy or do anything!

I am not talking about the polite salesperson who is kind and thoughtful! I am talking about the person who calls at inopportune times, who won't take "no" for an answer as he tries to browbeat or shame you into a sale.

So what are you supposed to do when the salesperson won't stop talking? Your first step is to interrupt them in a LOUDER voice than they are using. Say the following: "I am NOT interested now. I will NOT be interested later. So PLEASE NEVER CALL AGAIN!" Since they might call again (days, weeks, or months later), before you hang up, ask where the main office or headquarters of their company is based. Ask for the phone number. Ask for his supervisor. Try to get as much information as possible out of her. In order to do this, you must sound kind, pleasant, cooperative, and polite. If she is reading from a rehearsed script, tell her that before she sells you something, you need to know this information.

Chances are, she won't know it. Therefore, you will need to speak to her supervisor or to the supervisor's supervisor. No matter how you obtain it, get the information! Call the company's headquarters and get taken off their phone list. If they persist threaten them legally. Then hang up on them!

Slick Willy

Has anyone ever tried to sell you something over the telephone you didn't want to buy but did anyway? Maybe they intimidated you into giving money to charity or to a religious cause—perhaps even a great cause.

The person on the other end of the phone was such a great talker. Maybe it was his slickness or bravado. His voice sounded so rich and resonant, words flowing, full of enthusiasm, and confidence. How could you even dream of saying no? Before you knew it, you had pulled out your Visa and recited the expiration date on your card.

Before you start to max out your credit cards, STOP! BREATHE IN! LISTEN! Next, STOP! BREATHE IN! ASK! Ask questions. Ask about the product, the charity, the event. As soon as you have acquired enough information, tell the slick-voiced soul that you will be right back. LEAVE FOR A MOMENT! DON'T GET CAUGHT UP IN THE MOMENTUM! Get a drink of water, walk to the door, then walk back to the phone. Do anything. Just don't get sucked into a trance by his hypnotic, slick, all-knowing tones.

Tell him you'll call him or that you'd like to think about it. If he persists and tries to intimidate, pressure, or shame you, say the following: "Listen, I heard everything you said. You sound like you really know what you are talking about. I respect you for that. Now you have to respect me and give me some time to think about it and to let ME call YOU if I choose to get involved in this (charity, purchase, whatever).

Here is where you may start to see his true colors. The once-polite, slick-voiced, credible-sounding person may turn into a verbal monster with a mean staccato or harsh voice that sounds as though he is annoyed with you because you wasted his time. If you hear this voice, tell him you are through talking and need to hang up now. Then hang up the receiver.

Listen Up!

Be forceful with phone callers. There are times you truly don't have money to spare, and no matter how good the product sounds, its benefits won't pay your bus fare to work and back the next day.

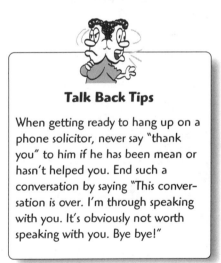

Talk Back Tips

When getting ready to hang up on a phone solicitor, never say "thank you" to him if he has been mean or hasn't helped you. End such a conversation by saying "This conversation is over. I'm through speaking with you. It's obviously not worth speaking with you. Bye bye!"

Unhelpful Helpers

Have you ever made a telephone call to someone to either obtain information or get proper service (discussed earlier in Chapter 16) who was doing neither? Did she have a snippy tone and a snotty attitude, as though she was doing you a huge favor just talking to you? Did the person frustrate you so much that you wanted to crawl through the telephone lines and choke her? Guess what? I can guarantee you that practically everyone else has felt the same way you have!

Be direct. Say "Please help me! Please, I really need help!" If she says, in her snippy, obnoxious little tone, "I m trying to help you!" say, "Well, I don't feel helped. I feel hindered." (Then go off on her as you continue to spew forth how upset you are.) "... I feel upset, I feel terrible, I feel frustrated. I feel like I am lost and that there is no way out! Help me! Please help me!" (This is even more effective if it is done in a crying or whining tone, as annoying as that may seem it seems to elicit more sympathy.)

This type of talk usually causes people to try their best to help you. They will try to hurry up and accommodate you just to get you off the phone. They may even get so weirded out by you that they may call their supervisor into the picture to help, which is what you wanted all along. Now at least someone with less of an attitude can perhaps solve your disaster.

Speaking of attitude, if someone over the phone has a bad attitude and is short or fresh or abrupt with you, you can bet that most likely it has nothing to do with you! Why would it? They don't know you. They can't even see you! Maybe they got into a fight with a boyfriend or wife. Maybe their tummy hurts. Maybe they spent their entire life savings on lottery tickets and lost! Who knows why? But just to make sure it isn't you, check in. Check in nice and friendly. As soon as they give you attitude about it, say "sounds like you're having...": a) "bad day," b) "a long day," c) "a stressful day," d) "a hard day," or say e) "a lot of these hassles are like mine today." Take your pick.

Talk Back Tips

Sometimes, just by acknowledging how the other person feels, you humanize her and her attitude towards you immediately changes for the better. Try it the next time someone gives you an attitude over the telephone, and see if you don't hear a 180-degree vocal change!

Another way to get results is to consistently maintain a sweet, polite, kind attitude with a pleasant tone. Usually, good outweighs evil, so you will see some positive changes in them after a short while. They usually do come around if you can stay strong enough and stay on your verbally positive course long enough.

Go Ahead—Blame It on the Phone!

The phone can be your best scapegoat in allowing obnoxious sounding people, like the annoying verbal abusers we discussed in Chapter 17, off the hook. It enables them to save face, while at the same time allowing you to get your point across so that you won't have to listen to their grating sounds: sounds as annoying as fingers raking across a chalkboard.

Oh No! I Need Some New Eardrums!

You feel as though you are in desperate need of an eardrum transplant after a loud talker blew your eardrums out with his booming voice on the other end of the phone line. What do you do? You blame it on the phone!

Had you known to do this before, you wouldn't have needed that eardrum transplant after all! The second your head jolted away from the phone receiver you should have blurted out, "Your voice seems to be coming across so loudly on this end of the receiver. It's probably the phone! Perhaps if you speak really softly I can hear you better." Whenever they speak in their loud tone, just keep blaming it on the phone until they speak softer. What you are in essence doing is conditioning them to speak to you in a softer voice.

See, you have been a diplomat! You have gotten what you wanted (healthy eardrums) and allowed them to save face at the same time. You have blamed their obnoxious tones on the poor technology of your telephone.

Huh? Huh? Huh? Huh?

What happens if the person talks too softly? Once again, blame it on the telephone. Tell them that your telephone is very sensitive (it's not a lie—all telephones are sensitive and require that the person speak directly into the mouthpiece). And *voilà*—you can finally hear the person. It's magic!

What in the World Did They Say?

You can't understand the person because she mumbles or speaks too fast. Whose fault is it that you don't understand them? Why, it's the telephone's, of course! Tell the problem talker that you don't want to keep asking to have things repeated and that your phone may not be able to pick up everything they say. This, too, is not a lie. Since they mush up their words or talk a mile a minute, how can you, on the other end of your phone, pick up what they are saying? When you tell them to speak extra slowly because you don't want to miss a word they say, their speech often slows down dramatically.

> **Talk Back Tips**
>
> You'll be amazed at how effective this "bad phone" technique can be. Suddenly, Mr. Fast Talker will become the most articulate communicator on the planet! And all his past verbal indiscretions can be blamed on the phone!

Help! I'm Gonna Drown in a Sea of Words!

What about those who are too wordy or who speak too slowly? When you notice them getting a bit too verbose, long-winded, or taking up too much verbal time, tell them that your phone lines can disconnect, so it's very important to get to the point a little faster than they normally would.

Once again, this is not a lie. Phones lines have been known to cut off, especially during a power outage, power surges, snow, hail, rain, or thunderstorms, earthquakes, tornadoes, heat waves, floods, fires, lightning, and other natural disasters. You never know when one of these disasters will actually hit and possibly cut off your connection.

They could be engaging in one of their long-winded tales and then where would you be? Unable to have heard their entire story, because your phone cut out. Who's to say that this wouldn't happen when you are talking to them?

By making them aware of the possibility of the phone line being cut off, you have accomplished your goal—to make them get to the point and not bore you to death! By the way, you don't have to go through *all* the preceding reasons as to the different possible reasons why the phone lines could be cut off.

I Gotta Go, I Gotta Go, I Gotta Go, I Gotta Go!

Before you get all bent out of shape at the poor person who won't get off the phone— the one who doesn't seem to ever want to hang up the receiver when they talk to you—you need to consider two things.

First of all, they might be suffering from a psychological issue known as "separation anxiety." This usually stems from a problem in early childhood, which may deal with early abandonment issues. Obviously this is not your problem and you don't have the time or the energy or the training to deal with this. The second reason is that they like you. They really like you! They like you so much that they don't want the moment to end. They don't like being away from you!

Why have I told you this? Because just knowing this often gives you a new insight so you have a little more compassion and may give them a little more "phone time" than you normally would.

What do you say to the person who won't get off the phone? You have told them a million times that you have to go and they turn a deaf ear to the phone line. Once again, you can blame it on the phone. This option is the same one you used with the person who talks too much. Say that your phone can cut off.

When you know that Mr. or Ms. Chatterbox has called, don't be rude to them. You just never know when they may be revealing something of major importance or value to you. You need to greet them in a cheery and upbeat tone and hear them out for a few moments. But set a time limit—let's say three minutes. When those three minutes are over, politely edge in the sentence "I'd love to spend more time talking, but I have to get ready to leave."

If you can't spit this phrase out because they are so consumed by what they are saying as they talk over you,

Talk Back Tips

Another option for dealing with the long-winded is to click your phone to imitate call-waiting. Tell them that there is another call, that important call you've been waiting for, and that you have to go. Then go!

keep repeating their name over and over in a calm tone. They will definitely get it. If you tell them enough times that you can speak to them only for a moment and really stick to your word, you will be conditioning them. They will eventually understand that when they call you, it's gonna be short and sweet.

I Got Your Machine! You Sound Silly!

Please, please, please! (I am really pleading with you—my hands are clasped together and there is a serious look on my face. My brows are furrowed and I look disgusted!) I, along with everyone else who has called your machine, has cringed when we listened to your answering machine message.

The joke on your machine you think is so funny? Well, guess what? It isn't. It's silly and makes you look ridiculous!

That song you think is so hip because you love the lyric? Well, guess what? Not everyone likes rap music forced down their ears, and surprise—nobody can even hear the lyrics!

I know that your happy little Johnny has finally learned to put some sentences together and how cute you think he sounds. But guess what? Nobody else thinks he sounds cute! They cringe at the sound of his high-pitched, drooly-wet, sing-song tone that nobody but you can understand. When we hear you coaching him to say "Goodbye, talk to you later," we are convinced that you should drag him to the nearest speech therapist as soon as possible!

Phone machines are not designed to reflect your personality or unique talents. We don't care that you can sing opera, play the flute or guitar, or do impersonations of famous people (most of whom are dead). We don't care about the bells or the whistles! All we care about is that you got the message that we called and that you will return our call when you hear our message. That's it! NO MORE! NO LESS!

Listen Up!

You might love the *Brady Bunch* theme, or even the National Anthem, but don't put it on your answering machine—keep it to yourself. I can assure you that you're in the minority. Not everyone shares your unique tastes. In fact, people may well get turned off before they ever meet you.

Time to Change the Message

You have to get this message across to the other person. Granted, this is not the easiest task to do, especially if someone has spent a lot of time perfecting their lousy, ridiculously embarrassing piece of laughable garbage they call a phone message.

Depending on the type of person they are, you may want to start with the humor approach. Try to make a joke out of it. Say something to them connected to their particular sick sense of humor that would make them chuckle. You are in the right arena when you try and match the humor that is similar to that on their phone machine. This often gives you a common bond and allows you entry into the door of the "verbally uncomfortable." Then you might want to say something like, "You know, you and I find this funny, but a lot of people out there don't share our great sense of humor. In fact most of them don't even have a sense of humor." The ignorant message producer will usually smile and agree with you.

Making a Great Message

Remember the old Saying KISS ("Keep it simple, stupid")? Well, do it! The two messages I'm about to give you are the only messages you need to use. They are simple and get the point across. You can expand on them by asking for the times and other necessary information but remember to keep it simple.

The first sample phone message is fairly personal. The second is less personal and more to the point. Choose whichever is more appropriate for you.

> Hello, _____(I, we, name[s]) am (are) not available to take your call at the moment, but if you leave your name, your number, and a brief message after you hear the beep (tone), your call will be returned just as soon as possible. Thank you for calling!
>
> It's not possible to take your call right now. If you leave your name, number, and a brief message, your call will be returned shortly. Please leave your message after the beep. Thank you.

Speak slowly, but not too slowly. Try to sound upbeat, which means don't record it when you are not feeling your best. Draw out each vowel for approximately one second as you flow one sound into the next. Doing this allows you to have more crisp and articulate speech as you record your message.

Talk Back Tips

As soon as you get people on the phone, ask "is it a good time to talk now?" This shows respect for them and their time. It preserves relationships and sets time aside for undivided attention.

Phone Munching

Let's say you have a chicken leg in your mouth when the phone rings. You pick up the phone and say "hello." The person on the other end identifies himself or herself. If it is someone with whom you must preserve a professional image or do business, spit the chicken out of your mouth immediately and then begin speaking. Do not, I repeat, do not, chew, swallow, or take another bite until your conversation is finished and you have hung up the receiver. Under no circumstances do you tell them that they just caught you with a chicken leg in your mouth. Ugh! No! Never!

On the other hand, if it's a friend on the other end of the line, continue chewing, swallow, and then say, "My, you caught me with a piece of chicken in my mouth. I was just having a little bite to eat. Do you mind if I eat while we talk or would you prefer talking later?"

Now, that's class! You have taken them off the spot and made it their decision. For some people, having someone chewing on the other end of the phone is not annoying at all. They never even give it a second thought. They figure, if you're hungry, no matter where you are or what you are doing, for goodness sake EAT! Food comes first! Go ahead. Enjoy yourself!

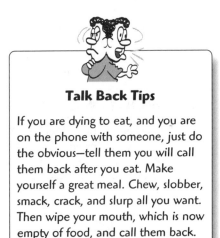

Talk Back Tips

If you are dying to eat, and you are on the phone with someone, just do the obvious—tell them you will call them back after you eat. Make yourself a great meal. Chew, slobber, smack, crack, and slurp all you want. Then wipe your mouth, which is now empty of food, and call them back.

On the other hand, there are those who find eating while on the phone appalling. They find all that smacking and gooing and chewing annoying, distracting, disgusting, ill-mannered, and distasteful. The bottom line is that when you are in business mode, never eat on the phone. When you are in friendship mode, check in to see if it's okay to eat over the phone. If it's not, don't hold it against them. Accommodate them. That's what friends do!

Choose—Them or Me?

People who talk to others while you are on the phone with them are playing some sort of a power trip with you, or they are so unconscious that you wonder what they are doing in your life to begin with. Businesspeople often do this to show you what a big shot they are.

Unless it is *truly* urgent, it is unconscionable and one of the rudest and most disrespectful acts to talk to someone else when you are on the phone.

Sometimes you have no choice. Interrupting the conversation midstream to tell your housekeeper to turn the stove off because you smell smoke in the kitchen so your house doesn't burn down is just fine. Scolding three-year-old Johnny, who thinks it's fun to stick his hands in the toilet or his fingers into a light socket, is understandable. What is not understandable is Johnny interrupting you every two seconds to ask you a question and you responding to every one of his questions—much to the irritation of the person on the other line.

While every book on child language development tells you to answer your child's questions and to respond to them verbally so that they will learn to speak well, they do not mean while you are on the phone talking to others.

If you are the recipient of this type of phone abuse, whether from a child or a third party, tell the person on the other end of the line that you have to go. Tell them that you will speak later. Don't even give them a chance to explain. In essence you are using negative reinforcement. You are punishing them for their rude, ill-mannered behavior.

If they do this over a long period of time, abruptly tell them you have to go and then get off the phone immediately. Believe me—they will finally get the message! When you are on the other end of the line, you can be assured that you will have their undivided attention!

A Return Call Would Be Nice!

Everyone is busy! Actors are busy! Athletes are busy! Mayors are busy! Mothers are busy! CEOs of Fortune 500 companies are busy! Brain surgeons are busy! These busy people still manage to *call back!* Probably the reason they are so successful and so well liked is because they respect others enough to call them back!

Listen Up!

Being "too busy" is no excuse not to return calls! Plenty of important people who have much more on their agenda than you take the time to call back! So if you don't want people to hate you, call them back.

Talk Back Tips

A survey of 100 women ranging in ages from 17 to 68 found that the number one thing that made them feel bad about men was when the man didn't call the woman back after he said he would call.

There is nothing that turns a person off in business or socially then someone who does not respond in kind to a call! It is both rude and inhumane. It creates hard feelings and can destroy business relationships and personal relationships forever.

If someone doesn't call you back and you need to talk to them, keep calling until you get them. If they are rude enough to not return your call, then they won't mind that you are being rude enough to keep calling until you get through to them.

After hearing that you have called for the umpteenth time, they will grudgingly take your call. At that time, you say, "I am so sorry to keep calling you. I am usually not this persistent, but since I never heard from you and I really needed to talk to you, I thought I'd call until I finally got a hold of you."

Stop Calling Already!

Even though they may annoy you, you can't get too upset with people who call too much because they might be lonely, they may really like you, they may be dependent upon you, or they value your judgment, opinions, ideas, and intelligence. Therefore, they regard everything you say as gospel. They want to tell you everything they are doing in their lives in order to get your approval. They want to take everything they are about to do in their lives and run it past you so that you can tell them what they should and shouldn't do and why.

In essence, they call you so much because you have been relegated to the role of surrogate "parent." They don't mean to be a pest, they just feel that they can't function without you.

The Least You Need to Know

➤ You don't have to be at the mercy of slick or obnoxious people who call you just to be "polite." They aren't thinking about you, so you don't have to be thinking about them. Be straightforward and speak back!

➤ If someone who is supposed to help you is being unhelpful, don't let them get away with it. Talk to a supervisor to get the right answer and proper help over the phone.

➤ If you are on the phone and can't understand someone because they mumble, talk too loud, soft, fast, slow, or too much, blame it on the phone (poor sound reception, for example). You'll be surprised at how suddenly their speech improves.

➤ Most people who bombard you with phone calls don't mean to be pests. They are just insecure and needy.

Chapter 21

Verbal Self-Defense in Sticky Situations

In This Chapter

➤ Handling humiliation

➤ Dealing with people who don't like you

➤ Handling those who embarrass you and get into your business

➤ Dealing with those who are opinionated, complaining, invasive, and cheap

➤ Talking to those who won't or can't speak the language

➤ Telling someone their smell offends you

Before I begin this section on what to say in sticky situations, I must warn you that these words are by no means the last word! They are merely designed to give you some general idea of what to say. You can follow them verbatim or you can modify these helpful comments to your particular situation.

As I have expressed several times throughout the book, it is imperative that you know exactly who you are saying these things to. Depending on who you're speaking to, it is sometimes a good idea to keep your mouth shut. But if you do decide to speak, you can be sure that using these words can give you confidence in defending yourself verbally.

Now you will have the words at your tongue's tip to spew forth so that you can say exactly what you meant to say. When people try to pressure you into something you don't want to do, ask you for money, or humiliate you in front of someone, they will be quite shocked by the person they chose as a "verbal victim." When they hear what you have to say to them, believe me, they will never mess with you again! They will have newfound respect for you!

I'm So Humiliated!

Whether it's done by a co-worker or a friend, there is no worse feeling than being humiliated in front of other people. You feel like crawling into a hole and never coming out.

When someone does this to you, it makes you feel two feet tall—like a child. In fact, being humiliated usually makes you regress back to your worst childhood memories—when you were feeling scared, unsure of yourself, unloved, and unwanted. You regress into that insecure, helpless, defenseless child who has no idea what to say. Sometimes, the insecure child decides to fight back and becomes rather defensive and even highly aggressive.

Listen Up!

Being humiliated can upset you so much that you revert to childhood feelings of insecurity. Your responses to the humiliation can also be childish—you fall silent or become highly aggressive. By being aware of these responses, you can learn better how to overcome them.

Now that we are adults, we are supposed to have more control over our emotions and how we handle people who try to embarrass or humiliate us—but we don't! We either hang our heads in shame and say nothing, or we lash out and attack back!

Ouch! Those Coals Are Hot!

When people rake you over the coals or try to berate you in front of someone, they are usually doing this in order to make themselves look good or to assert their power. What they don't realize is that when they do this to you in front of others, they usually end up making themselves look bad. The way they treat you might even influence whether others continue to do business with them.

I have known of several people who stopped doing business with others for this reason. For instance, they have gone to a business lunch with such a person. After hearing him berate a waiter, they wanted nothing more to do with him. So, one soothing factor when a person berates you is that it often backfires.

One thing you can say to a person after he has completely ripped you to shreds is to say "Now that that's over, do you feel better?" Another approach is to completely agree with him. When they say "How could you...?", you mirror right back "That's right, how could I?" Get even madder and sound even more irate and louder as you yell at yourself. Berate yourself more than they berate you. That will not only put a quick stop to their behavior, they will often come around to your aid. They will usually say "Well it's not all that bad!" They will try to comfort and appease you.

It's Not So Funny When It's Me!

When someone makes fun of something you did that you didn't find particularly funny, it can be just as humiliating as when someone rakes you over the coals. When you want to befriend and impress people, you don't want some idiot telling them about the day you looked ridiculous wearing shoes that didn't match and were so out of it you didn't even realize you had done it. You cringe because you don't want the listeners to think of you as a flake or a weirdo who does this all the time. You also don't want them to know the real story—that you were so hung over from the night before you had no idea where your shoes were, so you grabbed any shoes just so you wouldn't be late.

Another example. You are dying inside as you hear your sadistic colleague tell your potentially new supervisors about your *faux pas* at a presentation you gave at a board of directors meeting. She freely and loudly volunteers that instead of saying "that was the interesting part," you said "that was the interesting fart." Everyone was holding their sides, including you. The only difference was that they were holding their sides from laughter and you were holding your sides from nausea. You wanted your new colleagues to respect you, not to laugh at you and see you as a joke.

Since your colleague made you look bad in front of these colleagues, peers, or potential friends, it is best to laugh along with them and lightheartedly say something like:

➤ "You must have a touch of Alzheimer's. That wasn't me—that was your [sister, mother, wife, girlfriend, boyfriend, husband, son, daughter—take your pick!]"

➤ "You sure know how to show people the best parts of person's image, don't you?"

➤ "Excuse me, what's your name again? Do I know you? Are we friends? I don't recall any of my friends who would humiliate someone so badly!"

All the while, you make these statements, remember one major thing—SMILE.

If you didn't smile and gave these lighthearted yet biting answers (which are actually stinging retorts) and yelled, screamed, and accused, your potential new friends or business associates might see you in an unfavorable light. This light can shut both professional and personal doors for you.

Talk Back Tips

Why is it so important to smile in this situation? Smiling diffuses any hostility or defensiveness on your part, which makes you look more appealing in the eyes of others.

Burning Brunts of Jokes

Being the brunt of a joke is much like being the butt of a cigarette. They both burn! Both can destroy your life forever! One destroys you physically, while the other destroys you mentally and emotionally.

When one is constantly humiliated by being teased or made fun of, even in jest, eventually he comes to believe it, because it is constantly reinforced. Not only does the person who is teasing him or joking with him remind him of his shortcomings, but everyone around such a teaser follows suit. Why? Because joking around, no matter how hurtful it may be to the target of the joke, is contagious. Monkey see, monkey do!

One person sees another person making fun of someone, so the others think that person is an easy target. Then they follow suit, in order to amuse themselves, and proceed to verbally torture the person by making them the brunt of their jokes. That person is so overwhelmed (especially if he is a child), that he walks away, cries, and has trouble showing his face publicly.

As an adult, even though he may feel like crying, the minute he is in a group and is singled out as the brunt of a joke more than once, that is one time too many! If you are such a person, put a stop to it! And do it NOW!

Turn to the person who just made the "joke," and put on a huge exaggerated phony forced grin. Point your index finger directly at them. In front of all the other people, say in an upbeat, sing-songy, humorous, joking-like voice: "Now its your turn! From now on, the brunt of all jokes will be directed here!" (pointing to the person). You also have another choice, and that is to act like a disgusted parent. Wave them off by saying "Enough already! It's getting old!" Say it in a calm, bored, monotone with an accompanied bored look on your face.

Now if you want to be a little more high-drama, hold up your hand like a traffic cop does to indicate "STOP!" Say "STOP RIGHT NOW!" Then turn on your heels and leave. Go anywhere—to the bathroom, outside, anywhere. Just walk away. You will be away for only a minute or two to give them time to reflect on their bad behavior. Then you will re-enter the room. They will be in shock! There may be silence. It may be the same initial silence as when a king, queen, or rock star walks into a room! They can't believe you actually came back, especially after thinking you were so upset with them!

Now that you have thrown them completely off-guard, give a big hearty smile. Resume your conversation. Believe me—you'll never be a brunt again!

Listen Up!

When putting a stop to people making fun of you, immediacy is of the essence. You are conditioning others that they cannot speak to or about you in that way! And you're also sending a signal to anyone else who might have been following their lead.

You Don't Like Me! You Really Don't Like Me!

Smile, smile, all the while. Sometimes when a person can't stand you and you smile at her, she suddenly begins to be able to stand you more and more. Talking to someone who you know really doesn't like you is no fun! For some reason, perhaps a past transgression, a miscommunication, unwarranted gossip, or jealousy, she just is not receptive to you. Whenever you are around she gives you the cold shoulder, gives you that "look," or says something nasty, curt, cutting, sarcastic, or snippy to you. You can't make excuses for her any longer. It's way too obvious.

What do you do? Unless it affects your dealings with others or makes you so uncomfortable you feel like crawling out of your skin or pulling her out of hers, you need to bust her on it ! Be upfront! You have nothing to lose! She doesn't like you anyway!

Say something like this: "Look, I know you have some hard feelings towards me. I am not sure why you do. If you care to talk about why you feel so badly about me, I would like very much to get that out in the open once and for all. You never know, maybe there's been a misunderstanding we can clear up."

Notice that you are saying this in a very casual manner. There is no formality here. You are not giving the impression that you are reprimanding anyone or pleading with him. Instead, you are being open and honest and claiming to want to know what's going on.

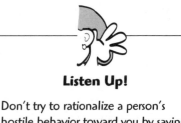

Listen Up!

Don't try to rationalize a person's hostile behavior toward you by saying "that's just the way she is," when she certainly is *not* that way with anyone else. You are only hurting yourself by thinking she is going to change her ways voluntarily.

It is very important to note that while you are making the preceding statement, you should not frown or act too serious or have a tense or uptight facial expression if you can help it. Instead, try smiling at her. Try to have a light and casual facial expression. This will help her feel more comfortable in your presence and even mirror back to your positive and open-faced expression. At least the door is open. She knows you know, and you know she knows. You were big enough to have made the first move, so if it works, you won! If it doesn't work, you still won!

By the way, if she doesn't want to talk about it or resists your efforts to be open and put the matter to rest, chances are she has no reason for not liking you. It's about what you represent to her, not what you actually did to her. So, now that you know your verbal adversary, be aware!

Verbal Vignette

When you know someone blatantly doesn't like you, try this experiment. Look right at him and smile. Keep smiling. Make it a sincere smile. Don't be uncomfortable. Think of something pleasant (obviously, not about him) as you smile at him. Usually, his facial expression will lighten up and he will return your smile with his own smile, as slight and faint as it may be.

When Someone Says Something Mean or Sarcastic to You

By now, after reading this book, you definitely have a good handle on why people say sarcastic and mean things to others, especially when they are unprovoked. The very best way to counteract these hostile words, especially when there was no apparent reason for the person to say them, is to respond in six simple words. The six words are "Excuse me, what did you say?" When one says these six simple words to other people, the other person always stops for a moment to regroup. They do it because they need that momentary pause to call upon the information stored in their brain cells. They need to rewind the imaginary tape of what they said and repeat it verbatim. Their brain goes into automatic, and then they usually go ahead and repeat what they said.

People who intentionally say something nasty or sarcastic to you definitely don't expect you to ask them to repeat what they said. In doing so, you have just gained the upper hand! You have just put them on the defensive in making them explain exactly what they mean by what they said.

Enjoy watching them sputter as they try to worm their way out of their sarcastic or lame comment, or tell you that ever popular lie that they were "only kidding!" Yeah, sure! I don't think so!

Oh No! Tell Me This Is Just a Bad Dream!

You go to a fancy dinner party with a new date. Many important people with whom you do business and socialize are there. You feel great until after you are seated for dinner and notice your piggish date with food slopped all over his face and crumbs and stains all over his clothes, as he talks with his mouth full and both elbows on the table to someone across the table. Moments later, you hear a shriek, which is really a laugh, as the two or them laugh at a filthy joke they are telling to an obviously annoyed gentleman seated between them. It's obvious that both of them are as drunk as skunks.

Talk Back Tips

Never get agitated with the agitated person—this will only excite him and may further exacerbate his already agitated state. By the same token, your calm often helps calm him down.

What do you say to the person who has embarrassed the daylights out of you because he is so out of control (whether out of anger, medicine, or drugs)?

What do you say to the people who have observed your having the daylights being embarrassed out of you?

With regard to the first question, you always must keep a calm and collected tone. Speak to him in terms of endearment by calling his name attached to "honey," "darling," "love," or "baby." This reassures him that he is still liked in spite of himself and his bad behavior. It helps to calm him down.

In the second situation, what you say to those who observed the two people embarrass you is the following,

"It's obvious they have a problem. I am going to try (keep trying) to get them some help." Don't go on and on about the specifics of what they did. Don't talk about other occurrences. Just say what I told you to say. Make it short and sweet and go on to the next subject. Everyone knows what's going on, so you don't have to go into great detail. Otherwise you are crossing over into the line of gossip.

Please, I Beg You, Please Don't Tell Them That!

What happens when someone you knew from the past (including a family member) or someone you may currently know starts to repeat a really humiliating event from your past?

Stop them in their tracks! Don't let them continue. Erase it. Say they must be mistaken or are crazy (in fact, they are absolutely crazy—crazy for bringing it up). If they persist, tell them they are insane. Talk over them. Never admit it. Say it was someone else. It is not a lie. It was someone else. You aren't the same person you were five years ago; you've changed completely.

There Are No Representatives in This House of Speakers!

What do you say to someone who has such a control issue that she takes it upon herself to speak on your behalf, even if you are right in front of her? Well, first hear what she has to say about you, just to see if it would be something that you would actually say. Then set the rules straight and do it quickly! Those rules are that absolutely nobody speaks on your behalf! *"You speak for yourself in the presence of others!"*

How do you get this point across? Well, humor is always a good way, for starters. You can say something like this. "You know, the last person who spoke on my behalf was my mother back when I was two years old and really couldn't speak for myself." Or you might want to say something like "I thought that only lawyers were supposed to speak for you, and only when you pay them!" Be sure to smile and chuckle for added effect as you make these quips. She should get the message.

However, there is always the chance that she won't get it. In that case, you might want to be more direct and tell her politely, "I really appreciate your trying to help me get my point across, as I know that you are as concerned about the matter as I am, but let *me* say what I have to." Usually that will take care of everything.

If she still doesn't get it, and now you are convinced that she is definitely unconscious, you might want to knock some consciousness into her brain by saying the following: "Thank you, but I

Talk Back Tips

As a rule, the calm and direct approach gets your point across. At the same time, you allow the "representative" to save face in front of others. No harm done—everyone is happy, everyone looks good.

don't need an advocate, I can speak for myself and I'm not invisible. I am here." Or "I have a brain, my faculties are together, and I am fully capable of speaking for myself, thank you." If she persists, interrupt her with the two words she probably hears most often: "SHUT UP!"

Hey! Butt Out!

When someone sticks her nose in your conversation and she has no business doing it, you can say the very same sort of things that you said to those who speak on your behalf, only phrase it something like this: "You must have a lot of time on your hands—otherwise you'd be living your own life." You can go the polite and kind route and say "Look, I know that you were probably just trying to be helpful, and I appreciate it, but I really can handle this on my own." If she continues to get involved, yell at her to "Get a life and get out of mine!"

You're Really Nice After All!

Many times you will find yourself talking to someone you don't like—someone against whom you have many prejudices. This is mainly due to someone trashing him. Someone told you all these horrific things about the person, so you end up having an attitude towards him. You are abrupt and cold in your facial and body language.

Talk Back Tips

If you notice a pattern where your direct experience of other people is radically different from what a certain person's venomous words would lead you to expect, take the time to reevaluate that person, and consider taking other judgments he makes with a very large grain of salt.

People have told you such awful things about him, which of course you believed. Now that you spent time talking with the person, you really like him. Your entire demeanor changes and he notices it. He mentions it to you!

What do you say? Should you just be honest and admit that you had heard some not very pleasant things and thought he was going to be a pain to work with? No. You just keep your mouth shut. Say something (which isn't a lie) like "I wasn't really all there when I first met you." It's true! You weren't all there. You had someone else's mind in you—their opinions and values. Now that you got your mind back, you are all there! You learned a valuable lesson and you learned it well.

Don't take anyone else's word for it! Make up your own mind!

You Said What About Me?

What do you do when you hear that someone has trashed you? It's the best scenario when you know that she trashed you and she doesn't know that you know. Let's say you are at a social gathering or even in a work situation. You go up to her and observe how she reacts to you. Is she standoffish? Super-friendly? Aloof? Downright hostile? All of these actions tell you a great deal about her character. If you are near her in a work-related situation, try your best to sit or stand next to her.

Make sure you look at her often and smile. This will make her very uncomfortable and feel very guilty (providing she has a conscience) for what she said about you. Find an opportune moment, preferably if you can get her alone for a moment, and break the news to her: "Hey, I hear you've been trashing me" or "I hear you've said [such and such]; that's not very polite of you." Watch her squirm. Watch her turn red. Watch her sputter and stammer. If you want to resolve any misunderstandings because she might make a good business relation, stick around. If not, adios ex-amigo!

Keep Your Opinions to Yourself!

There are people who are so nasty to be around. They make everyone feel uncomfortable because they are so opinionated. While having an opinion is a good thing, having too much of an opinion and not listening to the opinions of others is a bad thing. If someone is highly opinionated, you need to politely say "I appreciate your opinion. I can understand your point of view. Here's another point of view. What do you think about it?"

If he cuts you off and won't let you speak, if he won't give you a chance to present your opinion or puts your opinion down all the time, what you need to do is the following:

Put your hand out like a traffic cop would to stop traffic. If you are a woman, take out a mirror (a compact will do). Show him his face in the mirror. If you don't have a mirror, find a mirror or say "Go to the nearest mirror, and look in it." Then add, "The person looking back at you is the only person to whom you can tell your opinion, because he will always agree with you. You might as well carry a mirror around all the time and have conversations with yourself."

Are You Mute or Something?

Let's say you meet someone and he is not the talkative type. He is pretty reserved. He gives one- or two-word answers. Talking to him is like pulling teeth. He doesn't reciprocate and ask you questions in return. He just sits there waiting to be asked. He is boring. You sit in silence until you ask the next round of questions.

In order to get the conversation rolling you can try one of the following:

1. Ask him to ask you questions. Make it into a game. Have him ask you a question and then you ask him a question.

2. Tell him to describe the best movie he ever saw or the best experience he had or the most fun he had or the worst time he had. Just get him to say more than two words.

3. Tell him that you feel comfortable when people talk to you and that you would appreciate it if he could help you feel comfortable.

4. Sit in silence too. Say nothing. See who cracks first!

5. LEAVE!

Stop Kvetching Already!

After reading this book, you know what the word "kvetch" means. If people are always complaining to you, after you have tried to be kind and loving and supportive and giving them all the attention you can muster, then you need to refer them to others.

Talk Back Tips

Try this! Whenever a kvetcher complains about other people, say "Let's call them and tell them how you feel about them." That will put a stop to the griping right away!

For example, if they complain about their aches and pains, say "See a doctor." If they go into detail about how bad they hurt, say "Call the doctor now." If they continue, say "Let's call 911 and get an ambulance for you." What you say largely depends on what they complain about.

No matter what their complaint is, agree with them, take it to the extreme, and offer to take extreme measures to rectify the problem as I just illustrated. They will always stop you and this will in turn stop them from complaining—at least for a while. In essence, you are conditioning them to not complain, at least not to you!

Speaking in Different Languages

I give you a lot of credit for trying to communicate with someone who doesn't speak the same language as you. I appreciate your attempts at gesturing to them and drawing pictures, pointing to objects and saying words in their language. *But please don't yell at them. They merely don't understand.* They aren't deaf! Saying it louder isn't going to make them better understand what you want to say.

Verbal Vignette

Many of you might remember the story of how Chevrolet launched its new car, the Chevy Nova. As any car company does, Chevrolet had done extensive market research in advance to make sure that people in different cultures would respond positively to the car's overall design, special features, and name. Unfortunately, the folks at Chevy overlooked one key language problem: in Spanish, "no va" means "it doesn't go"!

Also, when you're attempting to speak their language, please make sure that you are familiar with key words and gestures so that you do not embarrass yourself and inadvertently make some obscene gesture. If you make the American "okay" sign to a Brazilian, you have just caused him to gasp by calling him an ugly word. And don't think you're safe just because a person from England or Australia speaks English. He or she has a different set of gestures and rules that mean different things as well. Saying the wrong word can really cause extreme embarrassment.

What Am I, a Bank?

Asking someone for money is one of the most invasive things a person can do. It can destroy friendships and cause anger and resentment. You really find out a lot about a person and his character when it comes to money matters. It can change and even end personal and business relationships. That's why we have business managers, CPAs, and attorneys to handle money matters.

If people are bold enough to ask you for money, you have to be bold enough to ask them to sign a document stating that the money is only a loan and that they will pay it back by a certain date. As obnoxious as you may think it seems, ask them to leave something of value like a ring or a piece of jewelry, a stereo—anything as collateral for the money. Otherwise, believe me, if they don't pay it back in time, you will be maaaaaad!

If they balk, blame it on past experience. You aren't lying. The past experience is what you read about in this book. Too many of my clients lost too much money but when they held items hostage in return for the money, they got repaid. If they start yelling at you and put you on the defensive, you can yell back "What do I look like, a bank?"

What Part of the Word "No" Don't You Understand?

Many people are so persistent that they often persuade you into doing things you don't want to do—anything from granting them a special favor to getting married! They do this by the Erosion Technique. It's the same one little kids use when they badger their moms to buy them that certain toy or take them to Disneyland. Like a broken record, they ask for it over and over and over and over again, never taking "no" for an answer and not relenting until they finally get what they want!

Tactfully Telling Someone About Body Odor

If someone has bad body odor or bad breath, you have a choice. Either tell that person, or suffocate! It's up to you! What you say depends upon who is doing the stinking! If it is your boss, you might want to say nothing, but send an anonymous care package of mouthwash, toothpaste, soap, cologne, deodorant, and a toothbrush. If it is someone whom you have to be around for a short period of time, who seems on the hostile or unapproachable side, hold your breath, do your business, and run. If you need to be there a while, say "I don't mean to offend or embarrass you, but I want to let you know that you have body odor (or bad breath), just in case you have to get close to a lot of people today." Just know that they might never speak to you after that and they might hate you because of their embarrassment. But in the long run you might have done them the biggest favor. If it's a friend or a lover or a family member, then you can go for it. Tell it like it is! But please be diplomatic!

Ask if maybe they ate something spicy or drank something to cause a heavy odor to come out from their pores. If they deny it, ask if they used a certain cologne or soap. Hopefully, by now they will get the message. They will see that you are trying to allow them to save face. By now they will have moved a few feet away from you or have retreated to the bathroom to brush their teeth or wash up.

Someone Who Never Gets the Bill

When you have been out to dinner with someone numerous times and he never picks up the bill or contributes to the bill, *speak up!* Don't you dare let him get away with it! If you don't speak up then you deserve him taking advantage of you! Don't let your anger stew and stew! It isn't going to do you any good unless you say something.

Listen Up!

Don't make excuses for the tight-wads. If they were truly unselfish people, they would offer to repay you in non-monetary ways, such as sitting for your child, cleaning your house, driving you someplace—anything!

Don't feel sorry for them because they can't afford it and then get upset when they don't reach for the bill. If they truly can't afford it, then they shouldn't be going out to dinner with you in the first place. Of course there is another group of people, many of them in the six- and seven-figure salary range, who are just plain cheap. Tell them to pay up! Don't be so quick to reach for the bill or rescue them from embarrassment. Say, "You know I always get the bill. Tonight, I'm gonna let you do it. Besides, I left my wallet at home." If they say "So did I," say, "Well, I'll wait here while you go home and get your credit card." If you live too far, get the waiter and be assertive. Speak on your friend's behalf. Say "my friend left his card at home, and he's going to give you his name and number and address and will call you tonight with the credit card number." SHAME HIM INTO IT! That will teach him! Of course you might never go out to dinner with him again.

The Least You Need to Know

➤ People who don't like you will humiliate you by making you the brunt of jokes or embarrassing you.

➤ Be very direct with people who speak for you, invade your life, or try to prejudice your opinions.

➤ Never be victimized by people who won't talk to you. Make them accountable for their speaking.

➤ Don't yell at people who don't speak your language. And learn their nuances and gestures so you don't unknowingly insult them.

➤ If people don't let you give your opinion, or they complain all the time, take extreme measures so that it has an impact on them.

➤ When someone smells bad, you are doing him a favor by letting him know about it.

Chapter 22

Verbal Self-Defense in More Difficult Situations

In This Chapter

➤ Breaking bad news to someone and helping them grieve

➤ Communicating with someone who is dying

➤ Dealing with people who lie to you

➤ Dealing with people who say obnoxious things

➤ Talking to people with physical and mental challenges

➤ Dealing with those who hurt your feelings

In Chapter 21, you learned what to say in sticky situations. In this chapter, you learn exactly what to say in even stickier situations—circumstances where you face a major dilemma. In some cases you may be damned if you do, and in other cases you may be damned if you don't. In any case, you have choices. You will learn exactly what to say and how to say it in situations you may have pondered and, perhaps, even dreaded.

Breaking the Bad News

In the days of ancient civilizations, those messengers who were unlucky enough to deliver bad news (sent by, perhaps, a neighboring king) were beheaded. Hence the expression "don't kill the messenger." One of the worst things in the world is to be the bearer of bad news. Even worse than that, of course, is to be the recipient of bad news.

Being the bad news bearer is not a position you seek out. It seeks you out! It just happens! Suddenly, there you are, in front of somebody you definitely don't want to be in front of, telling them something you definitely don't want to tell them.

Unless you are a therapist, physician, policeman, fireman, attorney, or minister, you probably are not trained in how to tell others something horrible or tragic has happened.

Dropping the verbal bomb on someone doesn't always involve telling them that someone has been maimed, fallen ill, or has died. It may involve firing someone, telling them they owe money, a relationship is over, or even that you've found someone else in your life. No matter what the message is, it is devastating, agonizing, and leaves the recipient in excruciating pain.

Thus, the messenger needs to break the news as gingerly as possible. Obviously you cannot be too blunt or direct, no matter how nervous you are, just so you can get it over with and not have to deal with the aftermath of emotion. Put yourself, your emotions, your fears, your hang-ups aside. Don't concern yourself with YOU for now; think of THEM! Don't be afraid to touch them, put your arm around them, hold them, caress them, or lightly massage their shoulder, back, or arm. Let them cry, scream, and wail. Don't say "please don't cry" or "don't scream so loud." Don't let their emotions affect you! Let them get all of their emotions out. Give them the freedom and the opportunity to grieve any way they see fit!

Talk Back Tips

Here's a simple tip for dealing with situations where you have to be the bearer of bad news. Always ask yourself, "how would I want to be treated if, God forbid, the situation was reversed?"

As the bearer of the bad news, you, unlike the messenger of ancient times, will not literally get your head chopped off—but it might be close. You need to prepare yourself for what's in store. Forewarned is forearmed. The person might cry hysterically, to the point that they hyperventilate and faint. You might even have to perform CPR or call 9ll or an ambulance. They might lash out at you and start hitting and punching at you blindly.

You're Not the Only One!

Telling someone their spouse has cheated on them is one of the most awkward and difficult things to do, because there's no way to anticipate in advance what is going on in the mind of the person who you think is being cheated on. For one thing, she may have an open relationship where such behavior is tolerated, so the information will not bother her, but you will have been upset with all the time you have spent trying (unnecessarily) to spare her feelings. Or she may not care. Or she may be glad because she herself is cheating or looking for an excuse to end the relationship. Or she may want to hurt or kill herself, her spouse, or the "other woman."

It is important to know for sure if you are going to reveal such information. How do you know that cheating was really going on? Did some gossip tell you? Were you actually in the bed with them? Did the alleged other woman or man spill the beans? If so, to whom did she spill them? To you? If so, are you justified telling this to the other spouse? And even if the other woman did tell you about the alleged affair, maybe she knows what a gossiping creep you are and just wanted to stir up a little trouble. As far as his admission, maybe he was just trying to impress you with his sexual virility. You might be wise just to keep your mouth shut and mind your own business in this case.

Listen Up!

Here's some golden advice for when you are wondering how to communicate unpleasant news to someone else: if the information is really none of your business, or if the source of the information is quite unreliable, you'll do yourself and the other person a favor by saying nothing. Butt out!

Wives and husbands often can tell whether their spouses have been true, so let them figure it out on their own. Otherwise you risk being verbally beheaded and banished from someone's life. They will usually be too embarrassed and the memory of the situation with be too painful a reminder for them to have you around anymore.

On the other hand, if you don't listen to me and tell, just be prepared to handle them as you would anyone who just found out they just lost a loved one and was beginning the grieving process.

Talking to the Grieving

When talking to someone who is mourning the loss of a loved one, remember that you will be interacting with them at various stages of their cycle of mourning. So they might be in their denial stage or "happy-go-lucky" stage, where it seems as though they don't care at all that someone they were with for 25 years just dropped dead. They are so cheery, making everyone coffee and serving cookies, handing out Kleenex and not shedding a tear. You will obviously talk to them differently than when their wailing stage hits—a day, a month, two years later.

You need to be tuned in and ready for anything. People grieve in different ways and for different reasons. Use soft and tender tones. Say comforting but sincere things. Let the bereaved know you are there for them and follow through on this! Be there when they call, even if it's 2 A.M.! They need you. You offered, so be there!

Dying with Love!

Perhaps the most difficult and heart-wrenching thing to do is talking to a person you know you will never see again alive. Although approaches to dying are highly personal, based upon people's religious and philosophical views, the commonality that embraces all humankind can be communicated through two modalities—sound and touch.

With regard to sound, it is very important to complete your relationship with the person you will no longer physically see. Through your voice, you must say everything you always wanted to, not holding back! If they are lucid, you will have given one another a gift no amount of money could buy.

Verbal Vignette

Music is another way to communicate and help a person die. As my father lay on his deathbed, I had his favorite singer sing his favorite songs. This made him so happy. He was at such peace, after being so restless. The singer massaged my father and held my father's hand as he sang to him, further demonstrating the power of touch.

Never overlook touch—it is one of the most powerful ways of communicating with the dying. We must hold up the example of certain African tribes, where people gather their entire village together when a person is about to die and take turns lovingly caressing, holding, hugging, cuddling, kissing, and massaging the person until they pass in peace. We need to communicate this same attention to those who don't have much time left on this earth.

Gotcha!

You caught someone in a lie. What do you do? It depends on what kind of lie and whom they were lying to. If it was an exaggerated truth said in front a bunch of friends and colleagues to make them look good, who cares? They tell you they made a six-figure income when they really made five. They tell you they went out with three gorgeous women on vacation in St. Tropez, when in reality they didn't even have a date. They know they were lying. You know they were lying. But most likely they don't know *you know* they were lying. As long as they feel they boosted their self-esteem after telling their little white lies, who cares?

On the other hand, suppose someone is doing business with you or you are in any type of social relationship with them (friendship or personal) and they are telling you a blatant lie. I say: BUST THEM! Who the person is and what the lie is should decide what method you use to let them know you caught them. At first, try letting them save face. Especially if you like them, smile, muster a little chuckle if you can, and say, "Come on—what's the real deal?" Usually they will respond with their own humor, returning your laugh, and coming clean with the truth.

Talk Back Tips

Try to think of other humorous things to say to the fibber, such as "You can't fool me. "I was born at night, but not last night." By using humor, you avoid backing the liar into a corner and increase the chances he'll give you the real story.

If they don't come clean, be more direct and serious. Confront them in a calm and civilized, non-accusatory manner, beginning the sentence with "I don't feel comfortable...," "It frustrates me that...," "I have a gut feeling...," "I'm not going to hold it against you...," "I'm not here to judge you...," "I'm not gonna yell at you...," "We all make mistakes...," or "Everyone slips up or does strange things once in a while...." You are giving them a gracious way out. You are letting them off the hook, allowing them to comfortably admit what they did with no severe repercussions from you.

Now, if they are cagey and still won't come clean, be blunt, bold, and insensitive. Don't worry about hurting their feelings. They certainly don't care about yours! Say, "Look, I know you're lying to me. Just admit it!" Or, "Why can't you just admit it? Stop lying! *You are a liar!* You are lying to me! Now admit it, if you have any respect for our relationship!" Usually, if they have any conscience and are not pathological liars or sociopaths or severely psychologically dysfunctional, they will admit it. If not, read on.

Liar, Liar, Pants on Fire! I'll Never Admit I'm a Liar!

We have all experienced firsthand the person who just can't tell the truth no matter what. They have all the evidence staring them in the face, and guess what? They still lie! It's obvious that this person has some major psychological problem they haven't yet dealt with.

You need to be direct and blunt and do so in an angry tone! This type of liar needs a lot of approval from others. That's why they lie. They don't want to look bad in anyone's eyes. So you need to shake a dose of reality into them. Look right at their face; give them an intense stare, because you do not break eye contact with them. In a loud, firm, unwavering tone, say "You are a liar. I caught you. I have all the evidence you lied."

Sweet Talkin' "Ear Candy"

While everyone loves to hear wonderful things about themselves, nobody likes to be manipulated or lied to, especially about themselves. Nobody wants to hear sweet words—"ear candy"—when the person is really saying those words with ulterior motives. They may say these sweet nothings (that is really what the words mean—nothing!) to many different people. They might say these things just to get what they want from that person. Their view: Give people a piece of "ear candy," and they will do whatever you want—go to bed with you, give you that job, give you gifts, anything your heart desires! Of course, the other person gets nothing in return, only a lot of ear candy.

Listen Up!

Like eating too much sugar, hearing too much ear candy will make you so nauseous you'll never want to hear those words again. In the future, whenever you hear sickeningly sweet words bombarding your eardrums, you'll know you are in the presence of ear candy and you should run as fast as you can!

Sexually and Racially Incorrect

When someone makes a racist or sexist remark in front of anyone, they are stupid for two reasons. The first is the obvious. They are showing how ignorant and backward and insensitive they are. Secondly, they are literally taking their lives in their own hands. People have been ostracized, families have been torn apart, people have been jailed, and, unconscionably, even murdered in the name of racism and sexism, as our history books show. This is not a joke.

Unfortunately, even in today's supposedly politically correct climate, many people are still not so politically (racially and sexually) correct. Prejudicial comments and sexist comments still bounce about disguised as humor. This should never be tolerated or condoned under any circumstance. If you are the target of such remarks, how you respond depends on whether it is said in front of you or in back of you.

Please read this carefully. Do not, I repeat, DO NOT GET PHYSICALLY VIOLENT—*ever!* Verbally violent? Well, that's another story, but physical violence is unacceptable.

If the comment was made behind your back, so much the better. Now you know who the clandestine enemy really is. If the comment was made in front of you, especially if others were present, you have a number of options, especially if someone was stupid enough to have made the comment at work. The repercussions—legal and otherwise— are enormous, so you could say nothing and let it be handled by the powers that be. On the other hand, if the comments were made socially or in other environments, here are some things you can say. To a racist:

"Guess what? We're exactly the same color under our skin, we're both blood red." If you really want to play with their mind, agree with their racist joke. Chuckle and say "Yeah, those _____ people (the group they were making fun, of which you are a member) sure are _____ (pejorative term). I'm sure glad you and I aren't one of them!" You will leave them with their mouths hanging open, because you are obviously one of that group and have been bold enough to let them see how obnoxious they are!

Talk Back Tips

There is one advantage to hearing about comments made behind your back: You now know who the person really is. And because the comments were not said directly to you, you can use the information in any way you choose, including not saying anything to the offender. This can be especially useful in business settings.

In response to a misogynist comment, ask "What century are you from?" or "If it weren't for us, there would be no you." You can also have some shocking fun! Let's say as a woman you hear an incredibly vulgar sexual put-down regarding women. Obviously this man does not respect you as a woman, so you shouldn't think twice about what you're about to do. Join in. Laugh real loud. They'll look at you strangely! Say "Yeah, those women—they sure do have great _____ (compliment about one of their anatomical parts that the joke probably referred to.) I liked it better when I was a man! I regret having that operation!" Watch them turn! Watch them squirm!

Come On! Just a Little Bite!

How appropriate that the word *diet* has the letters d-i-e in it, because you are dying to have something you aren't supposed to eat. With all of the pressures surrounding you, you are a hero if you stick to your plan. You certainly don't need anyone sabotaging your efforts, whether they mean to or not. Since it is so easy to give into a persuasive food pusher, you really have to muster up all your verbal and vocal strength as you say a firm and resonant "No, thank you!" If they insist, repeat "No, thank you!," only this time in a louder and stronger voice. If they still persist, say, "Look, I know you mean well, but I really cannot have any of this. I am under a strict program and my health depends upon it. You wouldn't want to be responsible for sabotaging my health, would you?" Most likely that will put a stop to it! Again, you haven't lied. Your health *is* in jeopardy. Besides the physical problems often caused by being overweight, you have to consider your mental health as well. Often people who are overweight are emotionally upset about it— otherwise, they would not be on a diet. People who are overweight are usually unhappy about it. Why else would they be on a diet?

Enough About My Weight Already!

Why is everyone so concerned about everyone else's weight? We live in a society that is obsessed by how much people weigh. How often have you run into a friend you haven't seen in a while and said, "Oh, you lost weight!" Or turned to another person and said, "It looks like she put on weight!" There are even people who will dare to ask, "Have you put on weight?"

If someone needs to lose weight, you don't need to say anything—believe me, they know it! They don't need you to tell them. They have a mirror to do that. But what about if someone moans and groans about how fat they are? What do you say? For starters, don't join their chorus. They can sing and groan it all they want to, but if you do, watch out! They will never forgive you. Never! If you are the one someone told to lose weight, say the following. "Why does my weight disturb you?"

Talk Back Tips

Isn't it amazing how people fawn over you and treat you differently when you look thinner? In my practice and personal life, I know many people this has happened to. But they completely ignore the flatterers. Their philosophy is, "if they didn't like me with a few pounds on, I'm not gonna like them with a few pounds off." And right they are.

That's My Friend You're Talking About!

What do you do if you're in a conversation and you overhear some people talking about another person who is your friend? First, keep quiet and listen to everything they have to say so that you have the entire picture. You may actually agree with them. You might want to join in and add to the conversation by providing a new and different perspective. This might give them insight as to why your friend might have behaved or reacted the way she did.

On the other hand, if they have nothing good to say about your friend, and much of it is based on lies, you have a responsibility as a true friend to stand up and defend! Say "Hey, that's my friend you're talking about!" If they say "So what," you may reply, "Well, I don't appreciate you talking about her that way!" If they are belligerent, you are better off not getting into it with them. You don't want to have any bloodshed over this! The fact that you defended your friend's honor is good enough. I will leave it up to you whether it's best to tell your friend about the incident. You may help them in the long run, although at the moment you are probably going to hurt their feelings.

You Don't Know What You're Talking About!

You have probably been in situations where someone is talking, but they really have no idea what they are talking about, even though they insist that they do. They insist that they are right. They insist that you do it their way. You know that if you do, you will have wasted a lot of time and money. But they are so stubborn, they just won't budge, no matter how hard you try to convince them that their way is wrong. You try logic. You write it down. You have all the evidence in the world. It doesn't matter. They are as stubborn as a mule. What do you say?

First of all, it depends on who it is you are talking to. If it's your boss and they are paying for the mistake, let them knock themselves out and go for it. If you have a lot invested in it, say the following, "You know, I really respect you, and I am sure that you feel the same. We are obviously at an impasse. I am going my way, and I know you will go yours for now. No hard feelings."

Verbal Vignette

Ralph Waldo Emerson once said, "If you do not believe as I believe and I do not believe as you believe, all it means is that I do not believe as you believe and you do not believe as I believe."

Talking to Those with Speaking Challenges

If you are dealing with a person who stutters or has any other type of speech impediment, the absolute worst thing you can do is to finish a sentence for them, even if you are trying to be helpful.

As uncomfortable as it may be for you to watch them struggle, repeat sounds, contort their faces, and even in some cases spray saliva, it is even more excruciating for them to have you speak on their behalf. (The exception is a stroke victim: You may be helping that person retrieve certain words from his or her damaged memory.)

Therefore, you must be patient. Try not to look away, even though you may be feeling embarrassed. Always keep in mind that they deserve to be treated with the same dignity and respect as you.

Talking to Those with Hearing Challenges

When speaking with the hearing-challenged, you obviously need to speak up, even if they are wearing amplification devices—but DON'T YELL! This can cause distortion and a squealing sound in their hearing device. Face them directly so that they can read your lips, and speak slowly so that they can try to understand everything you say to them. DO NOT speak down to them or treat them as though they are mentally challenged. Their intelligence has nothing to do with their hearing problem.

Talking to the Physically Challenged

Unless you have been exposed to many people with physical and mental challenges, you may well feel uncomfortable talking with such people. The key thing to remember is to treat them with respect and never talk down to them. The words of John Merrick, the Elephant Man, say it all: "I am not an animal—I am a man." Even though he was different, he was still a human being deserving of the respect of others.

Talk Back Tips

Don't be afraid to ask the physically challenged about their condition. As long as you do so with respect, you're not being invasive when you ask. In fact, most people with challenges will appreciate your directness and be glad you asked. Be sure to tell them about yourself as well—just as you would with anyone else.

The first thing to remember when you talk to anyone who is blind or paralyzed is never to yell at them or speak loudly or slowly in simple childlike sentences. They are not deaf or mentally challenged. Indeed, those with limitations such as blindness have often developed a sense of hearing much keener than that possessed by fully sighted people. Talk to them like you would to anyone else.

Talking to the Mentally Ill

People with mental conditions are among the most difficult people to communicate with, because you never know where they are coming from. Often you may think that a person is just being difficult or ornery, when in fact that is only the tip of the iceberg. Some are very psychologically disturbed. Some may have mood swings, going from elation to depression in a moment. Others may have sudden bursts of anger or impulsive behaviors that make them do things on a whim. Still others have compulsive behaviors that result in certain rituals, behaviors, or extreme irritation at certain things. And some sad cases are so out of touch with the real world that they hear voices.

Although people with mental conditions may be undergoing professional psychological treatment, there are some things you can do to communicate with them more effectively. It is important to speak in soft, consistent tones, try not to raise your voice. When you are explaining something or telling a story set limits and focus and get to the point as soon as possible. Make sure you limit communication to only basic information and avoid heavy, esoteric philosophical discussions.

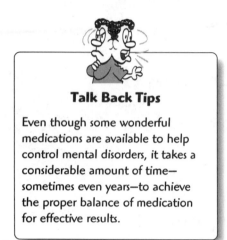

Talk Back Tips

Even though some wonderful medications are available to help control mental disorders, it takes a considerable amount of time—sometimes even years—to achieve the proper balance of medication for effective results.

No—Not You!

When you found out that someone you really liked or loved betrayed you, perhaps no words could express what you were feeling. Perhaps they betrayed a confidence. Perhaps in a moment of anger they threw back at you a confidence you shared only with them. You're numb! Speechless! You feel as though you got kicked in the stomach!

What do you say? After all, what can you say when respect is lost? That's exactly what you say. "I can't believe how I trusted you! This hurts me very deeply. Tell me how I can ever be able to trust you again. I am in a lot of pain right now!"

The key here is to never keep it in! Let it out! Say everything that you are feeling in your heart! Cry! Feel the pain! Speak the truth!

I Admit It! I Did It!

In our culture, the things we value above all else are honesty and integrity. We appreciate remorse. We are quick to forgive. We open our hearts to those who can take an honest look at themselves and see what wrongs they committed, admit them, and attempt to make them right. This is the basis of how we judge others and even more important, how we judge ourselves.

Listen Up!

When you are preparing to come clean about lying to someone, don't worry about her reaction. You can't control it. Focus only on doing what you know to be the right thing, which is admitting that you made a mistake.

Whether you are admitting you cheated, lied, or made a mistake, just remember that it takes a great deal of character and inner strength to admit you are wrong, make an apology, and have remorse for what you did. It takes an even stronger person to want to make amends for the situation. To admit you did something wrong, the first step is to not think about the other person's reaction. They very well might hate you and want never to deal with you again. But so what? You are a real person doing what you have to do. You came clean and you are a better person for it. You learned, and you probably won't make the same mistake again. If they reject you, tell them you understand, as painful as it is, and accept their verbal wrath. You've spoken your piece. You've admitted you're wrong. Let them vent! Whatever happens now is in their hands!

Don't Judge a Book by Its Cover!

What do you say when someone underestimates you? This often happens when people have known you for a long time. They don't realize that the soft spot in your brain has fused together since you were an infant, that you made it through kindergarten and actually have a Ph.D. in physics. But it doesn't make a difference. To them you will always be little Baby Jane, and babies don't have opinions. Let's say you are a female attorney and a male attorney is prejudiced against you and doesn't take you seriously, even though you graduated number one in your law school class from Harvard. Let's say you have a foreign accent. You are a highly qualified American board-certified foreign-born physician, but a patient doesn't want you to touch him. He thinks you don't know what you're doing. He underestimates you! What do you say?

First of all, you acknowledge their feelings. You embarrass them by busting open their prejudices so that everything is out in the open. There is nothing to hide. Then tell them why you are qualified (for example, list your credentials) and then ask if they will allow you to show them or help them.

For example, Jane says, "I know you still see me as little Baby Jane, but I have grown up, have a Ph.D. now, and know I can help you in this community project. I have worked on one similar to this one in Boston and it was very successful."

The female attorney says, "I know that some male attorneys still have an issue with female attorneys. They can't help it. I'm not making you wrong or putting you down. It may even be a natural competitive thing for some people. Maybe it's a personal thing with me. In any event, I feel that there's a lot of tension between us. All I want to do is contribute my expertise and do my best. If you are concerned about my abilities—I notice you always contradict everything I say—let me say that I have a very open mind, I am highly adaptive, and I learn fast. In fact, I graduated first in my class at Harvard. So let me help you help the company.

As for the physician, he needs to say the following. "I know that many people feel uncomfortable with foreign doctors, especially doctors who come from my country, because my country is very poor. You might wonder how a doctor from such a poor country came here to study. I've been in the

Talk Back Tips

Never underestimate the power of being direct with others. You might feel that you are just making trouble, but in fact the trouble is already there the moment they treat you inappropriately. All you are doing is bringing issues to the surface so that they can be dealt with intelligently.

United States for 20 years, I went to medical school here, where I also did my training. Now I am licensed in cardiology and have a faculty position at New York University. If you would like to check my credentials, you are free to call the medical board to verify what I am telling you."

Even though this might seem like a lot of work, there are no secrets. These three people have said what the others were thinking, so there were no "I think that you think" games, and everyone can get on with the business at hand.

The Least You Need to Know

➤ If you have to break bad news to someone, be prepared to take the brunt of their grief and allow them to act out their pain and initial shock in any way they choose.

➤ Words, music, and touch can be beautiful ways of communicating during someone's final days.

➤ There are all kinds of ways to deal with people who lie to you, depending upon their motives and how remorseful they are.

➤ Unexpected jolt humor is usually the best way to handle racial and sexual comments and weight insults.

➤ Never let anyone who betrays you off the hook without really letting them know how it has devastated your emotions and your trust in them.

➤ Get things out in the open when you did something awful. Even if you're embarrassed, 'fess up. If someone looks down on you or doesn't like you, let them know you know how they feel.

Chapter 23

Verbal Self-Defense Can Save Your Life!

This is one of the most vital chapters in the book because it can literally make the difference between whether you live or die! It tells you how to incorporate everything that you have learned thus far in the pages in this book and use it to your verbal advantage.

Everyone should know the information in this chapter! The split-second decisions you make about the verbal strategies you choose can change the course of your entire life within seconds! Although I cannot guarantee that these verbal self-defense techniques are foolproof, I can assure you that they can help protect you in most circumstances most of the time. You must be discriminating, cautious, aware, and alert, always using your own good judgment, so that you can avoid situations that put you in jeopardy.

In this chapter, you learn how to be more conscious of being in potentially disastrous circumstances. You learn how to possibly prevent disastrous consequences, from road rage, to being talked out of your life savings, to being mugged or raped. I have provided you with some very effective weapons to defend yourself against potential life-threatening situations. These weapons have saved the lives of others. Hopefully, you will never have to use them. But read and take heed!

Listen for Verbal Red Flags!

If you keep your mouth shut and really listen to what a person says, he will usually reveal just about everything you need to know about him if not more. If you just remain silent, as difficult and as uncomfortable as it might seem to you at first, you will be amazed at what you learn! You will clearly see who this person really is—not who you want them to be. In fact, this is one of the first things those in the law enforcement field learn. When interviewing, "Be quiet! Let them talk! They'll tell you what you need to know!"

When you keep your mind and ears open and pay close attention to everything the person says—every morsel of sound, every joke, sneer, cough, and tone—you will save yourself a lot of grief, emotional torment, money, and perhaps even your life. Let's say you are talking to someone you don't really know that well, or maybe just met. Just by objectively observing how a person talks and what he talks about during the course of the conversation, you can gain a lot of insight into his personality.

Talk Back Tips

The next time you meet someone, listen to him objectively with different ears. You might pick up things you ordinarily never would.

This happened with a client of mine. She met a business associate who talked about his wife ad nauseam and could never answer questions without saying "we" (even when not appropriate). My client pegged him as being henpecked. After finally meeting his wife, she learned she was correct. The moral of this story is that we know these things. It's not our sixth sense—it's our ears. We listened between the lines!

What You Hear Is Not Always What You Get!

One day a great looking, Armani-clad, well manicured, great-smelling gentleman came into my office. He said he was an "investor." He was referred to me by a dear friend who swore by him. Even though his outward image was a 10, upon listening to him, his inward image was beginning to drop into the 5 range. Being 100 percent alert to everything he said, I heard a lot of inconsistencies. He contradicted himself a lot. He lied about his background. At first, he told me that at ten years old, his parents were killed, so he lived with his grandmother, was dirt poor, grew up on the streets and made himself what he is today. Towards the end of our conversation, he said he came from a wealthy family in Connecticut, where his parents still live. He also joked a lot. When I asked him what it was that he as an investor actually did, he gave a hearty laugh and said in a joking tone, "I take people's money and run."

When my friend called me later to ask me what I thought of the "investor," I said that I wouldn't trust him in a million years. She got mad at me and told me I was stupid not to invest my money with him. After all, he was so well respected; all these prominent people used his services. She said he was a great investor. I told her that after listening to him, I thought he was a phony. He contradicted himself. And for someone who was supposed to be so savvy in the financial word, why did he mispronounce so many big words?

My friend got mad at me and stopped talking to me, until two months later. Apparently, that man in whom she had "invested" got "arrested!" He was a fraud! I knew it all along—just by listening carefully. I knew it by his contradictory stories. His last comment—his "joke"—said it all. As Sigmund Freud said, "there are no jokes, only truths." How right he was! "I take people's money and run!" He definitely told the truth here! It is no joke that he is doing time!

Listening Between the Lines

When you listen between the lines, here are some things to watch for and what they mean:

➤ Sarcastic jokes that have a ring of truth to them. This is a subconscious desire to confess or to let you know what is going on. The person is also testing you. By throwing out this comment, he is observing how you are going to react if it were to happen. If you return his smile or chuckle, he regards you as "safe" and feels more comfortable around you.

➤ Contradictory statements or inconsistencies. These are unconscious leaks in information, involving either letting down or putting up his guard, depending upon what truth or lie he tells you during the conversation.

➤ Bursts of anger. The person is out of control and angry because he is on the defensive and doesn't want to be found out.

➤ Going off on tangents. This is another diversionary tactic designed to distract the listeners in hopes that they will forget about the uncomfortable or touchy subject they are discussing. He is shifting the focus elsewhere.

Listen Up!

As paradoxical as it might sound, if someone gives you too much detailed information, he is probably covering up something. Nobody goes into minute, graphic detail unless he has something to cover up. It is a distraction or a diversion tactic.

Put a Lid on It!

As it says in the Bible, the power of life and death rests on the tongue. If you aren't conscious of what you are saying, you can destroy your own life and the lives of others. We are all too familiar with the devastation that occurs when someone gossips about us or betrays a hidden confidence. But what happens when we betray ourselves? What happens when our own big mouths leave the mouths of others hanging open because they are so shocked by what we have just revealed to them?

Unfortunately, a decade or two ago, the "Me Generation" was taught that there was no holding back and that we should let it all hang out. You could tell all—let the real you out at all costs—cry, scream, hit, regress, breathe, or chant as you verbally expunged yourself from the pain of all your inner demons. This is great if done in the privacy of your therapist's office, but not so great if it isn't. The fallout from it can be devastating.

Sure, you want to be open and honest, but some things are better left unsaid. We all have boundaries and some should not be crossed. No man wants to hear that you slept with 100 men before him, especially when you're lying there in the bed cuddled right next to him. No one has to know the details of your child's ill-fated vomiting attack during church.

I Wouldn't Mouth Off If I Were You!

Even though I am a firm believer in letting your emotions out (when appropriate), there are times when you just have to swallow your pride. Sometimes it is more appropriate to just shut up, swallow your words, breathe in, blow it out, shut up, clench your teeth, shut up, bite your lower lip, shut up, bite your tongue, shut up, shut up, shut up.... Why do I seem so adamant about trying to get this point cross to you? It is because I think that you will have a much better time at home or with your friends, rather than in a jail with a bunch of other inmates. It can happen to anyone, but don't let it happen to you. *Never* mouth off to a government official or to a judge (if you do, you'll probably never see the light of day).

So what do you do instead of getting a brain hemorrhage? You do the Tension Blow-outs combined with the Fantasy Technique and you'll be fine!

Your Speech Is a Loaded Gun

After reading this book, you know that words and tones can kill you emotionally. Saying the wrong words can break someone's heart and upset her to the point that she becomes mentally, emotionally, and physically incapacitated. Sometimes you know that your tone of voice can get someone all riled up or agitated or make her miserable. Other times you can say something unknowingly or something just to vent your own anger, which can cost you your life. In the next few sections I provide a number of scenarios on how violence was most likely provoked because of someone's unconscious action, being unaware of how she communicated to the other person. Since everything in life is based on stimulus and response interaction, if you are giving a negative or hostile stimulus (even unknowingly) by the way you are talking to someone, in most cases the response you get will not be very pleasant.

I'm sharing these examples with you to expand your awareness—to protect you, so that you don't end up making the same mistakes that the people in these scenarios do. Their mistakes cost them a great deal, including their lives! Perhaps by seeing what they did wrong, you won't do what they did, and that might just save your life!

Topics That, When Mentioned in Anger, Can Declare Verbal War

You can declare verbal war when, in anger, you mention another person's

➤ Mother or father

➤ Male or female companion

➤ Sister or brother

➤ Child

➤ Body part(s)

➤ Attitude

➤ Intelligence

➤ Honor

➤ Reputation

➤ Material things

Road Rage! Theater Rage! Outrage!

Take the everyday pressures people face, combine them with the time they spend in their cars, the increase in the number of cars on the road, the lack of courtesy and manners in so many people, and the different levels of driving skills, and what do you have? R-O-A-D R-A-G-E! Road rage is the buzzword of the year; all the magazines and talk shows are talking about it. Newspapers and news broadcasts report on the increasing number of road rage incidents.

Road rage is nothing new. It has been going on since the days of Henry Ford, when the automobile was first invented. You've seen those old silent films where one car is trying to run the other one off the road in the big "chase" scene. The only difference now is that people are more frustrated, madder, and meaner.

There is no question about it—with all of the pressures we go through in life in our complex society, there's a lot more stress. When you've had a bad day at work the only thing you really want to do is get home and relax. So, when someone gives

Bon Mots

Road rage occurs when people use their vehicles as instruments of anger—cutting people off, tailgating, sideswiping. In more extreme cases, people even use direct confrontation, physical fighting, and weapons.

Listen Up!

No matter what someone does to you on the road, scream, yell, or let them have it verbally in your car with the windows rolled up so they can't hear you. Never speak directly to them. Don't try to catch or provoke them. Your life is more important!

you a hard time on the road (cutting you off or tailgating you) it is only natural to get angry. However, the other driver might push you over the edge, to the point of road rage. In this case you might want to get out of the car, verbally confront the other driver (who usually reciprocates with as much intense anger), and doing some bodily harm (using fists or a weapon). If you follow your anger and not your head, the consequences could be dire!

Although road rage typically occurs in big cities such as LA, where there are millions of drivers, it has been reported everywhere, even in small rural towns.

So how should you handle an incident when it occurs? Let it go! Let it blow! Give 'Em Hell and Yell in your car—alone. Do Visual Fantasy, and Tension Blowout. Be done with it. Concentrate on where you have to go and on more important things in your life.

SHHHHHHHHHHHHH!

Just as road rage has recently plagued our society, so has "theater rage." Although I don't know of any reported deaths resulting from theater rage, that is not to say it cannot happen. Theater rage simply occurs when someone talks during a movie or play. They may be loving the movie as much as you are, but they are sharing their opinions, instead of waiting until the movie is over.

Unfortunately, in the age of television, VCRs, computers and CD Roms, many people don't go to movies very often and are, therefore, used to being able to talk during a film. Oftentimes these people have to be reminded that they are in a theater and are disturbing other people. People don't mind being told to keep it down, but they do mind being reprimanded like a whining child or a barking dog and told loudly to be quiet. So what do you do? Be real polite. Smile. Say "I'm sorry, but could you talk later? Thank you." Smile. Say this in a soft and pleasant tone. If you say it in a sarcastic or angry tone, you might as well have said SHHHHH. If they don't oblige, move! If the theater is crowded, tell the usher! Let them handle it. That is what they are there for.

I SAID NO TALKIN'!!

Gone are the days of Mrs. Smith saying "Johnny, stop it! I want you to stop talking and stop interrupting this class. You have always been a nuisance and cause the class to waste so much time. If I have to tell you again, I am going to send a letter home to your mother telling her how bad you are."

Teacher violence is on the rise. Teachers are getting beaten and even killed by their students left and right! Why? I wanted to know, so I asked a group of kids caught abusing their teachers. Ranging in age from 8 to 17, these kids gave me some pretty consistent answers. "She didn't respect me." "She dissed me in front of the class." "She picked on me all the time." "She hated me." I asked them what they would have wanted their teachers to have done. Every single one of them answered "Respect me." Although I was horribly against what they did, I can see their point. Had the teacher called them out of the room, spoken to them, and not embarrassed them in front of their friends, it would definitely have been a different story. So if you are a teacher or know any teachers, please share this information with them. It came directly from the mouths of the "teacher abusers."

Reason Before You Start Teasin'

Just as teacher violence is on the rise, so is school violence in general. The recent wave of school shootings, with children killing other children, is both shocking and appalling. But deeper investigation into the psychological profiles of these young killers indicates that they have something in common. They were all teased and tormented by their peers. Toxic words were hurled at them on such a continuous basis that it ripped their self-esteem to shreds. They lashed out!

Sometimes they lash in! With teenage suicides being at an all-time high, practically every suicide note contains some references to being cut off from people and being teased by others. This is a worldwide phenomenon, as such suicide notes have also been found among the belongings of teens in Japan and in Germany. All this because of mean, nasty, horrible words that insensitive people unknowingly use in their attempt to feel cool or superior to their unacceptable peers. The raw reality is that instead of using metal bullets they used verbal bullets to kill the "insides" of their peers. In their tortured and hopeless minds, all the kids had left to do was to finish the job, physically, and destroy themselves on the outside.

Verbal Vignette

Schools are becoming so sensitive to teasing that a program called *Bully-Proofing Your School* has now been taught in over 200 schools. More schools need to take it upon themselves to deal with this problem and teach children how to be nice to one another. Otherwise, there will be a lot fewer students to teach!

Tones Can Kill

Throughout this book I stress the importance of how you should say things. Your tone of voice can be a killer. If you talk to someone in a rough-edged, harsh-sounding, loud voice that gives the impression that you are angry, watch out! You might not even be angry, but the fact that you sound that way makes others feel like you are, and so you are in for their bad attitude. If you aren't aware that you sound the way you do, you are probably wondering why they are having a bad attitude. In defense you will probably return their bad attitude until a full-blown fight ensues.

This happens often with customer service representatives after a long day at work. They are in bad moods and have an attitude reflected in their tone of voice. You react in a hostile manner, they react to your hostility, and the cycle begins. So the next time you hear someone with a bad attitude, don't take it personally! Try to lighten them up through a kind tone, a kind word, and a smile. Always be aware of your tone when you talk to anyone, especially people you don't know who are in a position to be of service to you, so that you won't come across with "attitude."

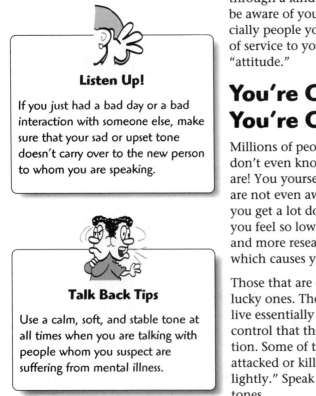

Listen Up!

If you just had a bad day or a bad interaction with someone else, make sure that your sad or upset tone doesn't carry over to the new person to whom you are speaking.

Talk Back Tips

Use a calm, soft, and stable tone at all times when you are talking with people whom you suspect are suffering from mental illness.

You're OK, I'm OK. OK, You're OK

Millions of people suffer from mental disorders and they don't even know it. They just think that's the way they are! You yourself might have a mental disorder that you are not even aware of. Sure, you get hyper, but at least you get a lot done. And then there are those days when you feel so low that you just can't get out of bed. More and more research shows that it is your biochemistry which causes you to suffer those mood swings.

Those that are diagnosed with mental disorders are the lucky ones. They can be treated with medication and live essentially normal lives. But some are so out of control that they can't afford or don't take their medication. Some of them are dangerous. Some have even attacked or killed people. The message here is "tread lightly." Speak to them in calm, non-jarring, polite tones.

Non-Words Can Kill

In some cultures, it is not nice to look a person in the eye and speak or initiate a greeting, especially for a woman. Touching a person is a no-no. Speech is abrupt, limited to business only, serious-faced and business-like, and perceived as not being very friendly. In other cultures, this behavior is unacceptable and perceived as insulting, condescending, and disrespectful. When these two cultures get together, the possible negative consequences of what can happen are inevitable. In fact, that has happened throughout the U.S. A number of murders have occurred in situations where people were simply ignorant of the social dynamics of a particular culture (such as handshaking, touching, warm greetings for males and females, smiles, openness, lots of friendliness, and social interaction). Since the universal language is warmth, smiles, and attempted verbalization, doing these three things with anyone, no matter where you are from, can save your life!

Your Mouth Can Save Your Life

Just as your mouth can kill you, it can also keep you alive. If you know what to say in the right circumstances, often circumstances that are beyond your control or are life-threatening, you can save your life. In the rest of this chapter, I show you how. I give you some life-saving speaking and vocal techniques. I also present you with some rather unpleasant scenarios in which you can use these techniques to thwart your perpetrator. Read this section several times. I want the information to stick in your brain. Just in case anything like this should ever happen to you (heaven forbid), you will be more likely than anyone else to survive! Above all else, remember that you still must use your good judgment and trust your instincts. This is merely an aid to help you in addition to doing that.

Verbal Kicks, Vocal Chops, Tonal Blocks

A verbal kick occurs when you push down on your abdominal muscles as though you are going to have a bowel movement and open your mouth and as loudly you can, drawing out each vowel clearly, and say "GET OUT OF HERE RIGHT NOW! I MEAN IT!" or "WHAT DO YOU WANT?" A verbal kick gives your voice the quality and resonance it needs to show someone you are not a weak person. You are a formidable opponent. You are not a victim and you mean business! Often it is all you need to get your perpetrator to leave.

Vocal chops occur when you speak in a staccato, marching-like abrupt tone. This is extremely effective in getting your point across, as it is like a series of verbal exclamation points or pellets being hurled at someone!

Tonal blocks come in handy when you just have to be quiet. You might want to scream your head off, but you know instinctively that it will get you killed. To control yourself, take a sip of air in through your mouth and hold it. Keep holding it for as long as you possibly can and let it out. Then do it again. This will at least stabilize you and keep you in control and level-headed as much as you can be under the circumstances.

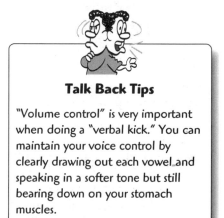

Talk Back Tips

"Volume control" is very important when doing a "verbal kick." You can maintain your voice control by clearly drawing out each vowel and speaking in a softer tone but still bearing down on your stomach muscles.

Be Nice!

This may sound weird to you, but be nice to your perpetrator. Doing so can often save your life. Speaking in soft tones and being friendly, even when the situation is the opposite of friendly, has saved many lives. When serial killers and murders were asked why they spared the lives of certain victims when they had the opportunity to kill them, they all said "they were nice to me." So, before you make the decision to do what you have to do, first be nice. Speak softly and kindly. It just may be the deciding factor as to whether the sicko spares your life!

To Catch a Thief!

Robbers case the joint to check out the premises they are robbing. In the same way, people are checking you out. Studies show that if you walk like a victim you'll be victimized. The same goes for talking. If you sound like a victim, you are more likely to be victimized. But now that you have all of the verbal self-defense strategies in this book, you don't have to be.

That's why a potential robber might ask something like "What time is it?" Engage them in conversation and look directly in their face, preferably in their eyes. Here is where you *do* look in their eyes as a sign of power. It signals "I will *not* be intimidated!" Then say, "You know, I'd tell you the time, but my watch never works. I need to get it fixed, but I have to get some money first because I lost my job and it's hard for me to work now because I've got a bad back and my sister's in jail and now I have to take care of her kids...." Believe me, he'll think you're a nutcase and try to find someone else to rob.

Listen Up!

Most of the time, you can't be sure whether people are carrying weapons or if they are stronger than you. So the best policy is usually: *get away.*

If he comes after you anyway and there are people around, give him a verbal kick, then Give 'Em Hell and Yell. Usually that will work and someone will come to your rescue.

If you caught him red-handed and you are sure he's not carrying any weapons, confront him, then Give 'Em Hell and Yell and a good verbal kick. Grab the goods. If he resists, do the obvious—run and call the police.

Rape

A client of mine shared this incident, which saved her from being raped. In essence, she turned the tables on her perpetrator. He had a knife to her throat as he told her to undress. In a soft, calm tone she said "don't worry, I won't hurt you." The rapist was so taken aback by what she said that he lost his footing. She ran and saved her life. This proves again that your life does rest on "the power of your tongue," as the Bible so eloquently puts it.

Once again, please take all the necessary safety precautions. Be alert. Use good judgment. When you see someone approaching you, if there are people around, confront them loudly or even sing. If they think you're a nutcase they usually won't bother with you.

Date Rape

A rape is no less a rape just because you know the person who raped you. In fact, it is more of a rape, because they know you, and you are not an impersonalized object, which a rapist can turn you into—you are a personalized human being to the date rapist, so they have even less regard for you than does the generic rapist.

Listen Up!

Additional strategies to prevent date rape: stay where there are other people, such as a restaurant, club, or mall. Also talk, talk, talk, and get to know, know, know. Don't be a victim!

This subject is so touchy because there are many semantics involved, as well as circumstances and possible miscommunication. The bottom line is that date rape may happen despite these efforts, but if you would never consider sleeping with the person, or if you would consider it but not until you were more committed, don't even put yourself in a compromising situation. Don't be alone with the person—not even in a car. If you are in a car alone with them, make sure you know the route you're taking and that you won't be stopping for anything. Also make sure that you have enough money to get home.

Sex Talk—Before It Gets Too Hot to Handle!

Even though everyone is preaching "safe sex," it is the last thing you want to talk about "in the moment." When things are getting hot and heavy and you've finally decided to take that final step with your partner, the last thing you are thinking about is an AIDS test! One of the hardest things to do is to bring up the topic of safe sex.

Talk Back Tips

In a recent survey among college students, only 40 percent admitted to using a condom during sexual intercourse.

In the heat of passion, especially when skin touches skin, you might feel so overwhelmed by desire that you find it almost impossible to break out of the moment and say anything. But let's face it, not talking about it and not doing something about it can kill you! So, here's what you say: "I feel so uncomfortable bringing this up, but in this climate of AIDS and all, we have to talk about it. I'm sure you don't have it, but I think we both should get tests so both of us will feel uninhibited." Then do it. You'll get the results the next day! After all, you've waited this long!

Listen Up!

Always use a condom that contains Nonoxynol-9, a chemical spermicide that has been shown to protect you from the AIDS virus. In addition, you may want to purchase some spermicidal gel that contains this ingredient and apply it according to the directions.

Wear a What?

We aren't embarrassed when it comes to getting stark naked in front of another person, but we are terribly embarrassed when we have to talk about using condoms! Obviously it helps prevent the spread of HIV, but you really have to be just as concerned about other sexually transmitted diseases that, if left untreated, can also ruin someone's life. So unless you have a 100 percent thorough clean bill of health, have had every test and every orifice checked and re-checked, are married, committed to one person, and *not cheating* (and I really mean it—no flings, no oral sex, not even a pat or a touch), then and *only* then can you abstain from wearing a condom. Otherwise you are playing with your life and someone else's. In the "Talk Back!" section, I will give you the excuses men use as to why they don't want to wear a condom and what his partner should say in return. The bottom line is that there should be *no excuses!*

Talk Back: Excuses for a Man Not Wearing a Condom

(Man) I never wear one.

(Partner) It's time to start now.

(M) I don't like the feel of it.

(P) The new ones are super thin; the sensation's exactly the same.

(M) It feels like you're taking a shower with a raincoat on.

(P) At least you'll have a super thin raincoat and you'll be able to feel the sensation.

(M) I don't have AIDS.

(P) I'm sure you don't. But there are other things you might not know you have that your last relationship passed on to you.

(M) That's insulting.

(P) The last thing I would ever want to do is insult you. I care about you and I am protecting the both of us.

(M) I can't believe you think I sleep around.

(P) I don't, but you've been with others in the past.

(M) I can't fit into one.

(P) You're in luck! Now they come in large and extra large.

(M) Let's not. (referring to wearing a condom)

(P) Okay, Let's not! (referring to making love)

(M) We'll be fine.

(P) That's right, because we're gonna have protected sex.

The Least You Need to Know

➤ Listen between the lines. Listen for inconsistencies in someone's story and listen to how he or she says things.

➤ Be conscious. If you don't control what comes out of your mouth, you can end up in jail or killed, or your words can destroy the lives of others.

➤ Road rage, fights, school rage, and other rages can be controlled by knowing what to say.

➤ The tones you choose and what words you use can often save your life in dangerous situations such as rape or robbery.

➤ There are no excuses for not having safe sex. Your life depends on it.

Chapter 24

Verbally Defending YOU Against YOU!

> **In This Chapter**
>
> ➤ Saying the right things about yourself to win others over to your side
>
> ➤ What to say to yourself to stop feeling uncomfortable around others
>
> ➤ Deciding what personal things you should reveal about yourself
>
> ➤ Why we reveal our personal details
>
> ➤ How to stop feeling bad about your past and feel great each day

You have learned what it takes to verbally defend yourself against all different types of verbal enemies. You now know what to say, how to say it, and who to say it to. You have the confidence to pull out any tactic you've now mastered. You are able to choose automatically the technique that is most appropriate to verbally slay your opponent. You know how to keep on going. You know how to slide from one technique into another, until one of them finally clicks and you come out the victor in verbal battle.

Now that you are an expert at verbally defending yourself against others, the time has come to learn to defend yourself against, perhaps, your most powerful and formidable opponent—YOU!

All too often in the art of verbal warfare, we are not our best ally. In fact, we can be our own worst enemy! Unfortunately, we know this all to well. Even though life is a series of losses and wins, when we win some of the battles, we are in such shock—we can't believe that we have won—that we sabotage ourselves and end up losing a battle we fought hard to win. We don't do it purposely. We do it unknowingly, out of ignorance. We do it usually because of some deep-rooted psychological issue concerning entitlement. We might not feel as though we are entitled or deserving of winning the battles in our lives, and so we find it impossible to relax and be peaceful!

What Did You Say? That's What They Think!

The best verbal self-defense you can use against your most formidable verbal ally is when you say nice things about you to you. When you speak highly about yourself, others will follow suit.

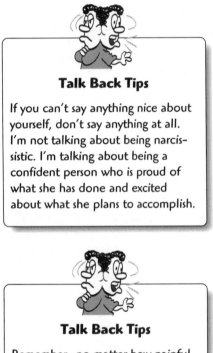

Talk Back Tips

If you can't say anything nice about yourself, don't say anything at all. I'm not talking about being narcissistic. I'm talking about being a confident person who is proud of what she has done and excited about what she plans to accomplish.

Talk Back Tips

Remember—no matter how painful it is, saying out loud what causes you pain does not make things worse. It is the beginning of resolving the issue.

As I said earlier in this book, when I was in college, we girls who lived in the dormitory and dated the college boys had a rule: "If a boy tells you that he is a jerk, believe him—he definitely is one." The same holds true with you. If you say you are a jerk, perhaps you are keeping a secret that others don't know. Maybe you are a jerk!

Maybe you might have a nice, pleasant, friendly exterior, but deep down inside you might be an awful, manipulating, seductive slime. Therefore, if you say you really aren't a very nice person, you probably aren't. After all, who knows better about you than you?

On the other hand, there are a lot of really nice people out there who, in an attempt to appear humble and not "big-headed," sabotage themselves by putting themselves down. Unfortunately, if you say "I'm such an idiot!" or "That's just my luck!" enough times, you might just be brainwashing yourself and creating a self-fulfilling prophecy. People will believe you are unlucky or an idiot and will stay away from you and expect the worst from you.

If you think you are fat and keep harping on it, or you have a big nose, are bald, or have fat thighs and constantly complain about it, you are conditioning others to focus on the features you find negative about yourself. Even if these things really are true about you, if you accept these things and even like these things about you, so will others.

Verbalize! No Complaints! Fix What You Hate!

Stop brainwashing yourself and others with these negative images. One of the best ways to stop saying things like "I hate my nose," "My teeth are crooked," "I'm so fat", "I hate my hair," and "I'm so short" is to get it all out verbally. But do this with those who can do something about it—you, your loved ones, and a professional who can fix it. By the way, with the advances in medicine today, things that were not changeable in the past—such as repairing certain facial deformities and the ability to walk, talk, and hear—are routinely fixed today. There are even ways to increase one's height—

something never considered as little as a half a decade ago! The bottom line is, "there is no excuse!" If there's something that really bothers you—figure out how to do something about it.

Look in the mirror. Really talk to yourself. Look at the thing about you that is the cause of your pain. Talk about it out loud when nobody is there. It's your personal business, between you and you. Talk about how much pain and grief this problem caused you, why you don't like it, what your life would be like if you didn't have it, and how doing something about it will change your life.

Now go to someone you are super close to and share it with them. Have a two-way conversation. Tell them what you told yourself. You might cry. You might even get talked out of having something done about it, but don't! Stick to your guns. Have them come with you only if they support you in your endeavor as you see the professional who can help you.

Verbalize everything you told yourself (and your loved one) to the professional and expect the best from him or her. If they don't pay as much attention to what is going on inside of you on an emotional level as to what is going on outside of you, do not have them work on you. There are too many other qualified professionals these days who can do both. They have to care about you and hear you as well as have the skill to help you.

Talk Back Tips

Like with any mantra, speak the words "I am entitled" both out loud and in your mind. Every time you say it to yourself, you will reinforce the idea.

Never Let the "Cat Get Your Tongue"

Now that you have fixed your outsides, you still have to fix your insides. You can do this through a verbal strategy I will teach you about in this section.

When you are overly quiet or shy or can't bring yourself to meet people or to see others, it is due to four reasons:

➤ You feel that you are inferior or less than other people.

➤ You couldn't imagine why anyone would want to be friends with you.

➤ You feel that the person might try to control you.

➤ You fear that the person might belittle or reject you. So, in order to play it safe, it is easier for you not to play at all, to sit on the verbal sidelines.

Well, guess what? You don't have to do that anymore. You have something to break you out of this syndrome forever, and it consists of three little words that you will repeat over and over and over and over and over in your head, even when you are being fed, even when you are in bed—all the time! These three simple words are "I AM ENTITLED!" Say it out loud, particularly when you feel these feelings of insecurity coming on strong. Then keep repeating it over and over to yourself silently.

You might think this sounds weird and think "how can saying one simple sentence make me feel less insecure?" That's what my clients asked me, but they were amazed when it actually worked. *It does work!* It starts to make you conscious of the fact that you are just as important as the next person—that they are no better than you are. The following methods are little tactics designed to remind you to not say bad things about YOU! Every time you say a bad thing like "I'm stupid" or "It's just my luck" or put yourself down, do one of these conditioning tactics so that you learn not to say it or feel that way again. As you do one or more of the things listed here, watch the negative statements you say about yourself become less and less frequent.

Quashing Your Negative Words About You

Do one or more of these 10 things after you say something negative about yourself. After a while you'll stop cutting yourself down.

1. Snap your fingers.
2. Blow air out of your mouth hard.
3. Bite your lower lip.
4. Bite your tongue.
5. Clench your jaw.
6. Slap your wrist.
7. Click your back teeth together.
8. Open the back of your throat like you're yawning, then yawn.
9. Clasp your fingers together.
10. Blow air in your cheeks.

Talk Back Tips

Usually, the way people talk about others in your presence is the way they will talk about you behind your back.

Observe What You Say to Potential Verbal Spies!

People remember! They don't forget! They do talk! They talk and they talk and they talk! They talk about themselves! They talk about others! They talk about YOU!

This means that if you tell them some good juicy tidbits about you, if you pour out your heart and soul to them, you can be sure that every drop, every word that you express, will be circulated among everyone you know and maybe even with those you don't know.

Loose Lips Sink Ships!

Sometimes you might think you are talking to a friend when in reality you are talking to a huge enemy—someone who really doesn't like you, is jealous of you, or who really wants to do you in. With the right verbal ammunition, they will destroy your reputation with their attempts to thwart your purposes.

Common sense tells you that you would never dream of giving your adversary any ammunition to use against you. But the reality of the situation is that you have already given it to them—straight from your mouth. This verbal bomb can explode in your face and kill you because it is so powerful. It comes completely unexpectedly from the "verbal enemy" you would least expect. The moral of the story is, "Never tell your best friend anything you wouldn't want your worst enemy to know!"

Verbal Vignette

As the late, great, reggae songwriter, poet, and musician Bob Marley said, "Your best friend can become your worst enemy." So watch it! Tell only a shrink about the deepest, darkest, dankest ditties that would be deadly if discovered!

Losing the Verbal War by Trashing Your Family!

Whether you like it or not, your family is just that—*your* family. You might hate everyone in it. You might not have spoken to them for 15 years. However, no matter what your relationship is with them, when you trash your family, especially to strangers and acquaintances, but even to people you know well, you trash yourself.

Almost everyone has family issues, and there are many different sides to these issues. When you start telling other people about your family issues, you are opening up your family, and yourself, to emotional pain. Most people aren't equipped to hear about other families' deepest and darkest secrets. If you open up to them they might, in their shock, tell two people who tell two more people, and so on and so on, and before you know it, people now understand why you act the way you do or feel sorry for you because of your background. You are suddenly "labeled"! The moral of the story is, tell only a professional about family tragedies. It won't go anywhere—for certain. Tell only a close, close friend or relative, and only after checking in with them to make sure they can handle such news.

Remember that you are taking a risk telling anyone but a professional, another family member who shares your plight, an intimate friend, spouse, or lover whom you trust with your heart and soul. Otherwise you put your reputation in jeopardy.

Winning by Letting It Leak!

Sometimes, you might not want a confidence kept. You might want this information out in the open for some reason. You consciously make this happen, knowing that not everyone can keep a confidence! However, this might not be all bad, as part of your own line of verbal defense strategies. In fact, politicians do it all the time. That's how we, the public, get information that is supposedly "leaked" to us from some unknown source. The information either enhances or embarrasses one side or the other. Sometimes this information is accurate; other times, it's a blatant lie. Sometimes the information predicts an event and prepares us for a pending disaster, other times it is just meant to scare us.

Whatever the case, it was calculated! It was an attempt to convey information by betraying a confidence.

How can you apply this verbal strategy to your own life? Let's say you want something to get out about you or your verbal enemy. It could be true information you want people to know about yourself or information that is a bit embellished. Your best bet is to tell the verbal big mouth and watch it spread like wildfire. You can exaggerate (kid around) or tell a tale. Once the Verbal Leaker hears the story, she is out of your control. (Right! And who told them to tell the world anyway?) In essence, they can become your best verbal weapon and PR agent.

Talk Back Tips

With all the Washington scandals recently, we've seen how people in the highest levels of government use leaks to their own advantage. You can use this very same strategy for yourself.

Losing the Verbal Battle by Recycling the Word

Remember that game you played in grade school, where one person would whisper something and then the next person was to repeat it to the next person, and so on and so forth down the line? By the time the 30th person repeated what the first person initially said, the story ended up being totally different and unrecognizable. This same thing happens in real life!

Things get distorted and embellished, but they don't have to go through 30 grade school children to get there. They can get distorted just by being filtered down through a few people who add their own spin or who bring their baggage or viewpoint to the story.

Let's say you go out on a date with John. You had an awful time. All he wanted to do was make out with you, and you just weren't attracted to him. You had no chemistry and he wasn't your type. You tell this to your co-worker.

She now tells her friend that your date was awful because you wouldn't have sex with him on the first date. Her friend tells another friend that your date is a sex maniac and won't date girls unless he has sex with them on the first date. Wow! Now the poor guy has a reputation he doesn't deserve, just because he kisses like a frog.

It's one of the casualties of opening your mouth and talking. It could have worked the other way too. You could have said you had a great time—that he was a great kisser. Your co-worker could have then told her friends that your date was a great lover. Word spread around that your date is so hot in bed and now every woman is dying to sleep with him.

So sometimes there is nothing you can do but be neutral and say "it was fine" or "okay," especially if you know someone is a "walkie-talkie" or Verbal Leaker.

Verbal Defeat Through Verbal Ecstasy—Why Tellin' All Feels Soooo Good!

Even if we know better, why do we still talk so much and gossip about ourselves, especially about our sexual selves? One reason is because it feels soooooooooooooo darn good.

It feels good to the talker. It's a release they desperately need. If they don't tell and talk about it, they crumble—literally. They suffer psychological, emotional, mental, and physical trauma. There is enough research in the medical literature to back up what I just said a thousand times over.

That is why therapists and clergy are so vital: people need to unload their problems to people who know what they are talking about in a professional sense. After they are done, it feels good. It feels even better if they are guided in the right direction and given the right advice.

Now let's take it a step further. Another reason we like to tell all, especially to our friends or to anyone who will listen for that matter, is because it feels good. As we talk about the experience and recall the minute details of the event (especially if it was a highly erotic event!), it is as though we are reliving the event and stimulating those same pleasure channels that felt soooo good.

Since, as far as the emotions are concerned, the brain can't distinguish between what's actually happening and what is being visualized, it is like you are there all over again! You take the listener along on this verbal magic carpet ride, and they too can visualize and empathize with you as though they were there. It's as though they were the protagonist in your detailed, erotic story.

When the story is over, the talker and the listener have both had a "verbal orgasm." Telling the tale over and over to as many people as will listen provides the teller with multiple verbal orgasms.

Talk Back Tips

In addition to being more health-conscious, eating better, and exercising more, one factor contributing to men's increasing longevity is that they are more verbally expressive than they were a decade ago.

Besides sex, people talk and talk in intimate details about negative experiences in their lives to purge themselves as well as to get someone else's reassurance. They tell the story from their side so that the listener will rally against their adversary and they will be "right." They feel better, you feel better, and you are entertained at the same time. Whatever the topic, there is a strong need for them to tell someone, and they chose you. So in some way that's flattering, but if you don't want to hear it, *don't*. Set limits. Say "I appreciate your feeling comfortable enough to tell me this, but I'm not comfortable listening to it." Smile. There is nothing to be mad at.

Don't Blame! Extinguish the Flame!

You need to stop restimulating your negative past! Of course, it might be interesting to hear about the hundreds of abusive lovers you've had, and how you were so poor when you were growing up that you had to eat dirt sandwiches and worms and live out of a cardboard box. But sometimes I wish I had a channel clicker so that if I heard one more disgruntled husband or wife complaining about their spouse, I could click them to a happy channel. Instead they could tell me how they got on with their lives and how their "dirty-doing mate" allowed them to move on find a better life, the right mate, and live in bliss.

Listen Up!

Nobody wants to hear the gloom and doom of your past. People don't ask you what you were like five years ago—they ask you what you are like now! So get over your past. Get into now!

Unfortunately, such a channel clicker hasn't been invented yet, but you can change your own channel. *Stop it already! Move on! Eight years is enough!* When you blame, you keep igniting the flame. You keep it going forever and ever. The less you talk about the tragedies and the people who "did you wrong," the more chance you will have to keep your eyes open to focus on those people who will be "doing you right."

Making Amends Verbally

The best part of Alcoholics Anonymous, Overeaters Anonymous, Narcotics Anonymous, Gamblers Anonymous, and other 12-step programs is that you get to make amends to people whose lives you were responsible for devastating! You get to say that you are truly sorry for the horrific and unconscionable deeds you inflicted upon them while you were under the influence of your particular demon. That is one of the beauties of the program.

Asking for forgiveness is one of the most wonderful and precious things you can do. It takes a big person to be able to do that. It takes a big person with a lot of courage and inner strength to approach another person and ask for forgiveness. But you have to do it if you are to be verbally effective. Honesty, sincerity, and coming clean are the basis of verbal self-defense. If you have those things, you have almost everything.

What do you say in order to say you are sorry?

Don't just think you can give a cursory "I'm sorry" and that's that! No way! You have to look directly at the person and tell them exactly why you are sorry. You have to tell them that you are sorry for what you did and how you think it made them feel. You have to listen to them wholeheartedly as they pour their heart out and tell you what your insensitive and horrible actions did to them, what scars your actions left, and what subsequent repercussions they had. You need to empathize with them.

Don't explain yourself and get defensive yet. Just sit there and listen!

Cry with them; empathize with them. Try with all your heart to feel what they must have gone through. Reach out to them physically. Try to touch them. Touch their hand. Ask them if they will allow you to hold them and caress them. If they won't, understand. Wounds take time to heal. They might forgive you now, sometime in the future, or never. Whatever the case, you verbally defended yourself so that you no longer have to wrestle with these verbal demons. You can finally put it to rest. You did the right thing from a verbal perspective!

No More Verbal Hypocrisy—a Clean Battlefield

If you don't want to do something or you don't want to be somewhere, then don't do it or don't go there. If you do, you will inevitably say the wrong thing to the wrong person, and this will always get you in trouble. People aren't dumb! They know when you are lying to them, want something from them, and are being manipulative.

Verbal Vignette

The days of lies are gone if you want to be a business success and a personal success today. In the new millennium, the only people who will make it are the ones who say what they mean and mean what they say. And people who don't verbally trash others or themselves are the ones who will come out the winners in the Communication Age.

Some people will even play along with your lie because it is challenging or fun to watch you trying to talk your way into something, such as into bed or into a business opportunity. You might think you are sweet-talking someone and getting ahead, but your empty words mean nothing, even if you succeed in getting the specific thing you want. You are ahead for only five minutes and then you are behind forever. You've gotta tell truths.

You never again have to be the verbal victim who is forced to say obligatory trite things! You no longer have to be a verbal hypocrite! Now you can sleep a lot better at night. Your conscience is clear as you have cleaned up your verbal battlefield once and for all!

Winning the War Through Verbal Gifts!

In order to win the verbal war, you have to use the most powerful verbal weapon, and that is the weapon of *love and kind words* given to yourself, your allies, and your adversaries.

Here is a list of verbal gifts:

➤ Words of endearment—"Honey," "love," "babe," "darlin'," "my love," "baby," and "sweetie"—go a long, long way and make people feel great.

➤ Lovely tones. Be upbeat and happy as though you are thrilled to see them. Have a tonal bounce, a song that says "I am so thrilled you are in my life, and I absolutely adore you!"

➤ Never take your verbal anger or attitude about someone else out on them. Never curse or damn the person, no matter how angry you get at them. Work it out! But work it out in a kind, loving, civil, and compassionate manner. No screaming and yelling!

➤ Apologize immediately and be the first to apologize when you've messed something up—especially if it's a little mess-up. Say it and mean it! Do it several times if necessary and use physical affection to reinforce it.

Talk Back Tips

If you want to feel great about yourself and make others feel great about themselves, win the verbal war by saying something sincere, kind, and thoughtful to someone each day!

➤ Say loving things to others unexpectedly.

➤ Never say petty things to people and talk about the small stuff. Always stick to the big picture.

➤ Tell people specific things about why you like, love, or respect them. Describe specific character traits, physical traits, behaviors, and incidents in great detail, and I mean in *minute* and *minuscule* detail. Everyone loves to hear that.

➤ Always encourage people in their endeavors. Explain exactly why you believe in them. Give your views about why you know they will make it and how you will never give up on them.

The Least You Need to Know

➤ When you say negative things about yourself, others tend to follow your lead and lose respect for you.

➤ If there are things about yourself you dislike, stop griping about it and do something to change it. You have many options available to you.

➤ People love to gossip, so be aware of whom you speak to.

➤ Even your best friend might reveal to others something very personal that you wouldn't want anyone to know.

➤ You never have to be a verbal victim again. You can say things to make you and others feel better and live a happier life.

Resources

Because I hold a Ph.D. in counseling psychology and a second Ph.D in the field of communication disorders, I have seen firsthand the positive impact that professionals in both of these fields have had upon people's lives.

The art of verbal self-defense requires that you feel good enough about yourself to deal with your emotional pain from your past, so that you have the confidence to handle any problem that presents itself. Using all the strategies I have taught you in this book will allow you to zip through any verbally toxic encounter. Thus, a qualified and competent counselor, psychologist, or psychiatrist is a plus to enhance your live. They don't have to be seen forever or cost you an arm and a leg. Often a good therapist will see you for short-term therapy just to help you with specific issues.

In addition to having the security of knowing the formula of what to say, it is equally important to know just how to say it. Sometimes you may not project the message as effectively as you could because of the way you sound or speak. Until you read this book, you may not have even realized that help was available to enable you to improve the quality of the way you sound. The added benefit to improving your speech is that you will also be improving your image and the way people perceive you. Therefore, I recommend a qualified speech pathologist who specializes in voice therapy with adults.

I recommend that you continue to read this book over and over again. Keep it! Save it as a reference book in your library. You will find yourself using it frequently, perhaps daily at first, then weekly or monthly until the techniques, strategies, and retorts become second nature.

You may need additional help as well. In addition to receiving additional material, which you can order directly from Appendix A, or engaging in a telephone session, you may need more extensive personalized treatment and counseling.

The following lists include sources of additional information and help.

References for Speech Pathologists

1. I do not recommend that you go to a singing teacher, but only to a speech pathologist who is licensed by your state, and who holds a Certificate of Clinical Competence from the American Speech Language and Hearing Association. This way you can be assured that you will be receiving treatment from a well-trained professional who knows exactly what they are doing and who will not harm your voice.

2. To find such a person, ask your friends who may know of one, or friends of friends who were helped by the person.

3. Check with several physicians (ear, nose, and throat physicians, general practitioners, and any type of dentist or orthodontist), so that you get a variety of names from which to choose.

4. Call each person and ask the specific questions listed in Chapter 17.

5. Contact the American Speech Language and Hearing Association at

   10801 Rockville Pike
   Rockville, MD 20852
   (301) 897-5700
   Fax (301) 571-0457

   They may be able to provide the name and phone number of the speech and hearing association in your state, which can possibly provide a list of names of speech therapists in your area who specialize in the treatmentof voice disorders.

References for Psychological Services

1. You may want to begin your hunt for a good psychotherapist by asking friends to refer one they or their friends have used.

2. Another option is to consult your clergy. Often they are excellent counselors. For many, sharing similar religious views can provide a great source of comfort, since they can address your particular issues and needs, perhaps in some cases even more effectively than a psychotherapist.

3. Ask several physicians and educators for any therapist they can recommend.

4. Just as one needs a speech pathologist who specializes in voice problems, you need a psychotherapist who is best equipped to help you with your specific needs. If you have a marital problem, a family problem, a drug or alcohol problem, an eating disorder, or a biochemical or personality disorder, you may want to seek out a therapist specializing in that particular area.

   To find this out, you need to ask questions. Just for the record, if you suspect that you or a loved one has a biochemical disorder (symptoms include mood swings or depression), the mental health professional you want to see is not a psychologist or even a psychiatrist, but rather a "psychopharmacologist."

5. You may also want to contact you local hospital to see if they have any outpatient psychotherapy programs or the nearest university medical center in your vicinity. In addition, public health facilities and mental health agencies usually exist on the city, county, state, or regional level. Often, these programs are much less costly.

6. Depending upon what issues you need to face, you can contact one or more of the following organizations. Perhaps they can refer you to someone in your area.

American Psychological Association
750 1st St., NE
Washington, DC 20002
(202) 336-5500
Fax (202) 336-5919

Divisions to Contact within the American Psychological Association:

Psychopharmacology and Substance Abuse

Child, Youth, and Family Services

Family Psychology

Psychology of Women

Society for the Psychological Study of Men and Masculinity

Society for the Psychological Study of Lesbian, Gay, & Bisexual Issues

Addictions

Adult Development and Aging

American Psychiatric Association
1400 K St. NW
Washington, DC 20005
(202) 682-6000
Fax (202) 682-6114

American Counseling Society
5999 Stevenson Ave.
Alexandria, VA 22304
(703) 823-9800

Association of Jewish Family and Children's Agencies
Box 248
3086 Hwy 27
Kendall Park, NJ 08824
(908) 821-0909
Fax (908) 821-0493

American Family Therapy Association
2020 Pennsylvania Ave. NW
Washington, DC 20006
(202) 994-2776
Fax (202) 994-4812

Association of Mental Health Clergy
12320 River Oaks
Knoxville, TN 37922
(615) 544-9704
(615) 544-8888

American Society of Pastoral Counselors
9504A Lee Hwy
Fairfax, VA 22031
(703) 385-6967
Fax (703) 352-7725

Black Psychiatrists of America
2730 Adeline St.
Oakland, CA 94607
(510) 465-1800

International Association of Counseling Services
101 S. Whiting St., Suite 211
Alexandria, VA 22304
(703) 823-9840
Fax (703) 823-9843

National Association of Alcoholism and Drug Abuse Counselors
3717 Columbia Pike, Ste. 300
Arlington, VA 22204
(703) 920-4644
(703) 920-4672

Parental Drug Association
7500 Old Georgetown Rd #620
Bethesda, MD 20814
(986) 986-0293
Fax (986) 986-0296

Asian Psychological Association
Department of Psychology
Slippery Rock, PA 16057
(412) 738-2274
Fax (412) 738-2098

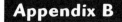

TO ORDER DR. GLASS' PRODUCTS

Fill out this form and include **VISA, MC, CHECK, or MONEY ORDER** to:

Dr. Lillian Glass
Your Total Image Inc.
P.O. Box 792
New York, NY 10021

OR YOU CAN PLACE A TELEPHONE ORDER

212-946-5729

OR SEND AN E-MAIL

info@drlillianglass.com

****ALL PRICES INCLUDE TAX, SHIPPING, AND HANDLING****

Emotional Feelings and *Mending Hearts* This set of 2 CD's of original songs which reflect every emotion you have ever felt. Some give you courage and help heal tender emotions while others stimulate your love and motivate you to climb the highest mountains.

Item	Price	Quantity	Total Amount
CD's (set of 2)	$45.99	_____	_____

Attracting Terrific People—How to Find and Keep the People Who Bring Your Life Joy! Never be lonely again! Find out how to attract and keep the best jobs, the best people, and have the relationships to allow you to have the most fulfilling life.

Item	Price	Quantity	Total Amount
Book (hardcover edition)	$32.99	_____	_____

Toxic People—10 Ways To Handle People Who Make Your Life Miserable Find out how to identify the 30 types of toxic terrors and use effective techniques that really work!

Item	Price	Quantity	Total Amount
Book (hardcover edition)	$32.99	_____	_____
Audiotapes (set of 2)	$32.99	_____	_____
Two Videotapes	$59.99	_____	_____

He Says/She Says—Closing the Communication Gap Between The Sexes Although men and women are different, there *are* things we can do and say to avoid fights, hurt feelings, frustrations, and pent up anger against the opposite sex throughout our daily lives, at work, and even in the most intimate moments. Now you will know what to do and exactly what to say to the opposite sex!

Item	Price	Quantity	Total Amount
Book (hardcover edition)	$32.99		
Videotape	$59.99		
Audiotapes (set of 2)	$32.99		

Talk To Win: 6 Steps To A Successful Vocal Image You don't ever have to hate the sound of your voice or be afraid to speak publicly again. Now you can use the same speaking and voice techniques used by Hollywood.

Item	Price	Quantity	Total Amount
Videotape	$17.99		
Audiotape	$59.99		

World of Words Never feel insecure about not understanding what another person is saying to you. You will learn the basic roots which allow you to figure out what most words mean, even if you've never heard them before. It's simple and easy, and takes minutes to learn.

Item	Price	Quantity	Total Amount
Audiotape	$17.99		

How to Deprogram Your Valley Girl It's classic, no matter what generation you're from! Humorous, cute, and funny, it has a serious message by explaining in easy steps how to teach your teen or child how to talk right.

Item	Price	Quantity	Total Amount
Book (softcover edition)	$10.99		

Speak for Success Now you will have the confidence to speak up, say what you've always wanted to say, and feel great about yourself!

Item	Price	Quantity	Total Amount
Videotape	$59.99		

Total Balance Due_____

Last Name_____First Name_____
Address_____
City, State, Zip Code_____
Phone Number(___)_____
Fax Number(___)_____
E-mail_____
Visa/MC Number_____
Expiration Date_____
Name as it Appears on Card_____
Signature_____

Index

W

X-Z

When You're Smart Enough to Know That You Don't Know It All!

THE COMPLETE IDIOT'S GUIDE®

For all the ups and downs you're sure to encounter in life,
The Complete Idiot's Guides give you
down-to-earth answers and practical solutions.

Personal Business

The Complete Idiot's Guide to Assertiveness
ISBN: 0-02-861964-1
$16.95

The Complete Idiot's Guide to Business Management
ISBN: 0-02-861744-4
$16.95

The Complete Idiot's Guide to New Product Development
ISBN: 0-02-861952-8
$16.95

The Complete Idiot's Guide to Dynamic Selling
ISBN: 0-02-861952-8
$16.95

The Complete Idiot's Guide to Getting Along with Difficult People
ISBN: 0-02-861597-2
$16.95

The Complete Idiot's Guide to Great Customer Service
ISBN: 0-02-861953-6
$16.95

The Complete Idiot's Guide to Leadership
ISBN: 0-02-861946-3
$16.95

The Complete Idiot's Guide to Marketing Basics
ISBN: 0-02-861490-9
$16.95

The Complete Idiot's Guide to Office Politics
ISBN: 0-02-862397-5
$16.95

The Complete Idiot's Guide to Project Management
ISBN: 0-02-861745-2
$16.95

The Complete Idiot's Guide to Starting a Home Based Business
ISBN: 0-02-861539-5
$16.95

The Complete Idiot's Guide to Successful Business Presentations
ISBN: 0-02-861748-7
$16.95

The Complete Idiot's Guide to Freelancing
ISBN: 0-02-862119-0
$16.95

The Complete Idiot's Guide to Changing Careers
ISBN: 0-02-861977-3
$17.95

The Complete Idiot's Guide to Terrific Business Writing
ISBN: 0-02-861097-0
$16.95

The Complete Idiot's Guide to Getting the Job You Want
ISBN: 1-56761-608-9
$24.95

The Complete Idiot's Guide to Managing Your Time
ISBN: 0-02-862943-4
$18.95

The Complete Idiot's Guide to Speaking in Public With Confidence
ISBN: 0-02-861038-5
$16.95

The Complete Idiot's Guide to Winning Through Negotiation
ISBN: 0-02-861037-7
$16.95

The Complete Idiot's Guide to Managing People
ISBN: 0-02-861036-9
$18.95

The Complete Idiot's Guide to a Great Retirement
ISBN: 0-02-861036-9
$16.95

The Complete Idiot's Guide to Starting Your Own Business
ISBN: 0-02-861979-X
$18.95

The Complete Idiot's Guide to Protecting Yourself from Everyday Legal Hassles
ISBN: 1-56761-602-X
$16.99

The Complete Idiot's Guide to Surviving Divorce
ISBN: 0-02-861101-3
$16.95

The Complete Idiot's Guide to
Organizing Your Life
ISBN: 0-02-861090-3
$16.95

The Complete Idiot's Guide to
Reaching Your Goals
ISBN: 0-02-862114-X
$16.95

The Complete Idiot's Guide to
the Perfect Cover Letter
ISBN: 0-02-861960-9
$14.95

The Complete Idiot's Guide to
the Perfect Interview
ISBN: 0-02-861945-5
$14.95

The Complete Idiot's Guide to
the Perfect Resume
ISBN: 0-02-861093-8
$16.95

Personal Finance

The Complete Idiot's Guide to
Buying Insurance and Annu-
ities
ISBN: 0-02-861113-6
$16.95

The Complete Idiot's Guide to
Managing Your Money
ISBN: 1-56761-530-9
$16.95

The Complete Idiot's Guide to
Making Money with Mutual
Funds
ISBN: 1-56761-637-2
$16.95

The Complete Idiot's Guide to
Buying and Selling a Home
ISBN: 0-02-861959-5
$16.95

The Complete Idiot's Guide to
Getting Rich
ISBN: 0-02-862952-3
$18.95

The Complete Idiot's Guide to
Finance and Accounting
ISBN: 0-02-861752-5
$16.95

The Complete Idiot's Guide to
Investing Like a Pro
ISBN:0-02-862044-5
$16.95

The Complete Idiot's Guide to
Making Money After You
Retire
ISBN:0-02-862410-6
$16.95

The Complete Idiot's Guide to
Making Money on Wall Street
ISBN:0-02-861958-7
$16.95

The Complete Idiot's Guide to
Personal Finance in Your 20s
and 30s
ISBN:0-02-862415-7
$16.95

The Complete Idiot's Guide to
Wills and Estates
ISBN: 0-02-861747-9
$16.95

The Complete Idiot's Guide to
401(k) Plans
ISBN: 0-02-861948-X
$16.95

Lifestyle

The Complete Idiot's Guide to
Etiquette
ISBN0-02-861094-6
$16.95

The Complete Idiot's Guide to
Dating
ISBN: 0-02-861052-0
$14.95

The Complete Idiot's Guide to
Trouble-Free Car Care
ISBN: 0-02-861041-5
$16.95

The Complete Idiot's Guide to
the Perfect Wedding
ISBN: 0-02-861963-3
$16.95

The Complete Idiot's Guide to
the Perfect Vacation
ISBN: 1-56761-531-7
$14.99

The Complete Idiot's Guide to
Trouble-Free Home Repair
ISBN: 0-02-861042-3
$16.95

The Complete Idiot's Guide to
Getting Into College
ISBN: 1-56761-508-2
$14.95

The Complete Idiot's Guide to
a Healthy Relationship
ISBN: 0-02-861087-3
$17.95

The Complete Idiot's Guide to
Dealing with In-Laws
ISBN: 0-02-862107-7
$16.95

The Complete Idiot's Guide to
Choosing, Training, and
Raising a Dog
ISBN: 0-02-861098-9
$16.95

The Complete Idiot's Guide to
Fun and Tricks with Your Dog
ISBN: 0-87605-083-6
$14.95

The Complete Idiot's Guide to
Living with a Cat
ISBN: 0-02-861278-7
$16.95

The Complete Idiot's Guide to
Turtles and Tortoises
ISBN: 0-87605-143-3
$16.95

Leisure/Hobbies

The Complete Idiot's Guide to
Baking
ISBN: 0-02-861954-4
$16.95

The Complete Idiot's Guide to
Beer
ISBN: 0-02-861717-7
$16.95

The Complete Idiot's Guide to
Cooking Basics
ISBN: 0-02-861974-9
$18.95

The Complete Idiot's Guide to
Entertaining
ISBN: 0-02-861095-4
$16.95

The Complete Idiot's Guide to
Mixing Drinks
ISBN: 0-02-861941-2
$16.95

The Complete Idiot's Guide to
Wine
ISBN: 0-02-861273-6
$16.95

The Complete Idiot's Guide to
Antiques and Collectibles
ISBN: 0-02-861595-6
$16.95

The Complete Idiot's Guide to
Boating and Sailing
ISBN: 0-02-862124-7
$18.95

The Complete Idiot's Guide to
Bridge
ISBN: 0-02-861735-5
$16.95

The Complete Idiot's Guide to
Chess
ISBN: 0-02-861736-3
$16.95

The Complete Idiot's Guide to
Cigars
ISBN: 0-02-861975-7
$17.95

The Complete Idiot's Guide to
Crafts with Kids
ISBN: 0-02-862406-8
$16.95

The Complete Idiot's Guide to
Fishing Basics
ISBN: 0-02-861598-0
$16.95

The Complete Idiot's Guide to
Gambling Like a Pro
ISBN: 0-02-861102-0
$16.95

The Complete Idiot's Guide to
Hiking and Camping
ISBN: 0-02-861100-4
$16.95

The Complete Idiot's Guide to
Knitting and Crocheting
ISBN: 0-02-862123-9
$16.95

The Complete Idiot's Guide to
Photography
ISBN: 0-02-861092-X
$16.95

The Complete Idiot's Guide to
Quilting
ISBN: 0-02-862411-4
$16.95

The Complete Idiot's Guide to
Yoga
ISBN: 0-02-861949-8
$16.95

The Complete Idiot's Guide to
the Beatles
ISBN: 0-02-862130-1
$18.95

The Complete Idiot's Guide to
Elvis
ISBN: 0-02-861873-4
$18.95

The Complete Idiot's Guide to
Understanding Football Like a
Pro
ISBN:0-02-861743-6
$16.95

The Complete Idiot's Guide to
Golf
ISBN: 0-02-861760-6
$16.95

The Complete Idiot's Guide to
Motorcycles
ISBN: 0-02-862416-5
$17.95

The Complete Idiot's Guide to
Pro Wrestling
ISBN: 0-02-862395-9
$17.95

The Complete Idiot's Guide to
Extra-Terrestrial Intelligence
ISBN: 0-02-862387-8
$16.95

Health and Fitness

The Complete Idiot's Guide to
Managed Health Care
ISBN: 0-02-862165-4
$17.95

The Complete Idiot's Guide to
Getting and Keeping Your
Perfect Body
ISBN: 0-02-861276-0
$16.95

The Complete Idiot's Guide to
First Aid Basics
ISBN: 0-02-861099-7
$16.95

The Complete Idiot's Guide to
Vitamins
ISBN: 0-02-862116-6
$16.95

The Complete Idiot's Guide to
Losing Weight
ISBN: 0-02-862113-1
$17.95

The Complete Idiot's Guide to
Tennis
ISBN: 0-02-861746-0
$18.95

The Complete Idiot's Guide to
Tae Kwon Do
ISBN: 0-02-862389-4
$17.95

The Complete Idiot's Guide to
Breaking Bad Habits
ISBN: 0-02-862110-7
$16.95

The Complete Idiot's Guide to
Healthy Stretching
ISBN: 0-02-862127-1
$16.95

The Complete Idiot's Guide to
Beautiful Skin
ISBN: 0-02-862408-4
$16.95

The Complete Idiot's Guide to
Eating Smart
ISBN: 0-02-861276-0
$16.95

The Complete Idiot's Guide to
First Aid
ISBN: 0-02-861099-7
$16.95

The Complete Idiot's Guide to
Getting a Good Night's Sleep
ISBN: 0-02-862394-0
$16.95

The Complete Idiot's Guide to
a Happy, Healthy Heart
ISBN: 0-02-862393-2
$16.95

The Complete Idiot's Guide to
Stress
ISBN: 0-02-861086-5
$16.95

The Complete Idiot's Guide to
Jogging and Running
ISBN: 0-02-862386-X
$17.95

The Complete Idiot's Guide to
Adoption
ISBN: 0-02-862108-5
$18.95

The Complete Idiot's Guide to
Bringing Up Baby
ISBN: 0-02-861957-9
$16.95

The Complete Idiot's Guide to
Grandparenting
ISBN: 0-02-861976-5
$16.95

The Complete Idiot's Guide to
Parenting a Preschooler and
Toddler
ISBN: 0-02-861733-9
$16.95

The Complete Idiot's Guide to
Raising a Teenager
ISBN: 0-02-861277-9
$16.95

The Complete Idiot's Guide to
Single Parenting
ISBN: 0-02-862409-2
$16.95

The Complete Idiot's Guide to
Stepparenting
ISBN: 0-02-862407-6
$16.95

Education

The Complete Idiot's Guide to
American History
ISBN: 0-02-861275-2
$16.95

The Complete Idiot's Guide to
British Royalty
ISBN: 0-02-862346-0
$18.95

The Complete Idiot's Guide to
Civil War
ISBN: 0-02-862122-0
$16.95

The Complete Idiot's Guide to
Classical Mythology
ISBN: 0-02-862385-1
$16.95

The Complete Idiot's Guide to
Creative Writing
ISBN: 0-02-861734-7
$16.95

The Complete Idiot's Guide to
Dinosaurs
ISBN: 0-02-862390-8
$17.95

The Complete Idiot's Guide to
Genealogy
ISBN: 0-02-861947-1
$16.95

The Complete Idiot's Guide to
Geography
ISBN: 0-02-861955-2
$16.95

The Complete Idiot's Guide to
Getting Published
ISBN: 0-02-862392-4
$16.95

The Complete Idiot's Guide to
Grammar & Style
ISBN: 0-02-861956-0
$16.95

The Complete Idiot's Guide to
an MBA
ISBN: 0-02-862164-4
$17.95

The Complete Idiot's Guide to
Philosophy
ISBN:0-02-861981-1
$16.95

The Complete Idiot's Guide to
Classical Music
ISBN: 0-02-8611634-0
$16.95

The Complete Idiot's Guide to
Learning Spanish On Your
Own
ISBN: 0-02-861040-7
$16.95

The Complete Idiot's Guide to
Learning French on Your Own
ISBN: 0-02-861043-1
$16.95

The Complete Idiot's Guide to
Learning German on Your
Own
ISBN: 0-02-861962-5
$16.95

The Complete Idiot's Guide to
Learning Italian on Your Own
ISBN: 0-02-862125-5
$16.95

The Complete Idiot's Guide to
Learning Sign Language
ISBN: 0-02-862388-6
$16.95

The Complete Idiot's Guide to
Astrology
ISBN: 0-02-861951-X
$16.95

The Complete Idiot's Guide to
the World's Religions
ISBN: 0-02-861730-4
$16.95

**Look for the Complete Idiot's Guides at your local bookseller,
or call 1-800-428-5331 for more information.**

You can also check us out on the web at
http://www.mcp.com/mgr/idiot

alpha
books